IMAGES
of America

HAWAIIANS IN LOS ANGELES

ON THE COVER: The togetherness, ingenuity, and community building tendencies of Hawaiian people culminate in the *Ho'olaule'a* (festival) at Alondra Park. The festival features many elements of Hawaiian culture, from mix plate lunches to shave ice, floral dresses to floral quilts, and civic clubs to health organizations. The Ho'olaule'a has been a staple in Los Angeles since the late 1970s. (Courtesy of the Rosero family.)

IMAGES
of America

Hawaiians in Los Angeles

Elizabeth "Nani" Nihipali,
Lessa Kanani'opua Pelayo,
Christian Hanz Lozada,
Cheryl Villareal Roberts,
and Lorelie Santonil Olaes

ARCADIA
PUBLISHING

ISBN 978-0-7385-9320-3

Published by Arcadia Publishing
Charleston, South Carolina

Printed in the United States of America

Library of Congress Control Number: 2011940894

For all general information, please contact Arcadia Publishing:
Telephone 843-853-2070
Fax 843-853-0044
E-mail sales@arcadiapublishing.com
For customer service and orders:
Toll-Free 1-888-313-2665

Visit us on the Internet at www.arcadiapublishing.com

In memory of Tutu Mary M. Pelayo,
a pillar to any community she is part of

Nani dedicates this book to her grandchildren,
so they can perpetuate the mana in them

CONTENTS

Acknowledgments

The publication of Images of America: *Hawaiians in Los Angeles* affords the opportunity to express the influence Native Hawaiians have in Southern California, specifically following the Kaio, Kuhia, Nihipali, and Pelayo families as their lives touch the lives of many transplanted Hawaiians in Los Angeles. This work could not have happened if it had not been for their part in the growth and interconnectedness of civic clubs and hula halau, who continue to share their culture, innovation, and pictures with Native Hawaiians, locals, and the Hawaiian at heart. Everyone in these groups and the people we have interviewed instinctively, if not intellectually, recognize the importance of sharing the culture of Hawaii and the culture of the Hawaiian diaspora in Los Angeles, which is as alive and as vibrant as a flower in Hawaii.

Nani, Lessa, and Christian recognize that their book, their story, and their personalities are due to the people and events that surround their lives. Acknowledging specific individuals would downplay the impact everyone they have shared a moment with has had on them. This story and book is as much yours as it is theirs.

Cheryl would like to thank Jesus Christ for giving her the opportunity to work on this project and her wonderful family—Jim, Emily, and Eloise—for allowing us to use our home as a meeting place.

Lore would like to thank God for bringing the coauthors together for this project. The combination of skills and perspectives of each member was needed in order to fully capture the spirit of the journey of Hawaiians from Hawaii to Los Angeles and their contributions to their "new" communities on the continent. She would also like to thank all the people who opened their lives and hearts to us by sharing their thoughts and stories.

We would like to acknowledge the editors at Arcadia Publishing, who spurred us to complete this project with sporadic reminders, questions, and comments throughout the writing process, and Florante and Rose Ibanez, who led us to Arcadia.

INTRODUCTION

In the words of Lilo from Disney's *Lilo & Stitch*, "*Ohana* means family. Family means no one gets left behind or forgotten." Disney could not have been more right when encompassing one of the most important Hawaiian values that Native Hawaiians maintain. Ohana, along with other ideas such as *kuleana* (responsibility), *malama* (to tend to), and *'aina* (land), are at the core of Hawaiian culture. Ohana, kuleana, malama, and 'aina do not quite mean the same thing as their English counterparts—family, responsibility, to take care of, and land—because in the Hawaiian version, family, land, and the world around us are always part of the same conversation. Throughout this book, we hope to show facets of this conversation, but at the core of this book is Native Hawaiian ohana: ohana related by blood, and ohana related by love. And through ohana, stories of kuleana and malama for history and ancestors, for each other, and for each other's culture will, we hope, become clear. In the end, we are trying to tell the story of recreating 'aina. However, to understand how Los Angeles became 'aina and why Hawaiians came to leave their so-called paradise, we have to take a quick look at Hawaiian history.

There is a creation myth that describes *kalo* or *taro* (a root and major food source in ancient Hawaii) as a sibling to humans. Thus, the foundation of Hawaiian belief, despite the influence of Western religion, rests upon knowing that the plants that we eat (and the ground they are from) are as vital as the people. In other words, the land and its people are twin skin; there should be little difference between one and the other. The Hawaii state motto shows how deeply this message permeates the culture: *Ua mau ke ea o ka aina i ka pono* (The life of the land is perpetuated in righteousness). This saying, coined by Kamehameha III when the islands were restored as a sovereign nation, has thrived through overthrows, coups, and annexation. It has lasted through Hawaii's history, when the nation lost its monarchy, became an American territory, and achieved statehood. The motto means that the fruitfulness of the land is tied to *kanaka* (human) action—tied to his or her ability to malama 'aina. But for diasporic Hawaiians, who are no longer physically connected to the islands, does ua mau ke ea o ka aina i ka pono apply? The question of what Hawaii is and who belongs is important to understand what it means to be Hawaiian in Los Angeles.

According to the 2009 American Community Survey, there are more Native Hawaiians and Pacific Islanders in California than in Hawaii. Unlike other migrating groups who are measured in waves and movements, Native Hawaiian migration to Los Angeles has been one consistent note since statehood in 1959. The reasons Native Hawaiians in the diaspora outnumber those who stay behind are complicated thrice over. First, the population of Native Hawaiians was ravaged by disease since Western contact, bringing their numbers from 300,000 to as low as 30,000. Second,

Hawaiians migrated to the continental United States following economic tides. Third, the definition of Hawaiian is slippery when Hawaii is the most racially diverse state in America.

In the late 1800s, the sovereign Kingdom of Hawaii had a reciprocity agreement with America, allowing Hawaiian sugar to enter the United States tax-free. This led to an increase in traffic between Pearl Harbor in Hawaii and Oakland/San Francisco in Northern California. With the increased traffic came more industrialization and diseases, like leprosy (Hansen's Disease) and small pox. Native Hawaiians had little resistance against both diseases. These diseases infected Hawaiians in waves, leading to the need for modernized hospitals to treat a dwindling native population. To take advantage of the booming sugar industry, workers from all over Europe and Asia immigrated to the sugar cane plantations growing across the islands. These waves of workers, representing countries such as Portugal, Philippines, Korea, and China, would come to play a large role in the development of modern Hawaiian culture and are depicted throughout the pictures that follow. Unlike the majority of America, which was recovering from a civil war and becoming more racially divided, Native Hawaiians accepted the Portuguese, Japanese, and Korean people wholeheartedly, making their food, language, and customs part of the ever-evolving culture of the islands and part of their ever-expanding ohana.

Hawaiian economics and industry shifted from the height of the sugar industry in the middle of the 19th century and ending in the middle of the 20th century. In that time, Native Hawaiians learned about private property and capitalism. Unfortunately, property and capitalism are not subjects for newcomers, and, with less than a century out of communal living, the natives were as new as they come. Native Hawaiians had a hard time understanding the concept of owning land while the Americans and Europeans instructing them through these changes took advantage of the situation and purchased acre upon acre. In the end, Native Hawaiians owned less than one percent of all lands in Hawaii.

As landownership shifted from the natives to American immigrants, so did the major industries of Hawaii change. Late in the 19th century, Hawaii was forcefully annexed by the United States, and the islands became a military installation and continued to grow in this industry through the Cold War. Throughout this period, and especially after annexation, Hawaii also became a tourist attraction. The problem with agriculture, military, and hospitality as staple industries is that they do not offer much of a future. Successful agriculture is predicated upon cheap labor. The military pays a living wage but not much more. Tourism needs more cheap labor than middle management. Combining the lack of property with these industries, Hawaii, for Native Hawaiians, became a tragic place to live and a hard place to succeed.

Even though Hawaii is a state now, it is important to recognize that Hawaii is limited in size and available industry. Native Hawaiian migration from the islands was necessary since available jobs were shared with new immigrants, and such jobs were labor intensive and low paying. The influx of Native Hawaiians to the United States goes back as far as the boom of the whaling industry in the 18th and 19th centuries. Back then, ships were at sea for three to four years and would pick up new crew members from places like Hawaii to make up for shipmates who were lost while chasing whales or jumped ship at the first available port. The work was grueling and dangerous, but whaling was a lucrative industry that helped build America. The Native Hawaiian migration trickle becomes emblematic of the Hawaiian diaspora as shown in the early families residing in Los Angeles who were attracted by various economic booms. These Hawaiians were not here for one boom or bust industry like sugar; they were here to make something lasting. They wanted to perpetuate 'aina and necessarily Hawaiian land.

When Hawaiians came to Los Angeles, they brought with them the need to recreate ohana while maintaining kuleana for their history and culture and holding true to the charge to perpetuate the land through righteousness. However, how do you perpetuate your land on a different shore? Like all the best answers, the answer is spiritual and simple. Through ohana, Native Hawaiians recreate and refashion California into another version of Hawaii. Yet this version, composed in a land already loud with unfamiliar music, must have a more constant *mele* (song), one that can carry across the Pacific and one that carries descriptions of loss and longing for the islands and the fulfillment and contentment gained from building a new home. The Los Angeles mele describes the diasporic Native Hawaiian's firm grasp on tradition in this new land. At the same time, the mele also describes the significance of being Hawaiian.

At this point in our story, Native Hawaiian and Hawaiian is a mixed experience. Today's number of Native Hawaiians is upwards of 235,000 in the United States, with most of them identifying themselves as mixed race. Defining what it means to be Hawaiian or "Hawaiianness" is a challenge because of the influx of other cultures through the history of the islands and the intermarriages that have resulted from the collection of other cultures at home and abroad. A population of 30,000 is what was left when the missionaries took a census in the early 1800s, which was not even 100 years after white explorers first came in the late 1700s. The combination of mixing races and dwindling population and the confused identity that ensues, defining what we mean when we say Hawaiian and other Hawaiian words in this book is necessary. (Please note that the absence of ʻokina in the following Hawaiian words represents the transitional period much of this book describes; its presence denotes current uses by the groups depicted.)

Native Hawaiian: A Native Hawaiian is someone who can trace their ancestry to the Hawaiian Islands before the arrival of Europeans in approximately 1778 (Captain Cook's Arrival). While Native Hawaiians are indigenous like Native Americans, they do not have the same official designation as indigenous peoples of America except in the State of Hawaii. Unlike Native Americans, Native Hawaiians have no reservations or sovereignty. When their country was annexed, they simply became subjects of the United States.

Local: A local is someone born and raised in Hawaii who shares the modern culture of the Hawaiian Islands. Local culture is a combination of Hawaiian, Portuguese, Filipino, Japanese, Korean, Chinese, and other ethnicities that have come to Hawaii to work during the sugar plantation days. An example of local culture is the plate lunch, which is a Japanese bento box with foods from any or all of the above cultures.

Diasporic Hawaiian community (our focus): The diasporic Hawaiian community consists of people who have left Hawaii for the continental United States. These people are, while sometimes being Native Hawaiian, often mixed-race due to the high rates of intermarriage and the strong presence of local culture in Hawaii.

Hawaiian at heart: People who are Hawaiian at heart are those who maintain the values of Hawaii by being part of and perpetuating the Hawaiian culture.

ʻAina: Land, earth
Ali'i: Chief, chiefess, officer, ruler, governor
Auana hula: Contemporary hula
Haku: a lei made by braiding or plaiting the flowers
Halau: Meeting house for hula, hula school
Haumana: Student, pupil, apprentice
Hanai: Foster child or adopted child
Honu: General name for turtle and tortoise
Ipu: Bottle gourd
Kahiko hula: Ancient style of hula
Kahili: Feathered standard, symbolic of royalty
Kane: Male, husband, masculine
Kokua: Help, aid, assistance
Kuleana: Responsibility
Kumu: Teacher, tutor
Lokahi: Unity, agreement

Makua: Parent or any relative of the parents' generation, mature, older, senior
Mana: Supernatural or divine power, authority
Mele: Song, anthem, or chant of any kind; poem, poetry; to sing, chant
Mo'opuna: Grandchild; relatives two generations later
Mu'umu'u: A loose gown, sometimes with short sleeves
Ono: Delicious, tasty, savory; to relish, crave
Po'maika'i: Good fortune, blessedness, blessing, profit, prosperity
Ui: To ask, question, appeal, turn to for help or advice
Wahine: Woman, lady, feminine

One

Bringing Ohana to the Continent

Why Hawaiians Came

About 90 percent of the flora and fauna in Hawaii is unique to the island chain. Many of these plants and animals were brought by the natives or arrived from distant shores, and all of them bear a distinct imprint from life on the islands to the point that success becomes difficult when new species are introduced. It is no wonder that the state motto and some of the most common phrases, such as *malama*, *ohana*, and *kuleana*, can be linked to an overall desire to conserve. Conversely, with little land of their own, many Native Hawaiians had to take this mindset to the continent. The kanaka arrived in Los Angeles with a desire to conserve their morals and create new families or ohana on land that can be their own.

The years after World War II were a vibrant time in Los Angeles, and Native Hawaiians, no longer subjects of a territory of the United States but American citizens, found themselves members to a larger country. In search of economic opportunity, the kanaka found themselves on the continent taking part in various burgeoning industries. The most common connection between Hawaii and the continent was the massive military complex (namely, the Navy) that created a fleet big enough to patrol the Pacific Ocean. Despite losing their country through deception, kanaka showed an unwavering loyalty to the concept of freedom the United States offers. This loyalty is instilled through the charge to malama 'aina, to take care of the land. The difference after World War II is that the 'aina was extended from sea to shining sea.

During the 1950s and 1960s, diasporic Hawaiians were too busy rooting themselves in this unfamiliar land to leave a distinctive imprint on the California landscape, but the roots of their influence can be seen in various industries, from engineering, to education, to the military. While they influenced business, they formed relationships, built families, and called ohana on the islands to a new gathering place. The pictures that follow contain promise, loss, reunion, unions, and partings all at the same time.

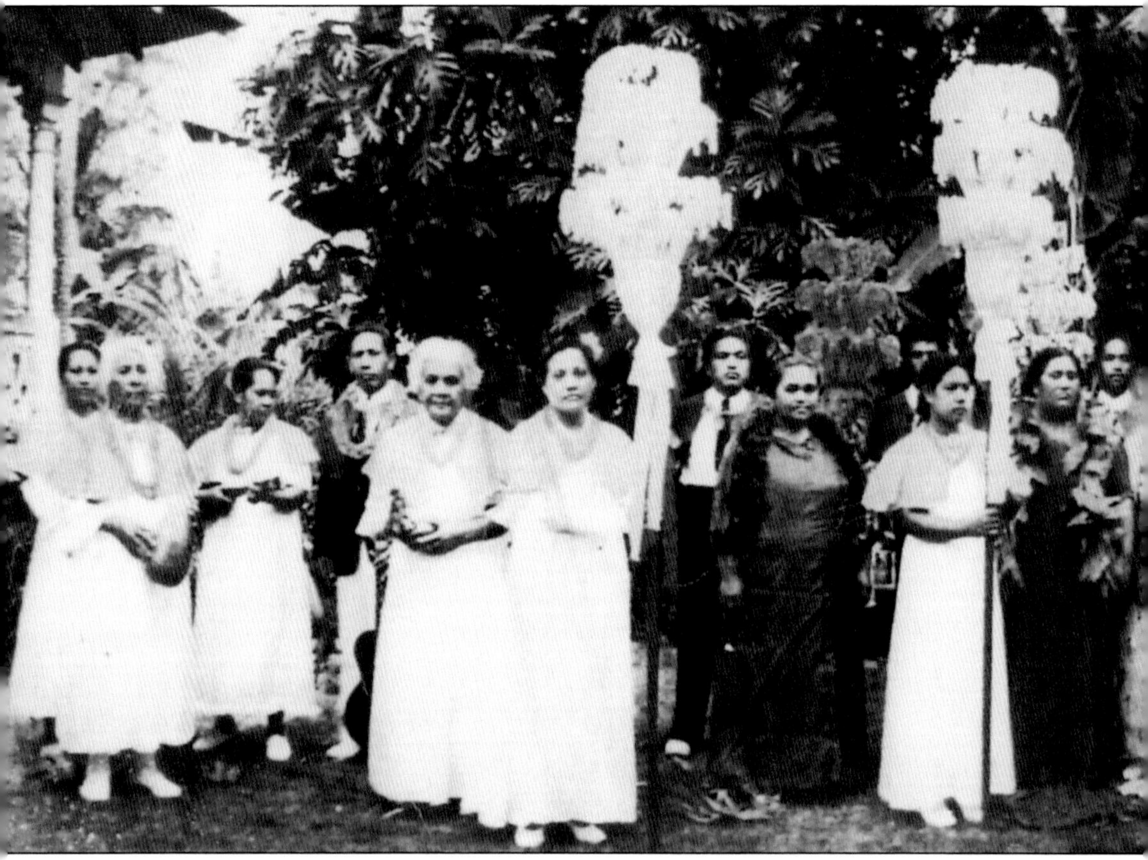

Members of the Kaio family are pictured celebrating Jubilee, a celebration of the Hukilau, which is reminiscent of May Day in Hawaii. Lei Day, as it is also called in Hawaii, is a celebration of many aspects of Native Hawaiian culture. One tradition is to reenact the royal court. The purpose of the reenactment is to emphasize Hawaii's history as a modern kingdom as well as encourage the

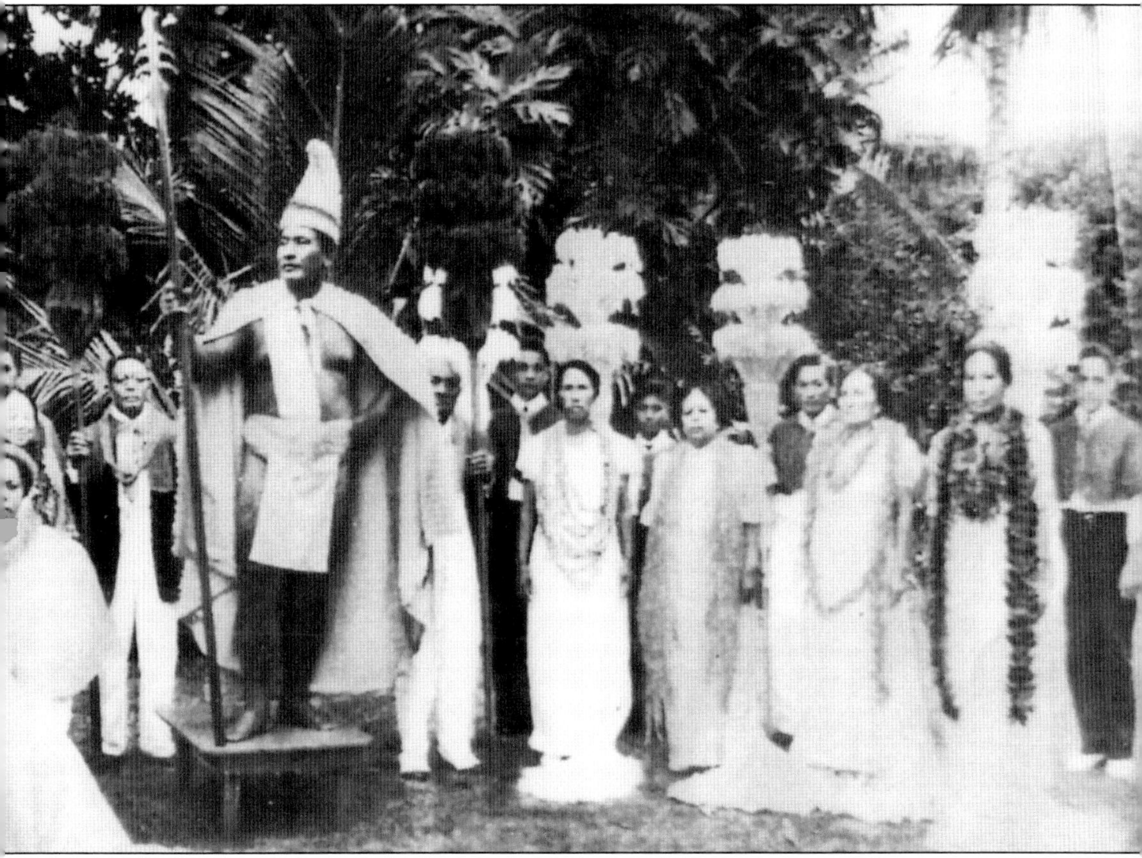

spirit of resiliency that characterizes Native Hawaiians. Much of the costuming and ornamentation is handmade. While this photograph of Native Hawaiians was taken in Hawaii, many of the individuals depicted here eventually moved to the continental United States for various reasons. (Courtesy of Elizabeth "Nani" Nihipali.)

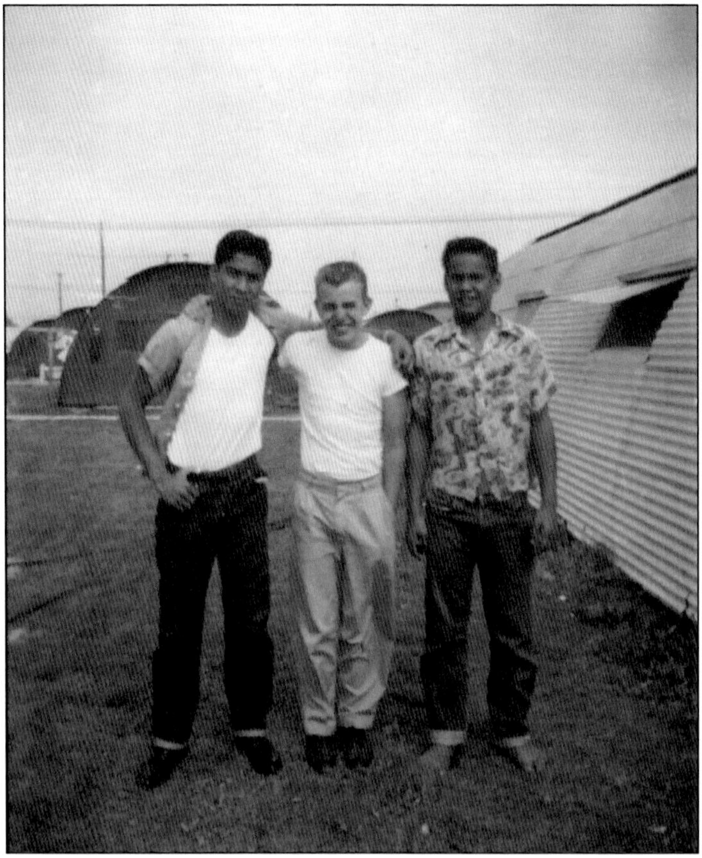

Born and raised in the sugar plantation town of Aiea, Gus Keolanui (left) and brother Norby (right) arrived in California with their mother and stepfather in 1954. Like many Native Hawaiians arriving here, the first part of their life was filled with temporary elements. The Keolanuis spent the summer living in a Quonset hut in San Pedro. The huts, the height of permanent-temporary housing, was made of corrugated iron and had no ventilation system (much less air-conditioning). Soon after, their family moved to permanent Navy housing in Long Beach. The young man in the center is not identified. (Courtesy of Gus Keolanui.)

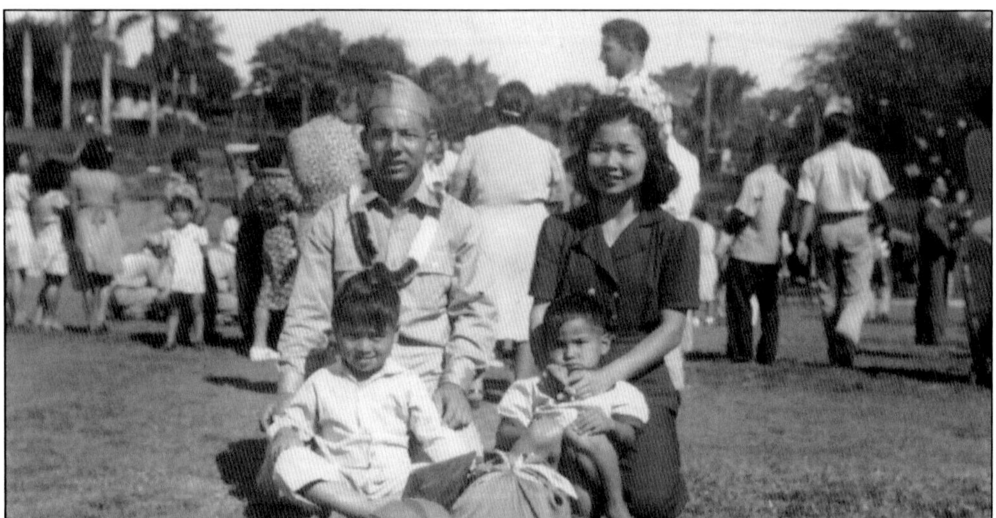

This photograph features the Keolanui boys with their mother, Harriet Bittenbender, and her brother Toshiyo after he returned from World War II, serving in the 442nd regiment. (Courtesy of Gus Keolanui.)

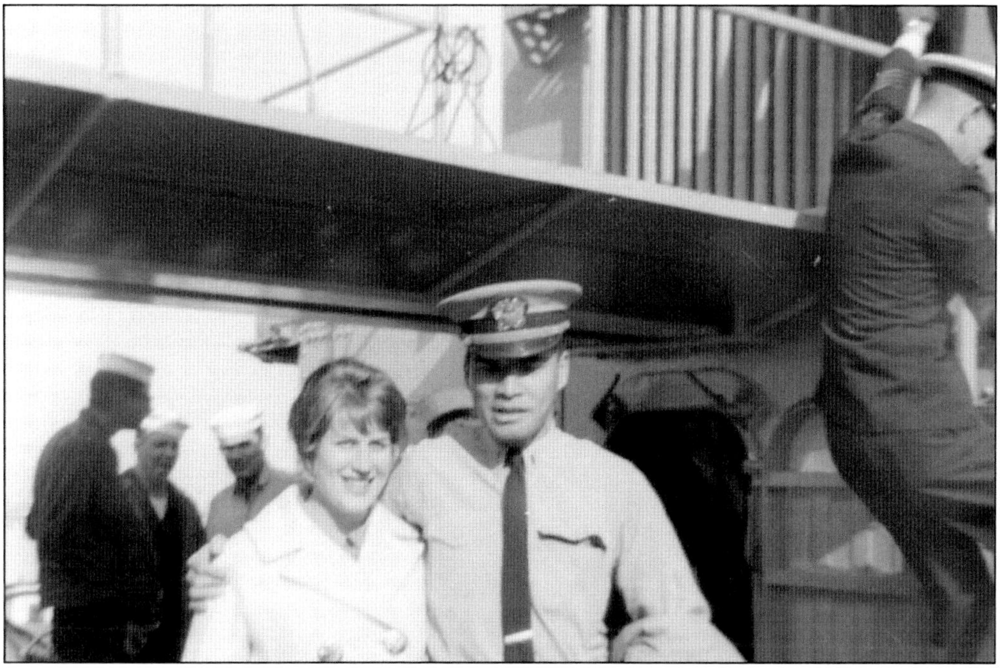

Gus Keolanui (right) and his wife, Geri (left), met in Long Beach while Gus was an officer in the Navy. Some Native Hawaiians found that outside of Hawaii they were capable of building relationships outside of those dictated by blood and race while others felt it necessary to, as the last Hawaiian king, David Kalakaua said, "Ho'oulu lahi," or "Increase the race." With each relationship, Native Hawaiians created a stronger connection to their new 'aina and new ohana. (Courtesy of Gus Keolanui.)

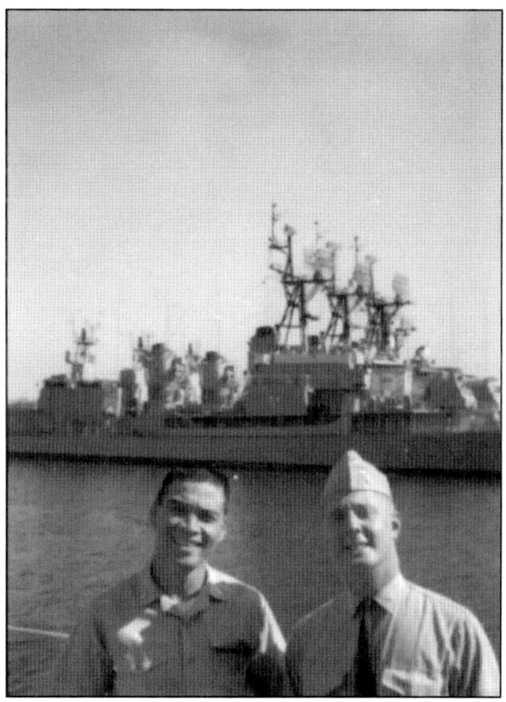

Seen here, Gus Keolanui (left) and his shipmate stand in front of a destroyer berthed at the Long Beach Naval Base. Gus spent four years in the service, which included four cruises in north and Southeast Asia and a promotion to chief engineer. His last cruise was in 1964, where he bunked on the destroyer USS *Brinkley Bass*, which patrolled the coast of North Vietnam. He left the Navy as a lieutenant commander. (Courtesy of Gus Keolanui.)

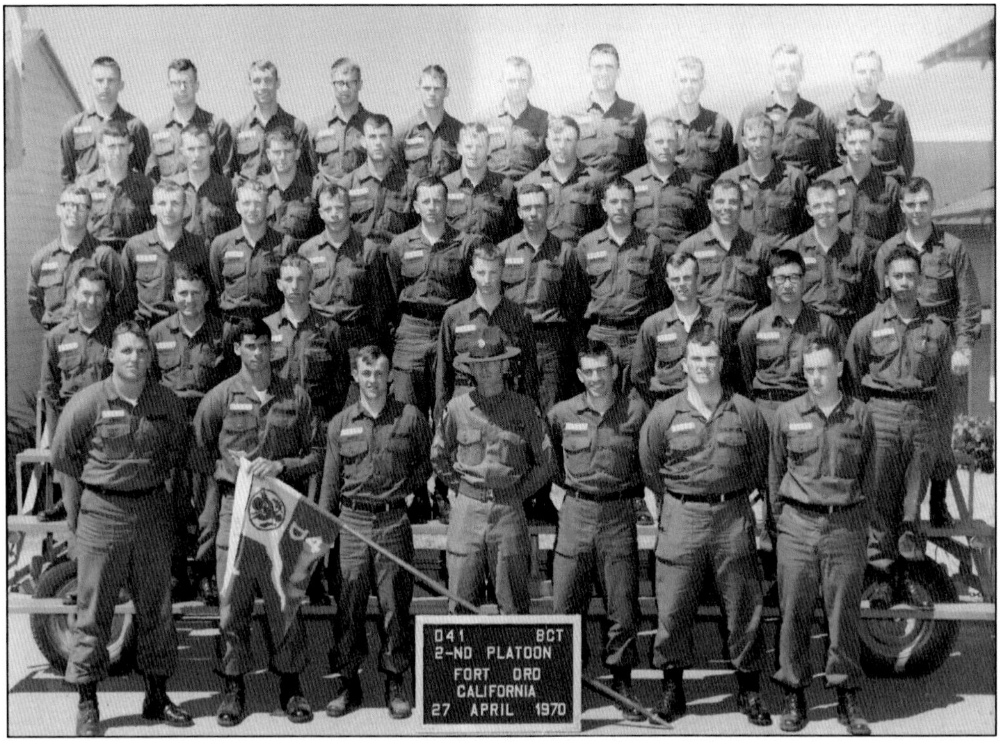

At the age of 15 and after the death of his mother, Lincoln Ke'aloha Kaio chose to go to San Pedro, California, and live with his aunt in 1965. Moving an ocean away from home at such a young age was made possible for Kaio through his ohana. Lincoln relied on the strength of ohana and stayed with his extended family on the continent. Four years later, in 1969, Kaio (on the second row and far right) was drafted in 1969 to fight in the Vietnam War. The photograph below shows Lincoln in Vietnam while serving. After the military, Lincoln returned to his family in San Pedro. (Both, courtesy of Lincoln and Sissy Kaio.)

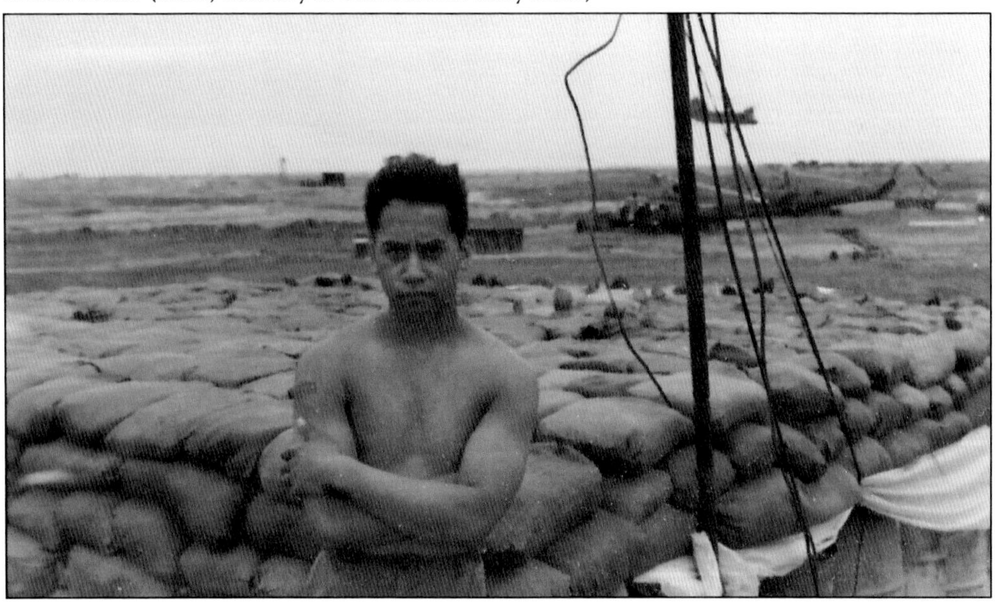

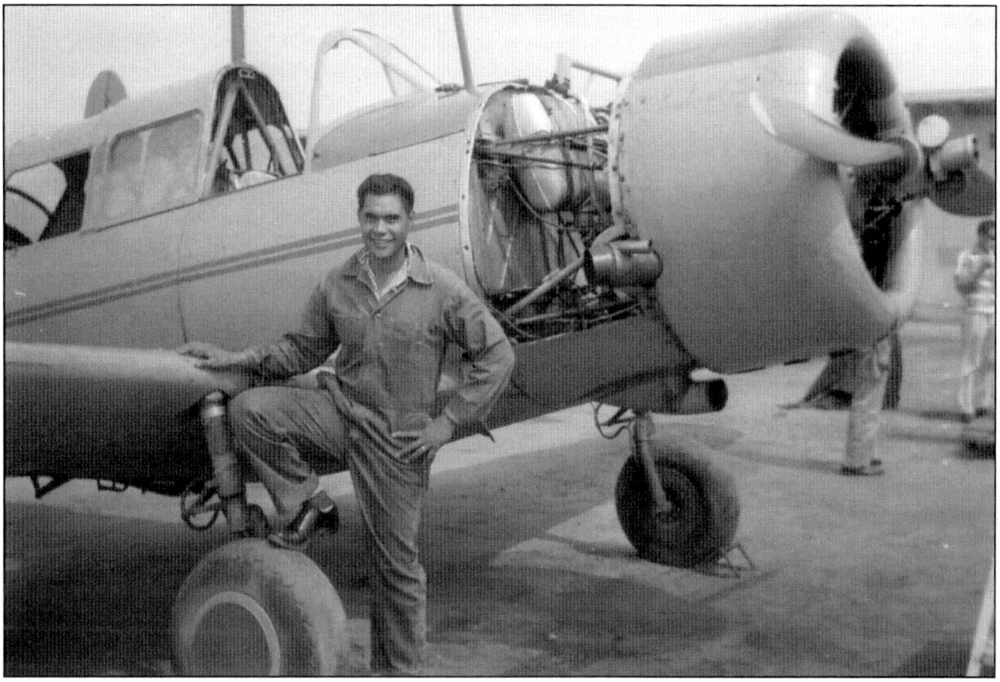

After World War II, powerful Los Angeles families led by Harry Chandler, one-time president of Los Angeles Times, used cheap land and sunshine to attract aerospace companies like Douglas Aircraft Company, Northrop, Jet Propulsion Labs, and Boeing. Aerospace offered an opportunity for a career and an education unavailable in Hawaii. Through research and innovation, these companies continue to put people into space. Shown above, Alcario "Sonny" Pelayo was a student in engineering in 1949 heading toward a career that lead toward work on space shuttles (Courtesy of the Pelayo family.)

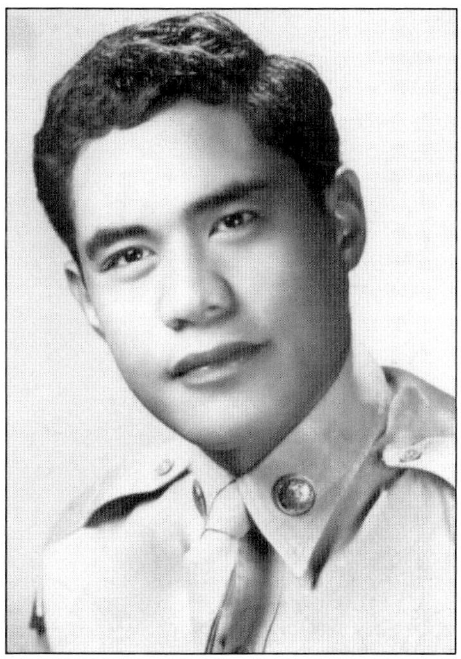

Alcario "Sonny" Pelayo is pictured in his ROTC uniform at Kamehameha School. In Hawaii, military life was ingrained in its children, and it is evident in the high number of Native Hawaiian men and women who enlist and serve in the US military. Pelayo served for the US Coast Guard in the Korean War. (Courtesy of the Pelayo family.)

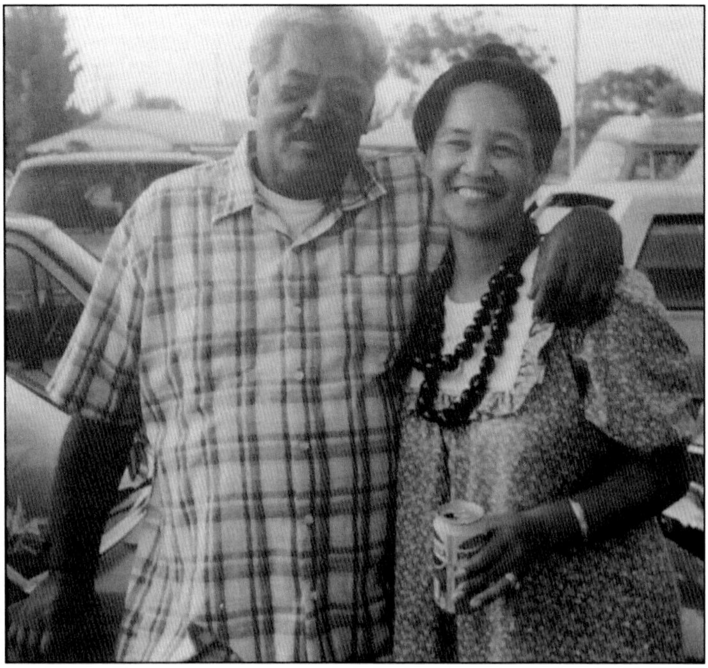

For many Native Hawaiians, Los Angeles was not their first stop in California. Historically, the entrance to America on the West Coast was Oakland or San Francisco. Paul and Elizabeth "Nani" Nihipali arrived in San Pedro, California, by way of Northern California in the 1960s. The Nihipalis were attracted to the growth of unionized construction work that was occurring during a Los Angeles growth spurt. (Courtesy of Elizabeth "Nani" Nihipali.)

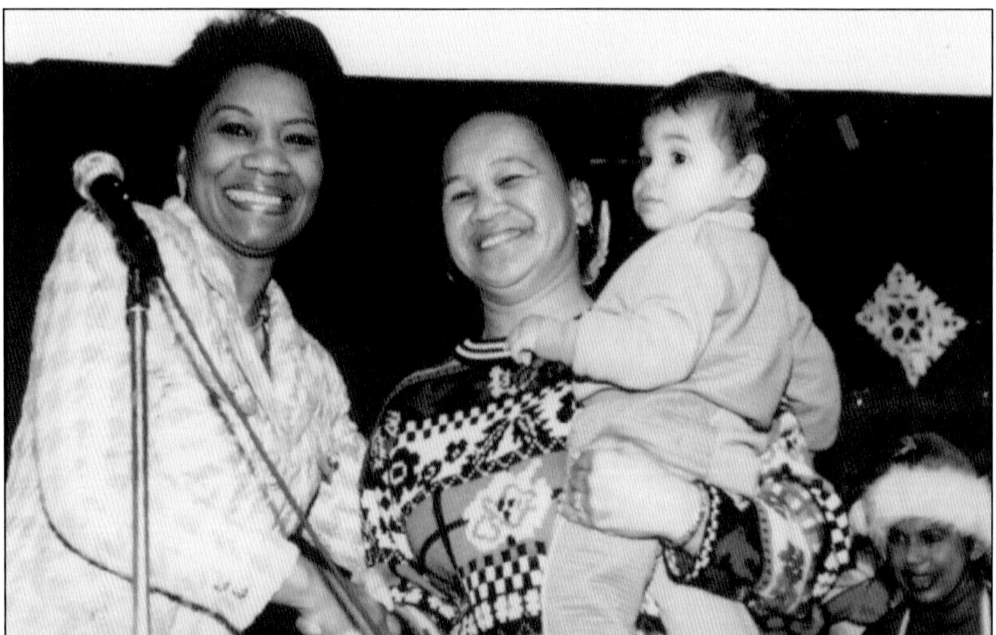

To support her children and grandchildren, Nani volunteered time with different community organizations. Her involvement led to leadership roles, such as president of the City of Carson Early Childhood Parent, Teacher, and Student Organization; commissioner of the City of Carson Parks and Recreation Department; and commissioner of City of Carson Human Relations Department. (Courtesy of Elizabeth "Nani" Nihipali.)

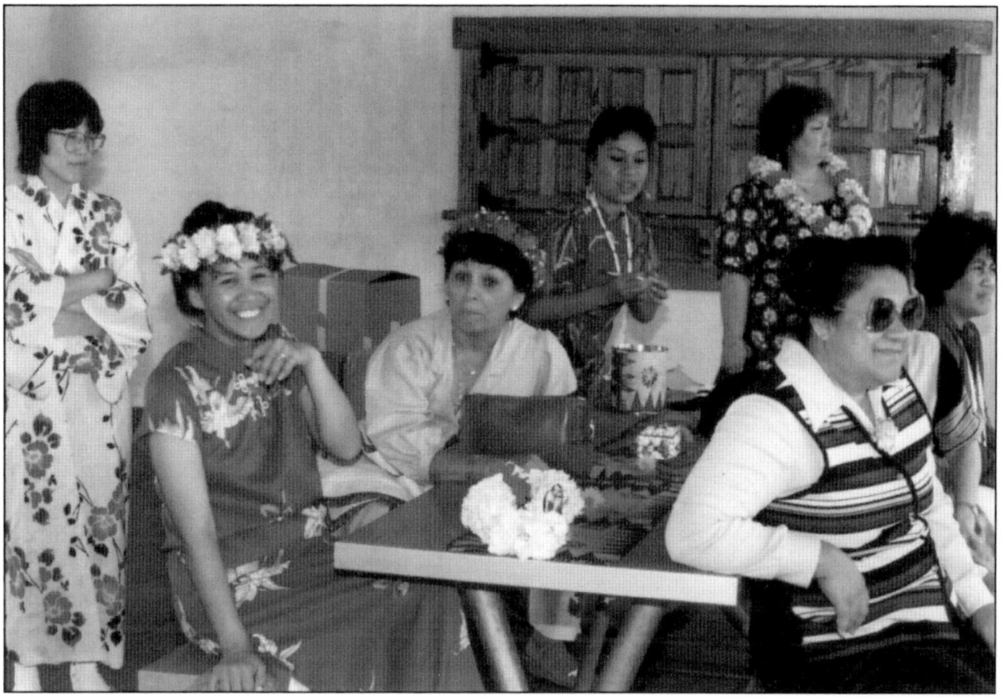

Hawaiian culture is matriarchal. This is especially evident when it comes to *kokua* (helping) to make ends meet. Above, Elizabeth "Nani" Nihipali (second from left) works at the Terminal Island Immigration office. Here, she excelled by embracing the inclusive nature of Native Hawaiian culture by participating in activities that encouraged and celebrated the various cultures of America, including her own. She also received many special awards for her work. (Courtesy of Elizabeth "Nani" Nihipali.)

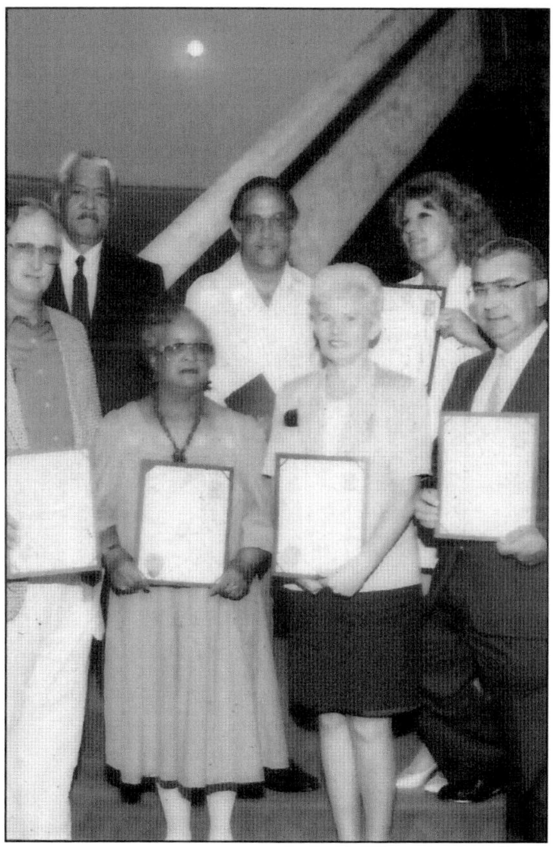

In 1993, due to his expertise with construction work, roads, and paving, Paul K. Nihipali (pictured in the back row, far left) was appointed to the City of Carson's Public Works Committee. (Courtesy of City of Carson Public Information Office.)

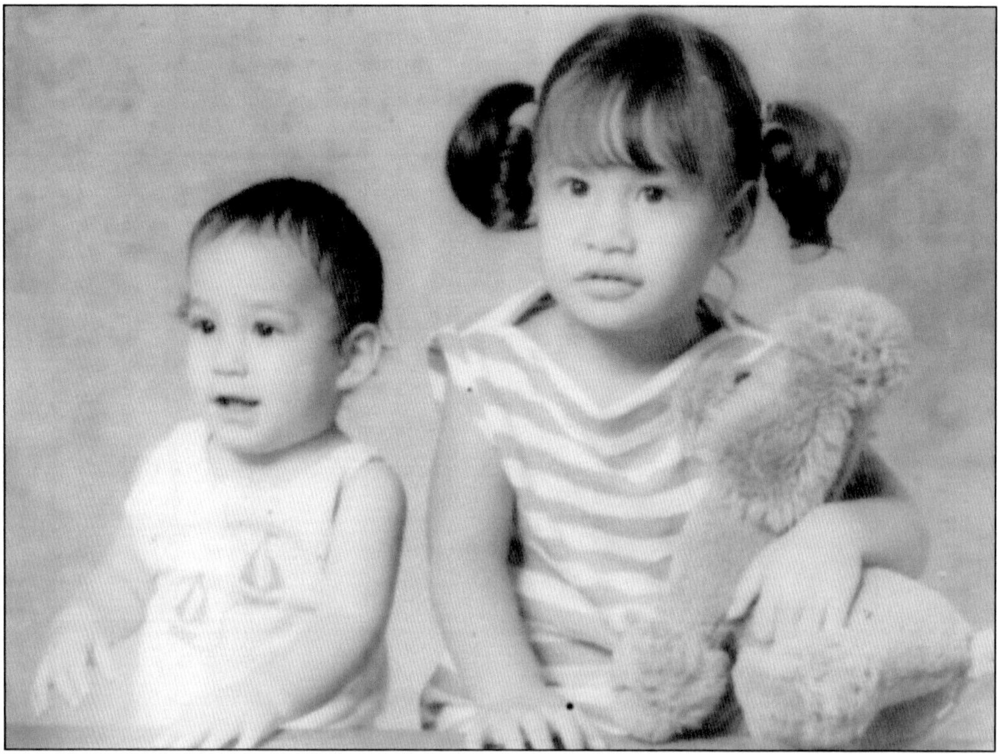

Pictured around 1972 are Frank (left) and Amber Kanani Reed (right) in Honolulu, Hawaii. Frank left Hawaii in 1982 for the continent with his father, although Amber stayed behind to live with her aunt. Frank lived in Van Nuys when he passed away of HIV complications in 2008. Despite not liking this state, Amber moved from Kalihi on Oahu to California in 2001 and settled in the City of Gardena. (Courtesy of Amber Reed.)

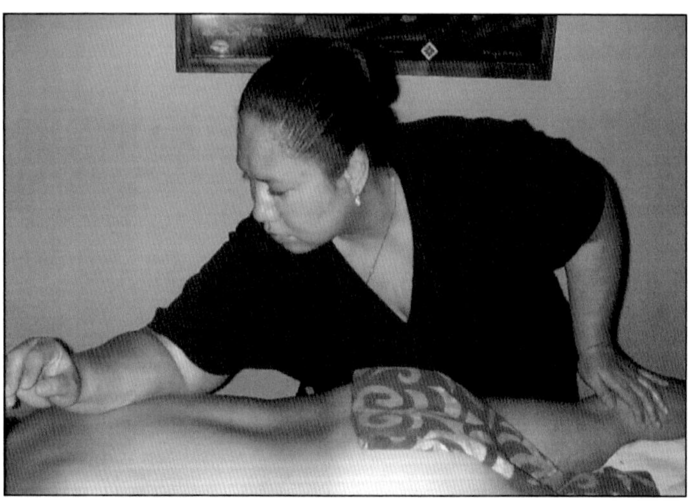

Amber Kanani Reed lived in Kalihi before coming to Los Angeles. She became a Lomi Lomi massage therapist because it was her belief that all ailments or conditions in the body stem from a blockage of proper flow of energy and a misalignment in its structure. Here, Amber demonstrates her massage technique on her significant other, Eric Chang. (Courtesy of Amber Reed.)

Duke Kaleiali'i Brown (right) comes from a line of Hawaiian-Chinese ancestry. He is pictured with his partner, Mark Williams, and their dog Honey Girl. His mother named him after surf pioneer Duke Kahanamoku. Duke came to Los Angeles in 1994 and has worked in the airline industry for nearly two decades. Duke is also the founder of Duke's Designs, a company that designs and creates handbags and accessories. His handbags are influenced by Hawaiian culture and its reverence for beauty in nature. Many of his designs showcase images of tropical flowers, wildlife, and landscapes from the islands. Island design combined with simplicity, utility, and durability provide the foundation of Duke's style and an homage to the islands. Pictured below is a sample of one of Duke's totes, a brown canvass accented with a wooden hand carved *honu* (turtle). (Both, courtesy of Duke Kaleiali'i Brown.)

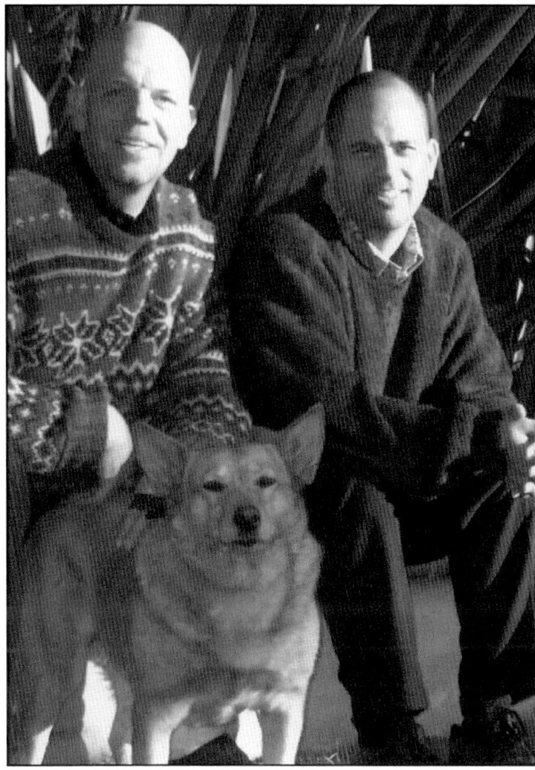

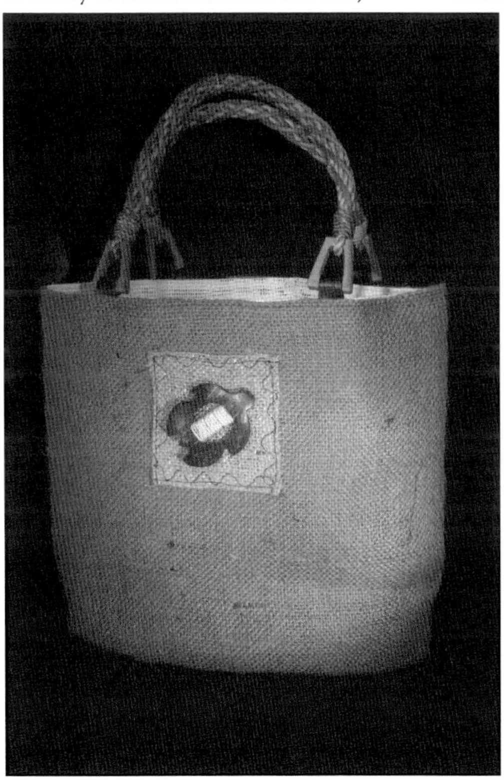

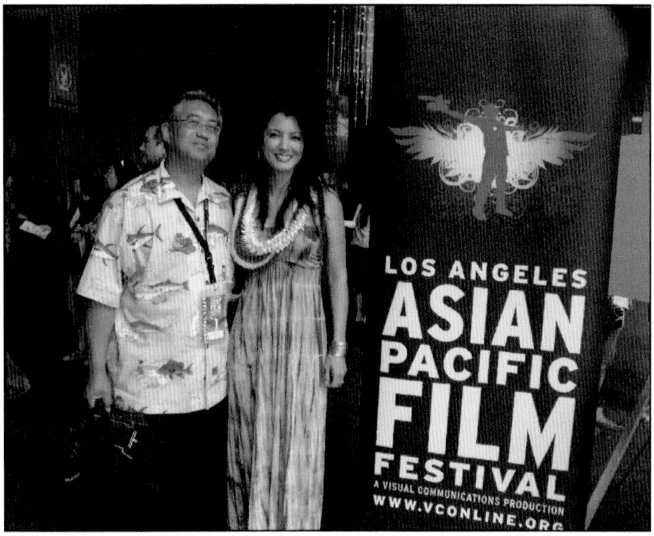

When it comes to working in Hollywood, Native Hawaiians occupy an interesting place. Because many are mixed race, they can portray multiple roles. Pictured above, Kelly Hu (right) is an actress and model born in Honolulu, Hawaii, and is of Native Hawaiian, Chinese, and English descent. Florante Peter Ibanez (left) is a community photographer, author, and 2010 president of the Asian/Pacific American Librarians Association. (Courtesy of Florante Peter Ibanez.)

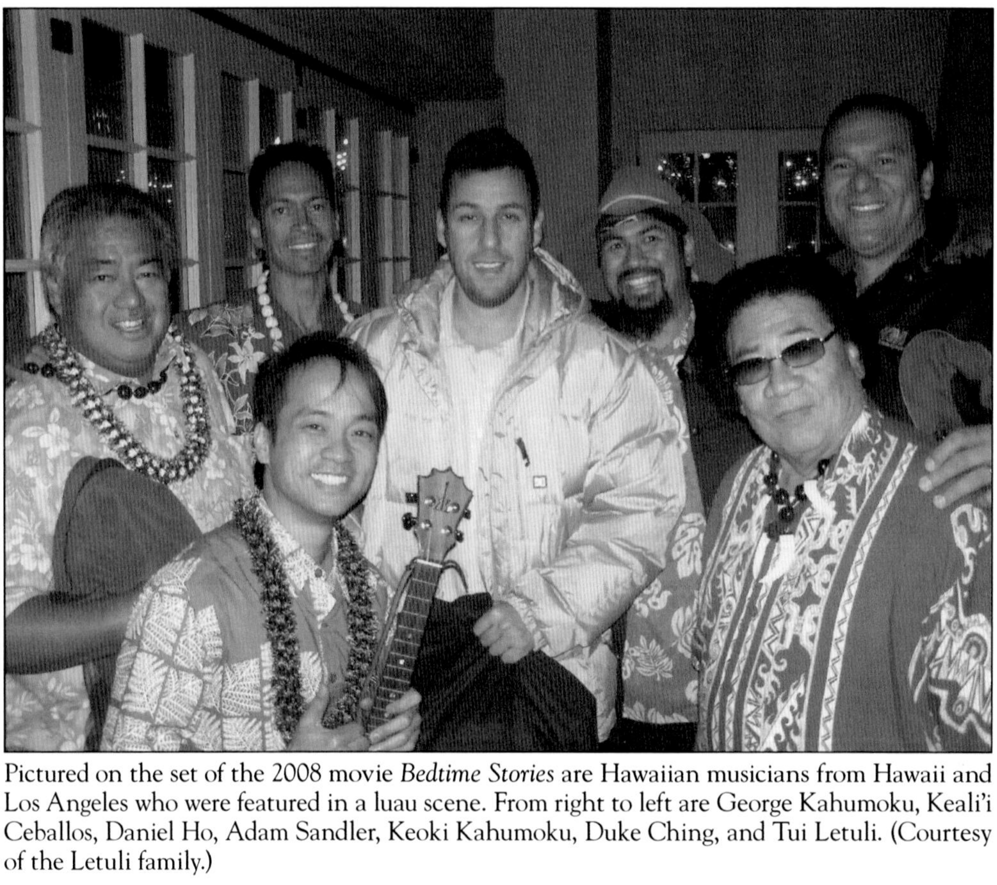

Pictured on the set of the 2008 movie *Bedtime Stories* are Hawaiian musicians from Hawaii and Los Angeles who were featured in a luau scene. From right to left are George Kahumoku, Keali'i Ceballos, Daniel Ho, Adam Sandler, Keoki Kahumoku, Duke Ching, and Tui Letuli. (Courtesy of the Letuli family.)

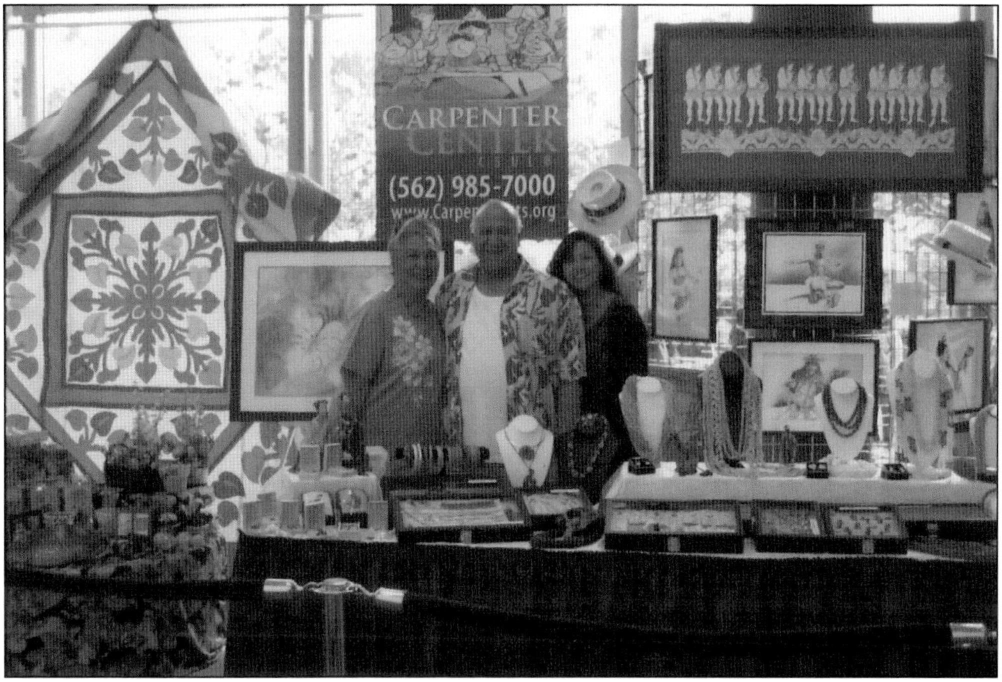

Alice Richmond turned her heritage into a business by selling the crafts she made as well as other Polynesian pieces. She prided herself on making historically accurate *Hawaiiana* (a popular term of academia used in reference to history and various aspects of Hawaiian culture) available to diasporic Hawaiians. She would pride herself on her ability to recognize a fellow native and offer them a price they could afford. Her booth, Hawaiian Connection, has been a staple at the Alondra Park Ho'olaule'a since the 1980s and continues after her death through her goddaughter Maile Pelayo Letuli. Below is a photograph of her merchandise acting as artifacts at the Long Beach Aquarium of the Pacific's Polynesian Festival. (Both, courtesy of the Letuli family.)

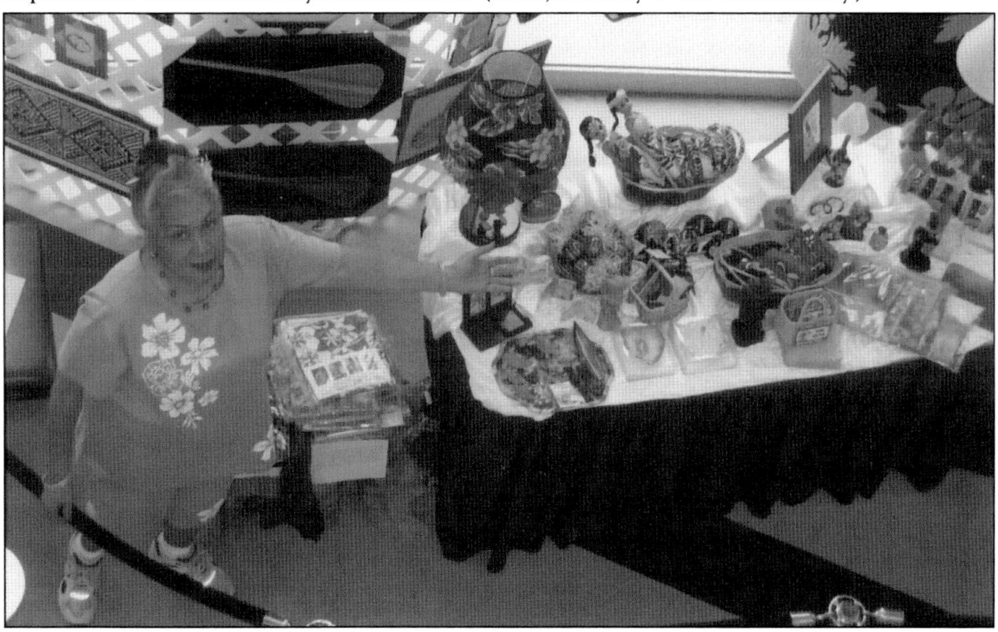

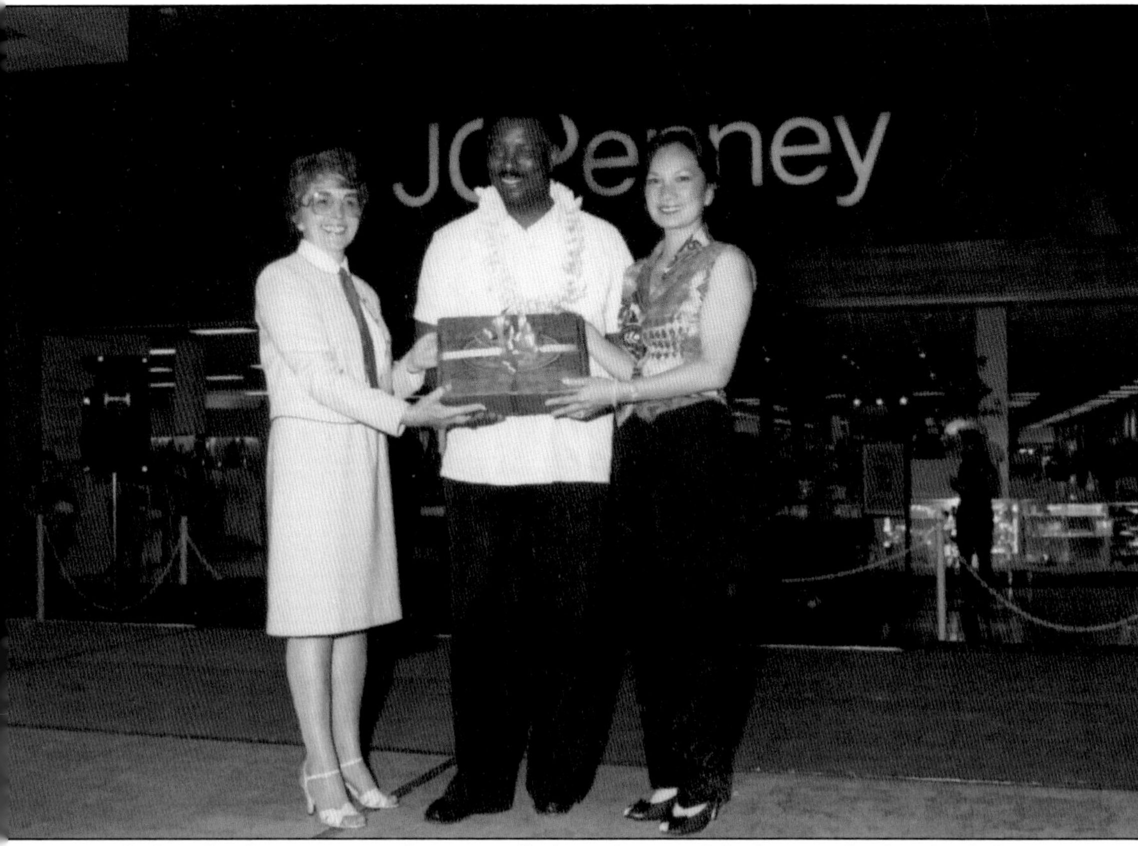

The benefit of growing up with a sense of *kuleana* (responsibility) is a work ethic that helps Native Hawaiians excel in their workplace. Arleen Laimana (right) came to California from Honolulu, Hawaii, in November 1959. As community representative for Bank of America, she maintained a high profile in the Carson community by supporting business ventures through corporate sponsorship and fundraisers. Arlene became a major resource for Hawaiian civic clubs, such as Sissy and Lincoln Kaio's halau, Na Pua Me Ke Aloha, and Mary Kovich's Lei Hulu of California. (Courtesy of Lincoln and Sissy Kaio.)

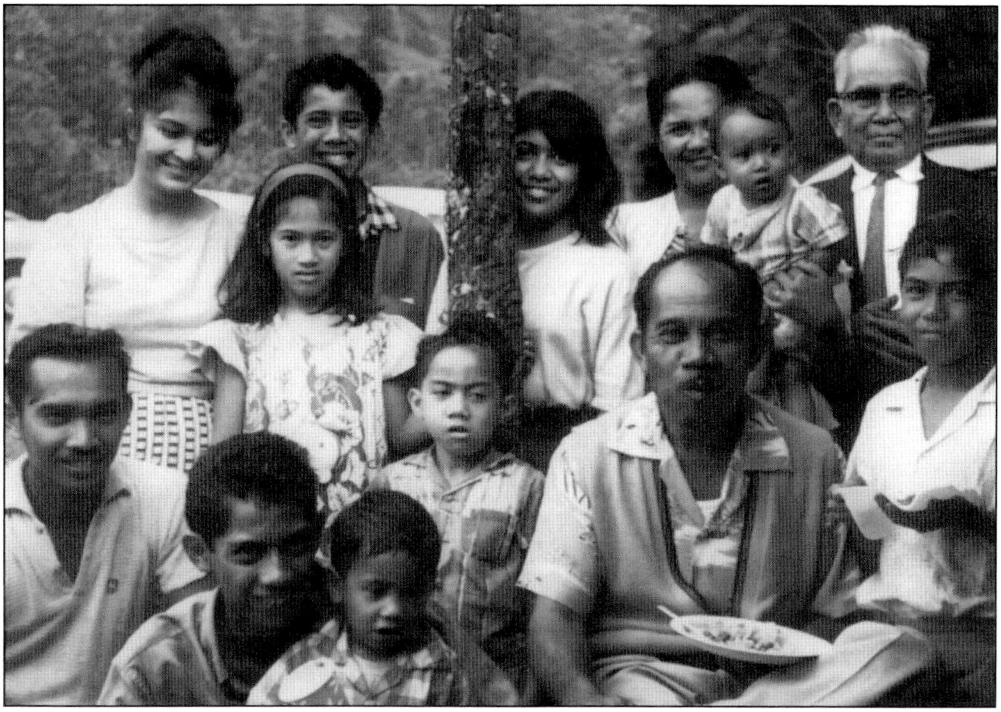

The Brigoli family has been in charge of the official design and distribution of the Alondra Park Ho'olaule'a T-shirt since 1977. Wally Maxilom (married to Sharon Brigoli) owned Wally's Creative Designs in Carson, California, and was the first to get involved with Ho'olaule'a. In 1990, when he and Sharon left to go back to Hawaii, Tony Brigoli, Wally's brother in-law, took over. His print shop was run out of the garage of his home. Since 1993, when Tony went back to Hawaii, the honor and the rights were passed to Albert (pictured above in the first row, second from the right) and Laydeen Brigoli. Pictured above is Albert Brigoli's family after a church get-together in Kaneohe, Oahu. Pictured on the right is a Ho'olaule'a T-shirt designed by the Brigoli family. (Above, courtesy of the Brigoli family; below, courtesy of Christian Hanz Lozada.)

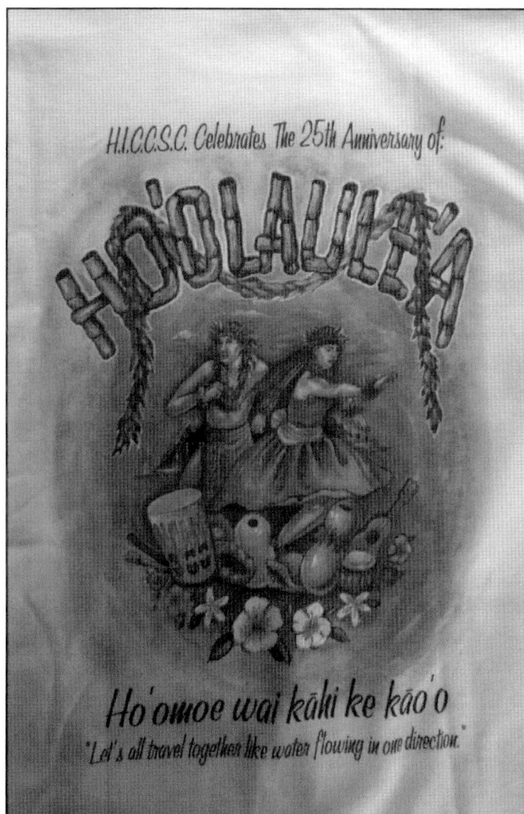

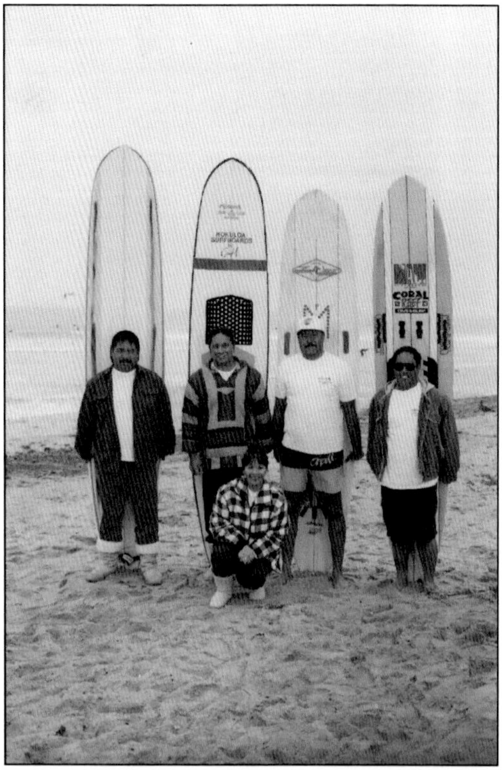

Carson resident Anthony Marasco Jr. was one of the founding members of the Surf Club of San Onofre. In the late 1980s, Raymond Patterson, Anthony's friend from San Clemente, passed away. Raymond's wish was to "take friends who haven't been to Hawaii to San Onofre and show them the aloha spirit." To fulfill that wish, Anthony started the surf club. Pictured from left to right are Sandy Kanaeholo, Kalani Akui, Helen "Ahoi" Marasco (kneeling in front), Frank Anthony Marasco Jr., and Alfred Kuhia. (Courtesy of Frank A. Marasco Jr.)

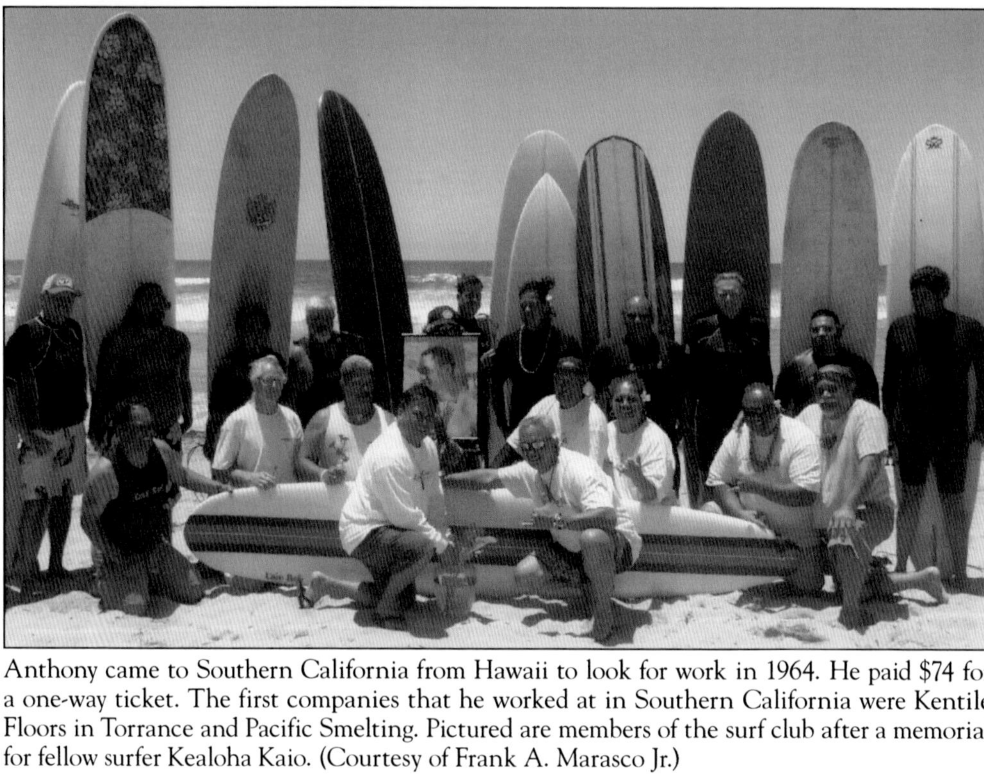

Anthony came to Southern California from Hawaii to look for work in 1964. He paid $74 for a one-way ticket. The first companies that he worked at in Southern California were Kentile Floors in Torrance and Pacific Smelting. Pictured are members of the surf club after a memorial for fellow surfer Kealoha Kaio. (Courtesy of Frank A. Marasco Jr.)

Being so far from home and isolated in many cases, Native Hawaiians started to connect with other Native Hawaiians when possible and with locals when it was not possible to connect with other natives. Building upon this distance and coinciding with the changing times, these relationships crossed racial boundaries that had been looked down upon in the islands. On the right, Helen Kekauoha and Ahin Kahawaii are celebrating their marriage in 1979. Ahin later started Western Waste Management. (Courtesy of the Kekauoha family.)

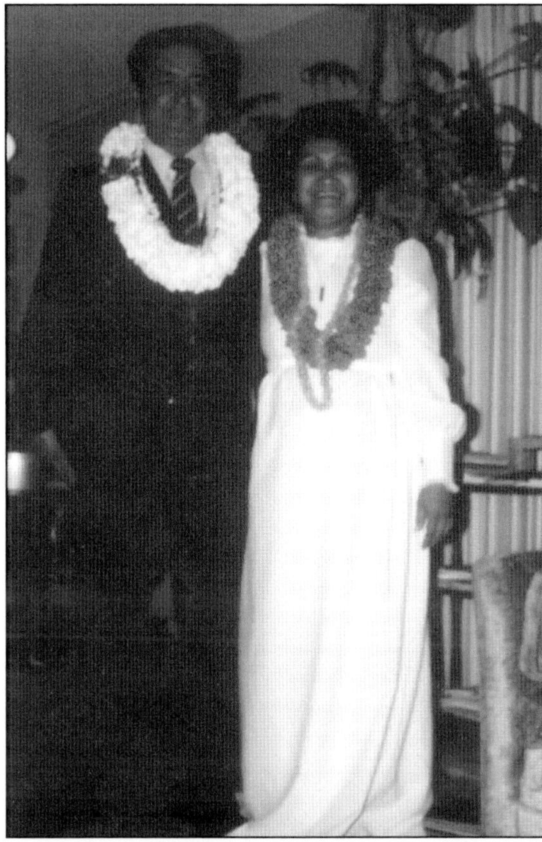

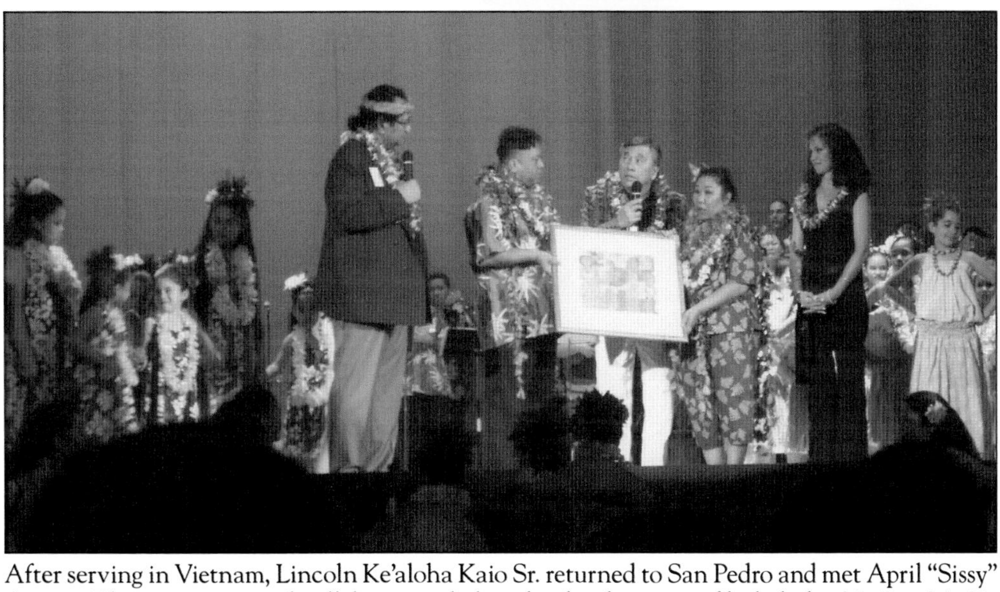

After serving in Vietnam, Lincoln Ke'aloha Kaio Sr. returned to San Pedro and met April "Sissy" Aguon. Their marriage and collaboration led to the development of hula halau Na Pua Me Ke Aloha. Building upon their shared cultural heritage, strengthened by aloha for each other and their students, Lincoln and Sissy's hula halau has become a staple in the South Bay. (Courtesy of Lincoln and Sissy Kaio.)

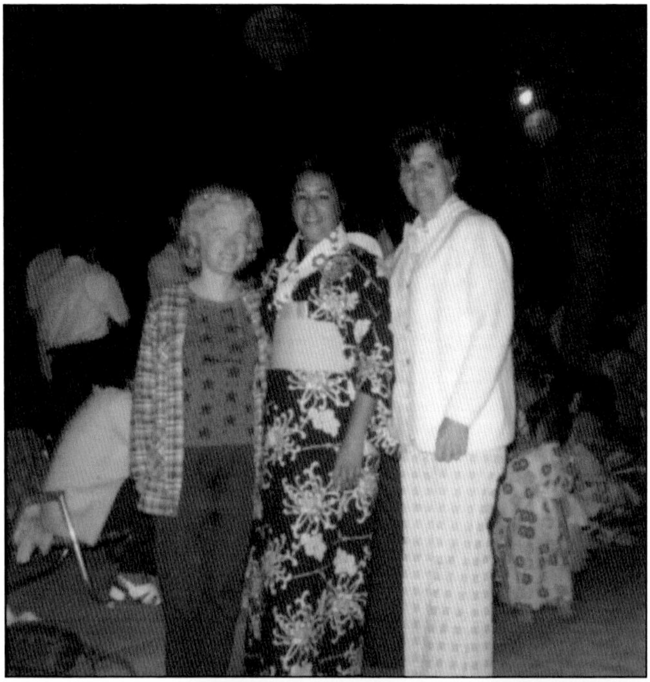

As relationships between races opened up, the tendency for Native Hawaiians to accept and celebrate other cultures became more visible. As ohana expanded, so did Hawaiian culture. Pictured here, Mary and Alcano "Sonny" Pelayo took part in the Obon festival with the South Bay Japanese Cultural Institute. (Both, courtesy of the Pelayo family.)

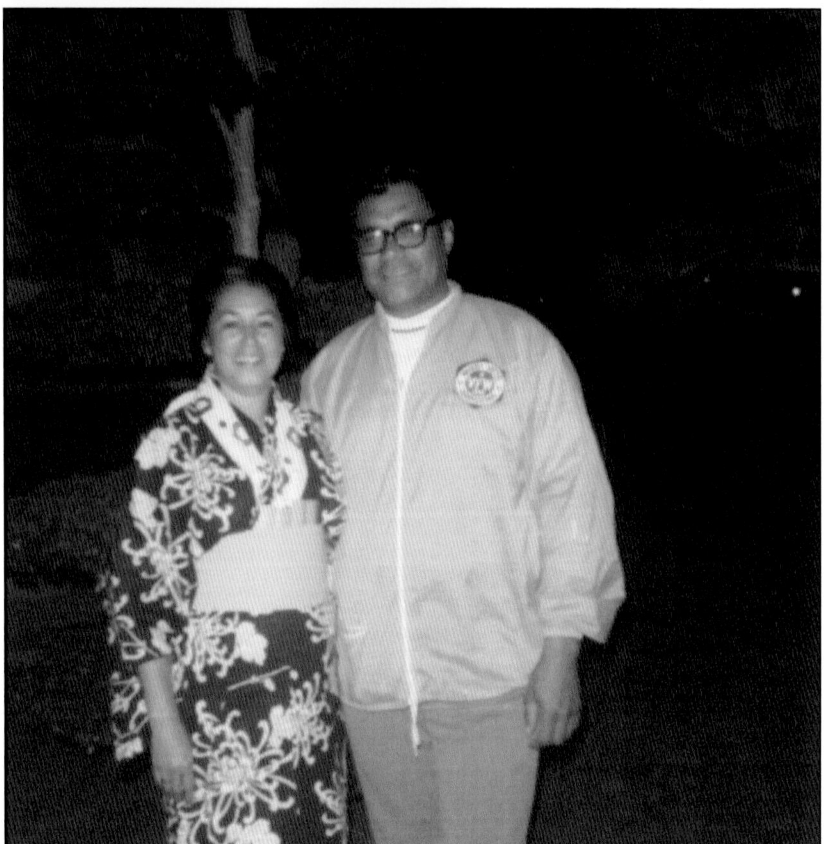

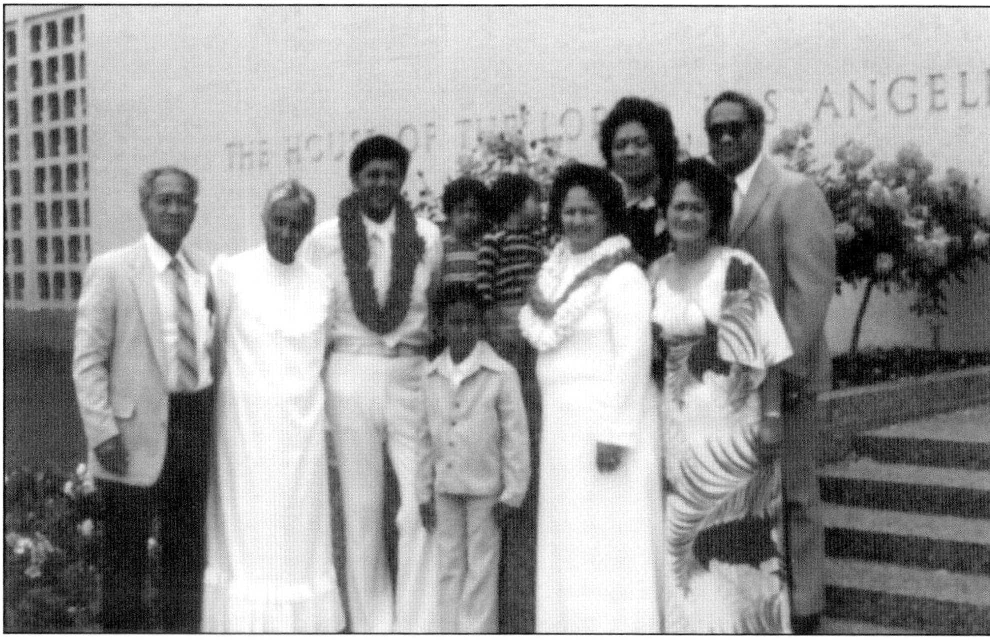

As much as expanding ohana embraces other cultures and traditions, Native Hawaiians sometimes adhere to devout belief systems that can be strengthened on the continent. Shown here is the Kekauoha family at the sealing of Hosea and Maile Kekauoha (also shown below), which took place at the Santa Monica Church of Jesus Christ of Latter-day Saints Temple. (Both, courtesy of the Kekauoha family.)

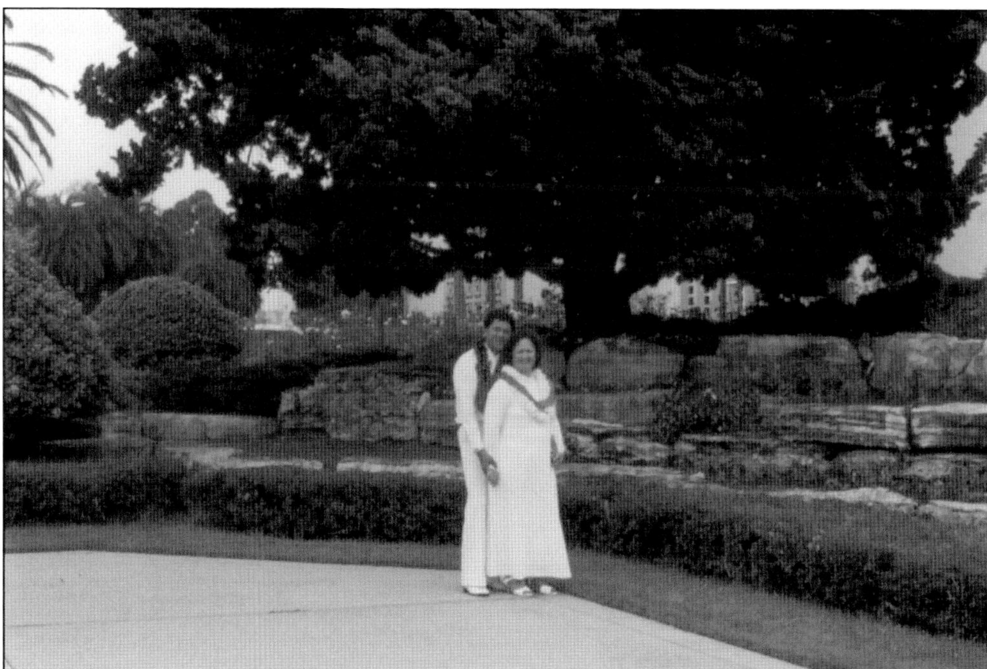

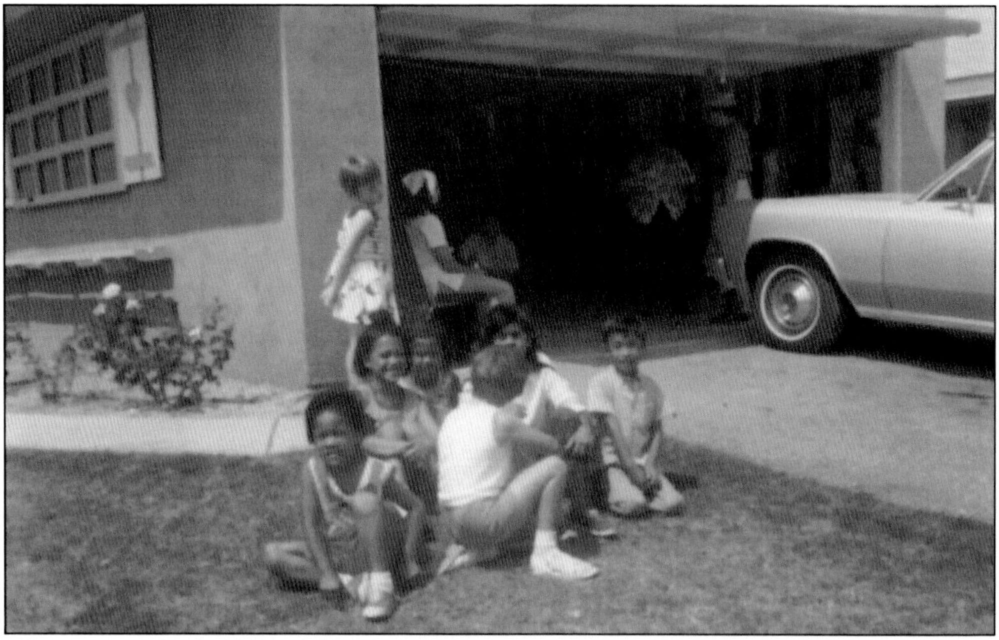

The economic foothold afforded by the growing industries in California allowed Native Hawaiians to root themselves in the Los Angeles landscape. One of the biggest rites of passage for any Angeleno is purchasing a single family home on the outskirts of the city. Shown above are the children of the Tanemura and Pelayo families with other *keiki* (children) playing in the front yard of the Tanemura home. Shown below from left to right are Branscombe and Alice Richmond, Al Sonny Pelayo, and John Chave standing in front of their new garage. (Above, courtesy of the Tanemura family; below, courtesy of the Pelayo family.)

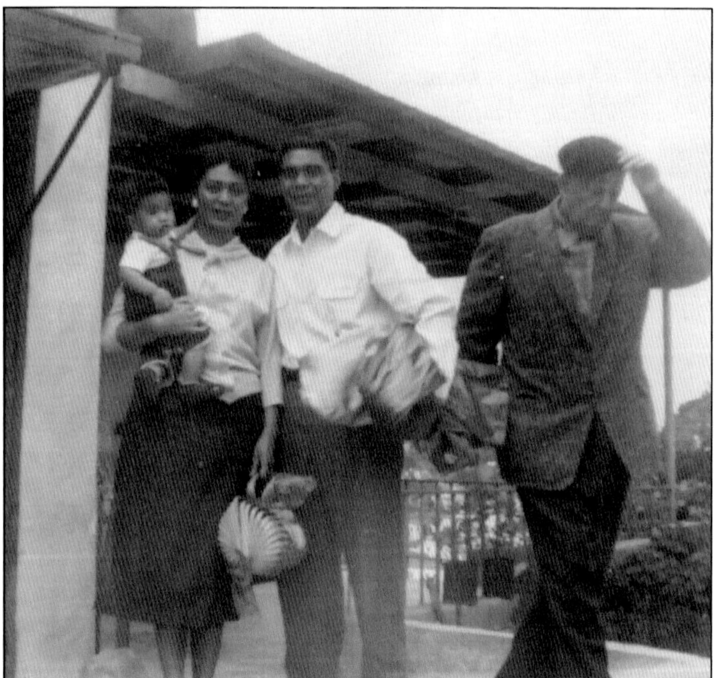

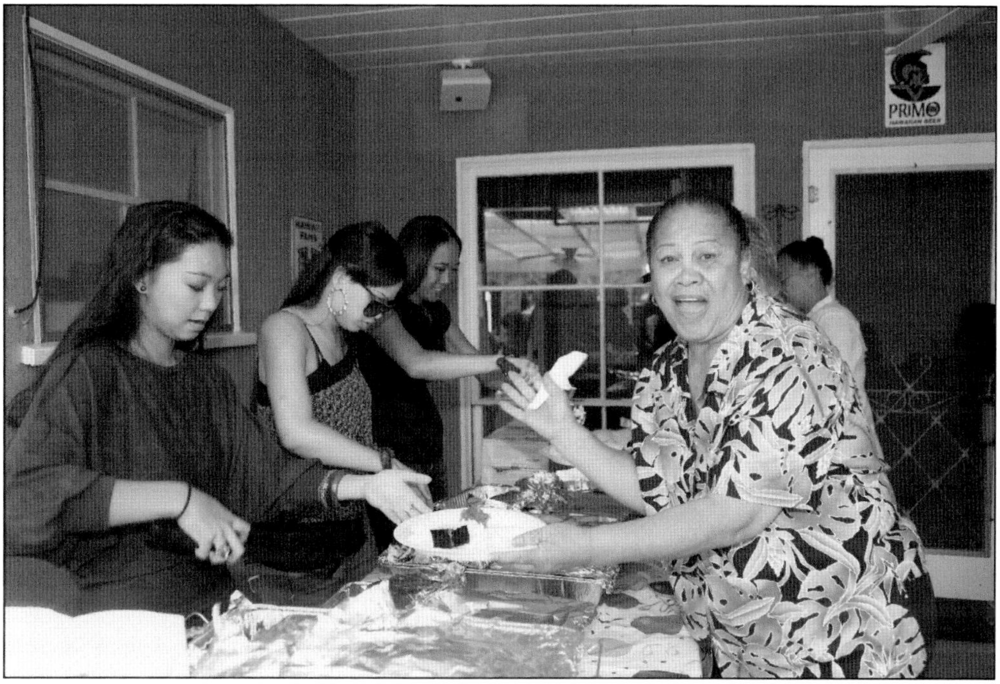

Having a home means being able to spread aloha in a way that cannot be done in an apartment or on one's own. Having a home means that one's ohana has a place to gather, and once together, the family can reaffirm who they are, where they come from, and where they are going. In the pictures above and below, the Nihipali family holds large family gatherings in their backyard. The events may look catered, but the food is made by ohana, and the large quantities are necessary to feed the guests who cycle through the home for hours on end. (Both, courtesy of the Nihipali family.)

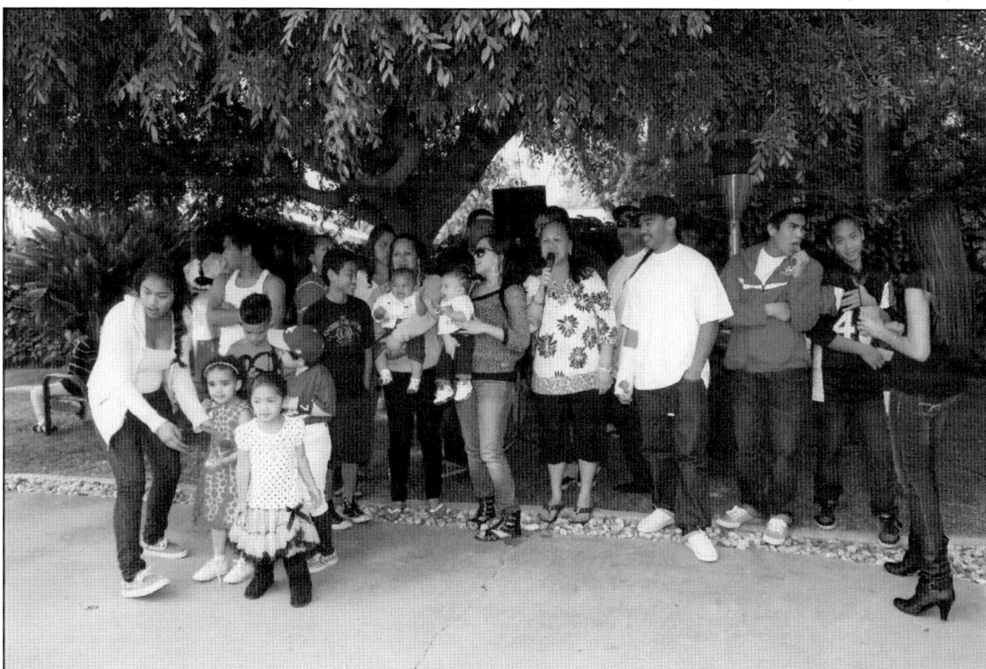

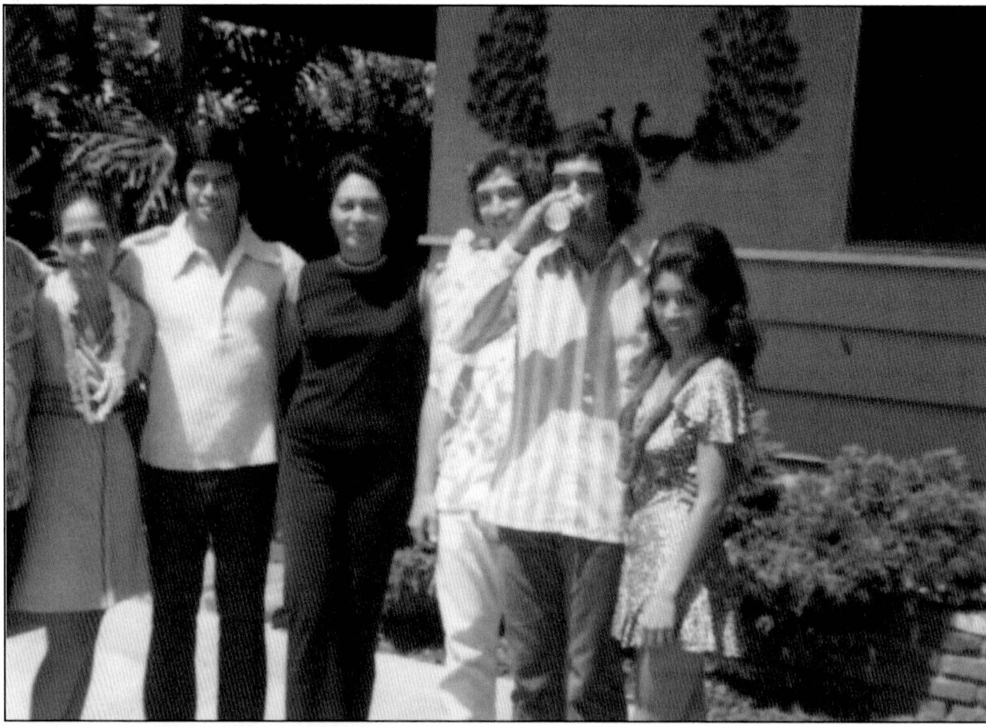

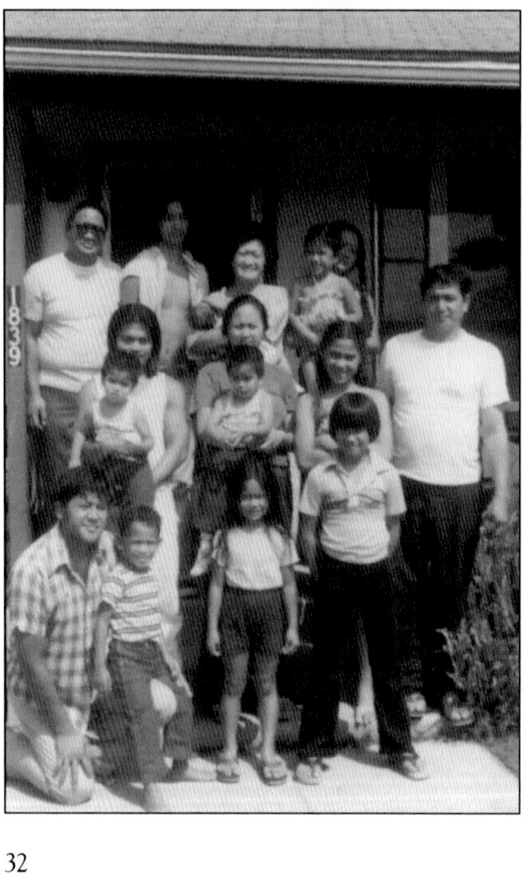

After the original Native Hawaiian migrants made a home in Los Angeles, they could celebrate their aloha by extending it to family in Hawaii. Shown above are Ipolani and Palani Vaughn (far left) from Oahu staying at the Pelayo home in Torrance, California. On the left is a photograph of the Kekauoha's extended family. Ohana and kuleana make it almost unacceptable to allow visiting family to stay anywhere else other than a relative's home, if not the relative's own bed. (Above, courtesy of the Pelayo family; below, courtesy of the Kekauoha family.)

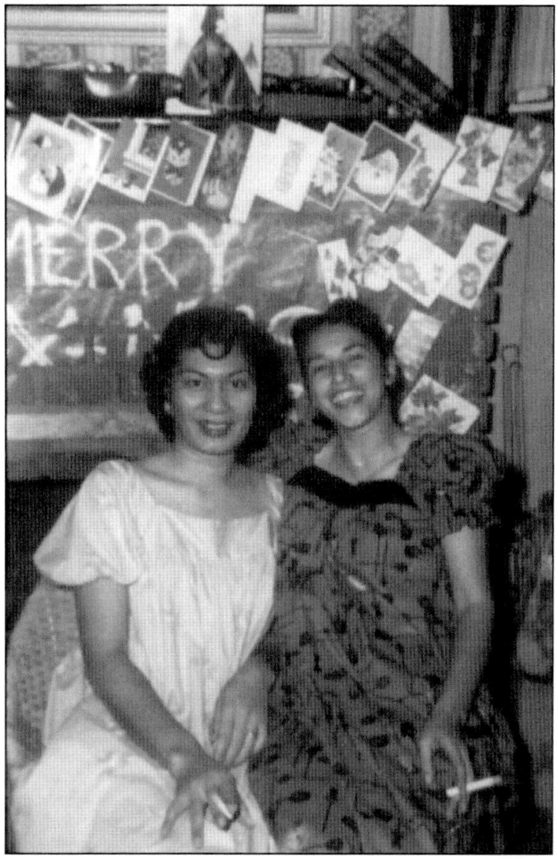

With more possibility for financial success and stability, Native Hawaiians gathered family around them near and far for two very specific occasions: holidays and babies. Their success in the 1950s also enticed family to make the jump over an ocean. Alice Richmond (who moved to California after her brother, Alcario "Sonny" Pelayo) is pictured on the left with Mary Pelayo. The sister-in-laws knitted their families together by reinforcing aloha. In this sense, aloha means love and generosity because their homes were open to each other. (Courtesy of the Pelayo family.)

Below is Mary Pelayo entertaining Rose Kalei Pelayo, her mother-in-law, from Oahu. (Courtesy of the Pelayo family.)

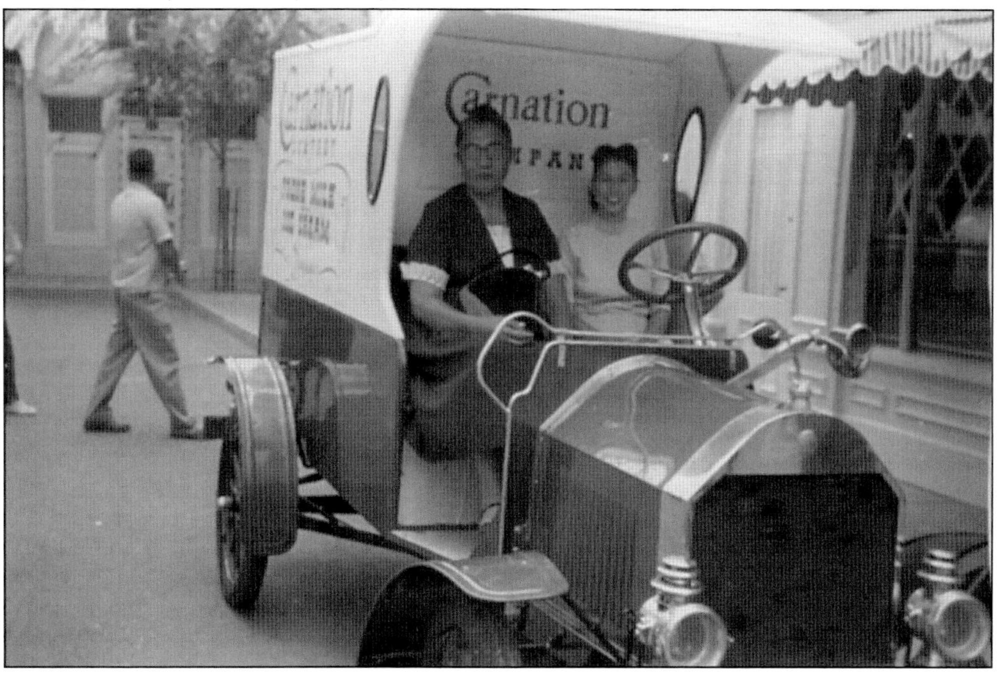

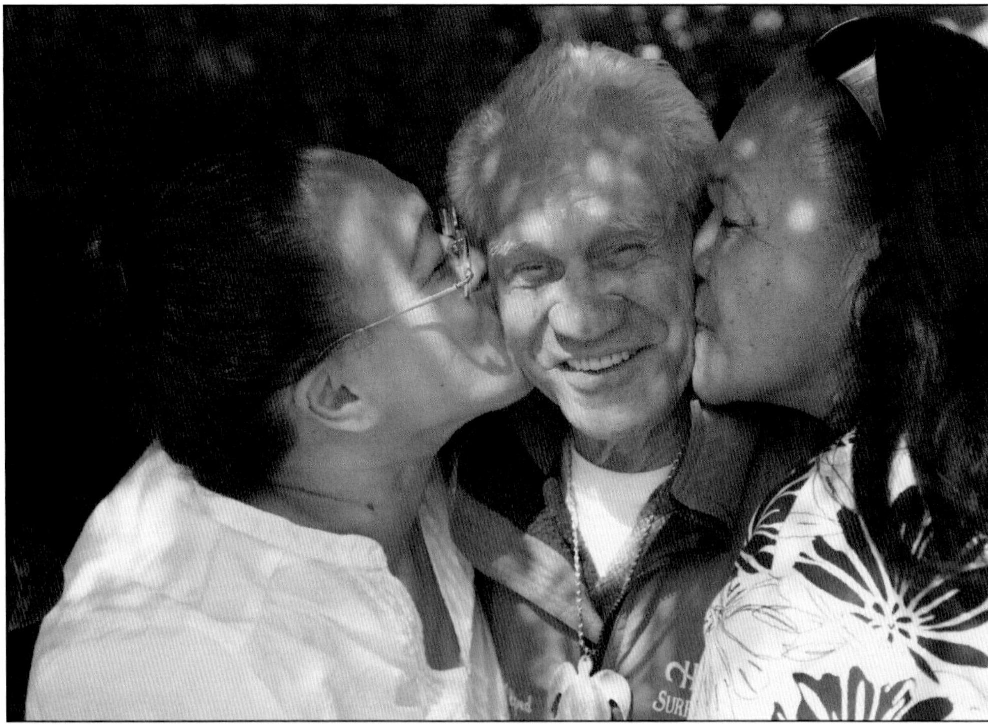

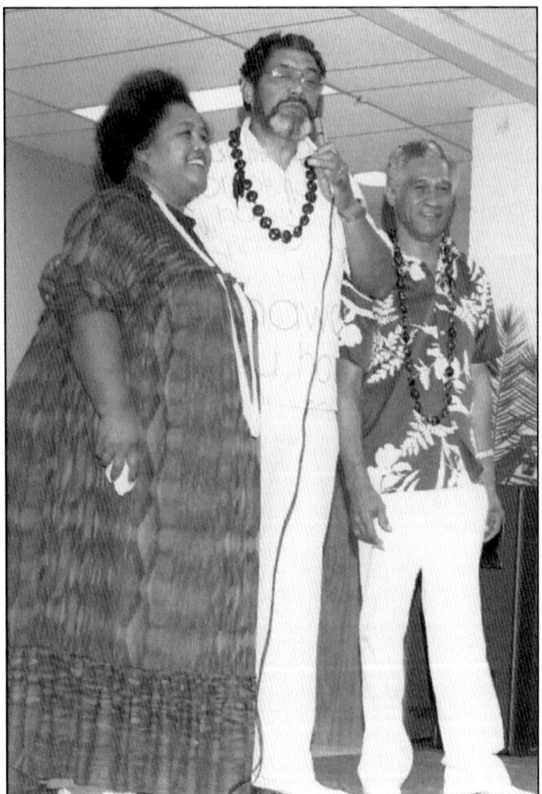

Pictured below from left to right are Elizabeth Kuhia, Alcario "Sonny" Pelayo, and David Kuhia. The Kuhias followed their daughter Nani (above, on the right) to Northern California and then to San Pedro. Their primary motivation was to help raise their first grandchild, Laydeen (above and on the left). The Kuhias had to decide between continuing life on the islands or following their children to the continent. Hawaii makes this decision difficult because one will lose much more than one will gain. The family one embraces is more intimate but smaller compared to the family one leaves behind. The home one creates has so much less history than the land one abandons. In keeping with Native Hawaiian tradition of hanai, Laydeen was given to her grandparents to learn kanaka tradition. Growing up, Laydeen learned how to perpetuate Hawaiian tradition through hula and civil service. (Above, courtesy of Elizabeth "Nani" Nihipali; below, courtesy of the Pelayo family.)

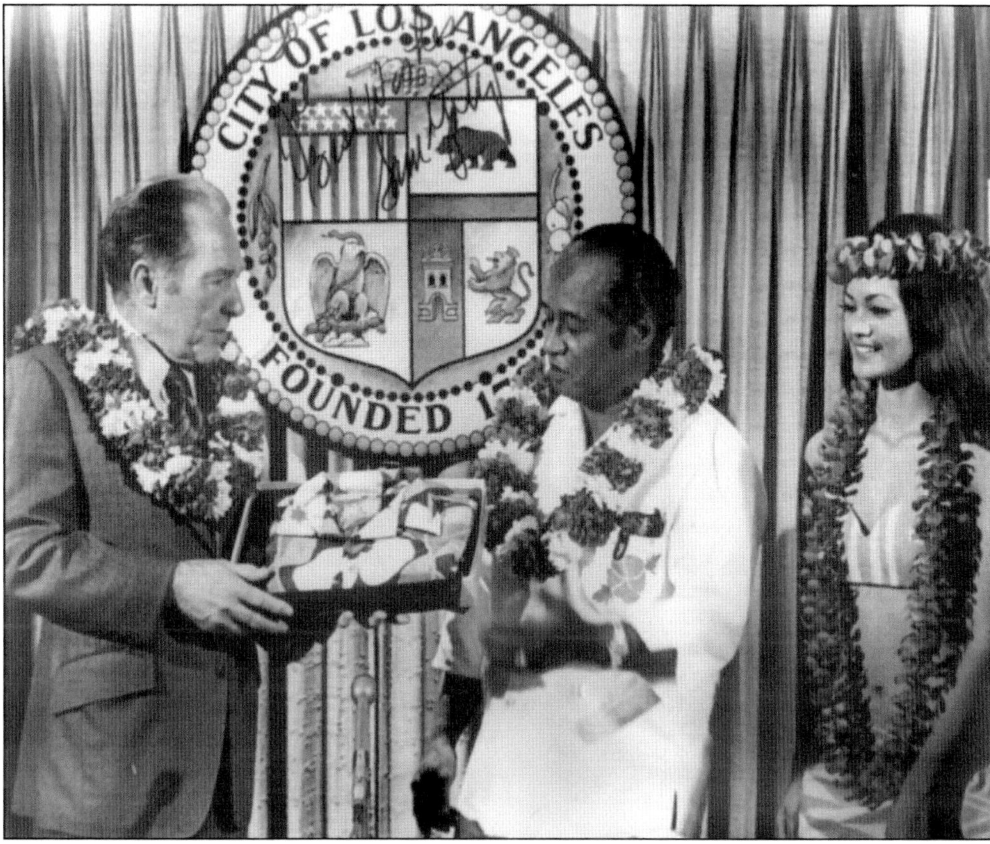

To reinforce the idea of being a distinct people, the first generation Hawaiians in Los Angeles started news outlets to keep the diasporic community informed of events in Hawaii and in the new Los Angeles Hawaiian community. The *Voice of Hawaii*, started by Bobby and Mary Chun, was one of those outlets that became a staple for Hawaiians abroad and not just in Southern California. Pictured above is Joe Keawe, president of the Polynesian Society, receiving an award for his work in the Los Angeles Hawaiian community. Below, from left to right are Joe Keawe, Luana Kuni, Ralph Nagao, and Doris Keawe. (Both, courtesy of Charmaine Kuni Keoho.)

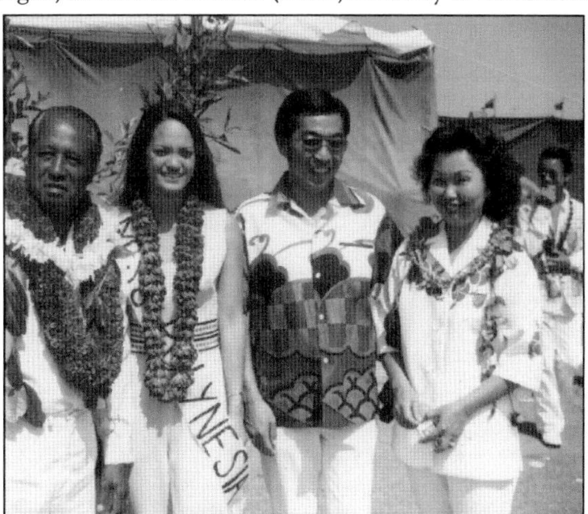

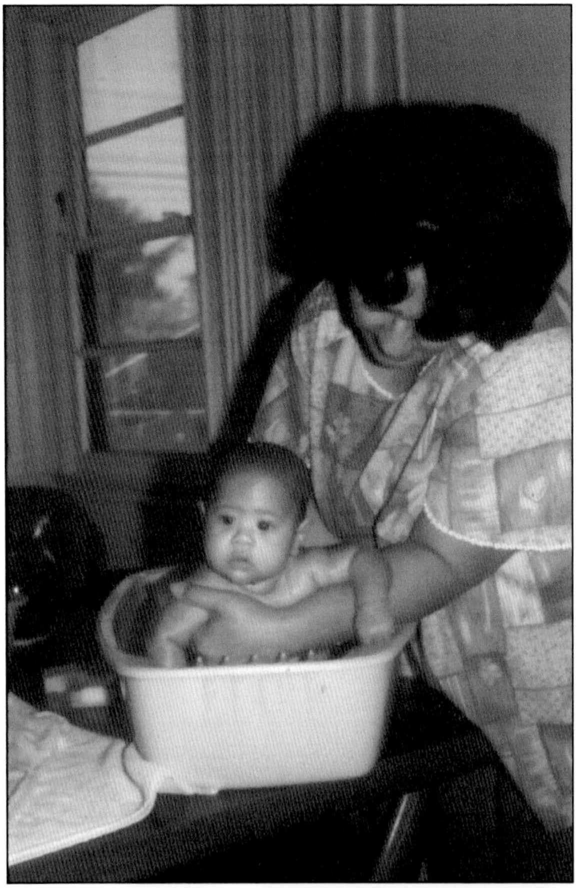

There is more than one way to grow ohana. As Native Hawaiians formed relationships and marriages on the continent, they naturally started having children. One of the Kekauoha children is pictured on the left enjoying a bath. Below, Alena is pictured with his mother, Jeraldine Tanemura. Having children is an important step for Native Hawaiians because of the twofold isolation on the continent. Daily life in Hawaii is a smaller scale; it is common to run into family and friends often. In the sprawl of Los Angeles, it is common not to run into family and friends for weeks or months on end. Native Hawaiian children help remedy this loneliness by attracting distant relatives, combining resources, and teaching the values of ohana, kuleana, and malama. (Above, courtesy of the Kekauoha family; below, courtesy of the Tanemura family.)

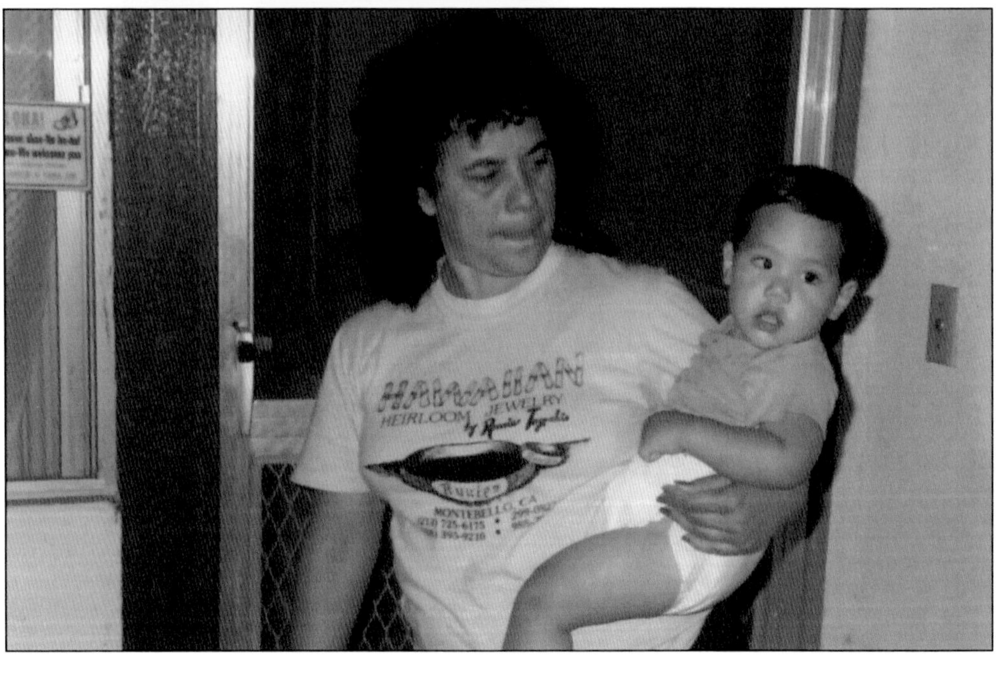

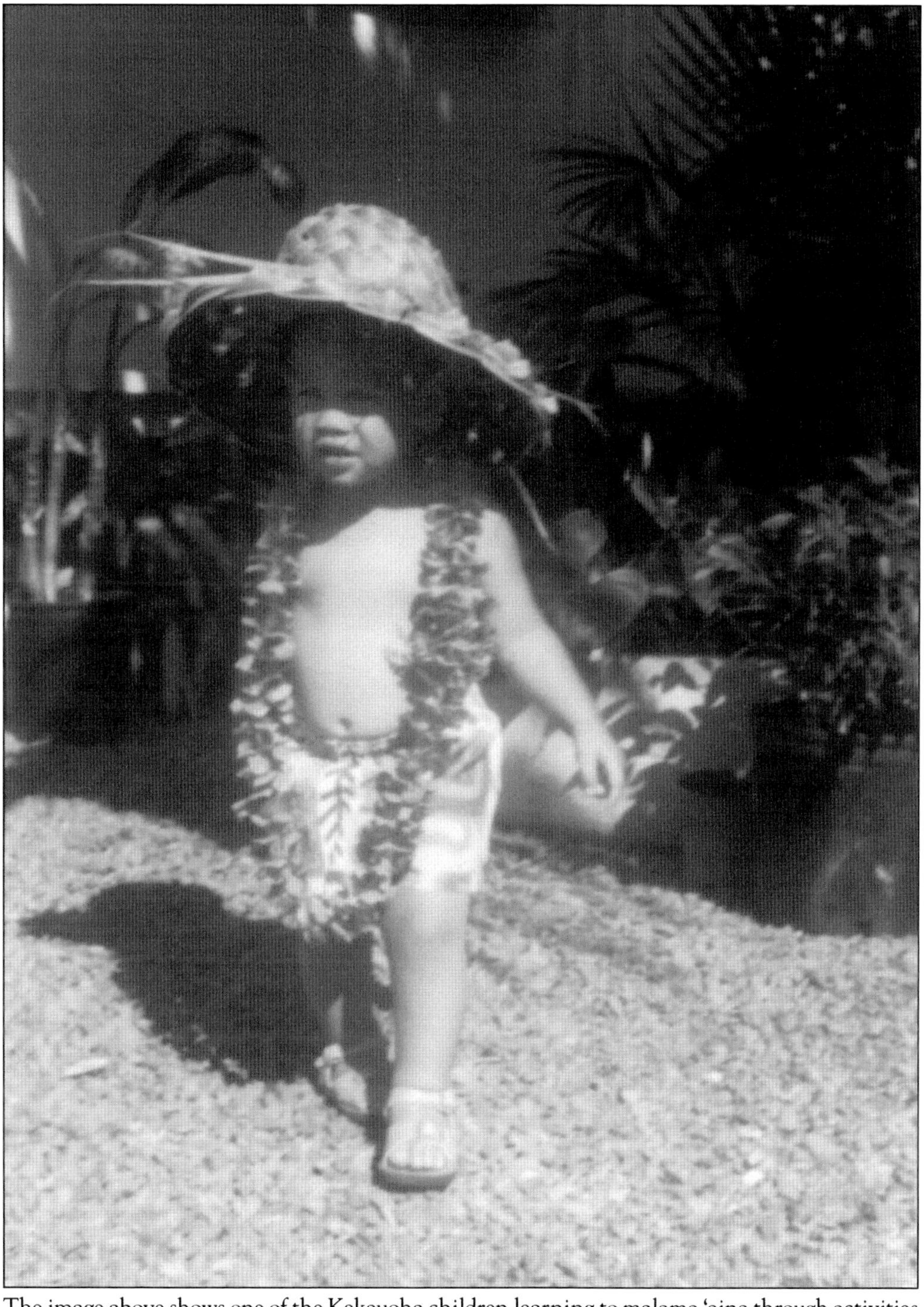

The image above shows one of the Kekauoha children learning to malama ʻaina through activities associated with Hawaii but universal to all peoples. His hat, the lei, and the garden show just how much kanaka try to recreate Hawaii in their own backyards. Like others who migrated to California, the first generation of Hawaiians in Los Angeles started establishing families and making Southern California home. (Courtesy of the Kekauoha family.)

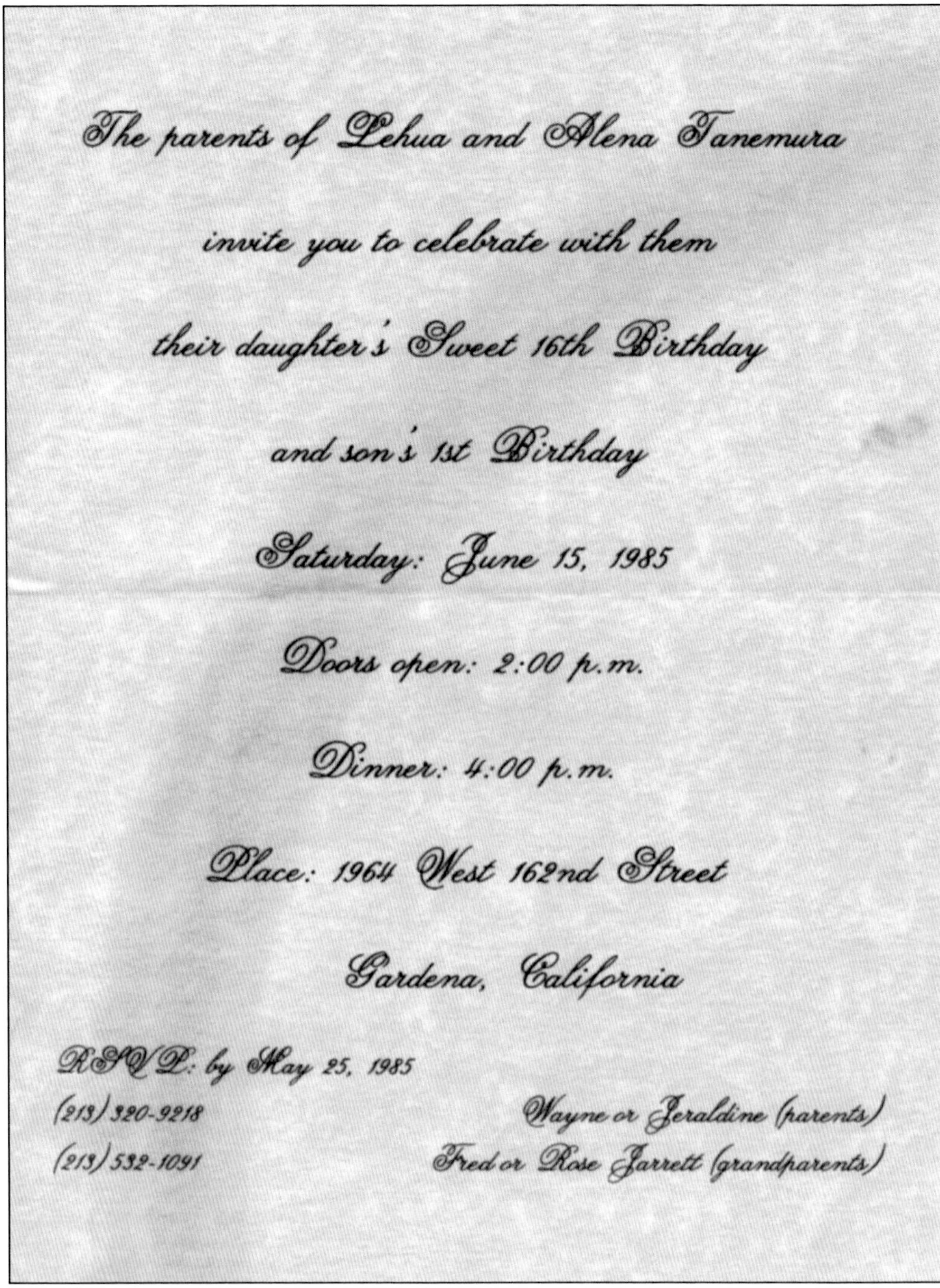

The parents of Lehua and Alena Tanemura

invite you to celebrate with them

their daughter's Sweet 16th Birthday

and son's 1st Birthday

Saturday: June 15, 1985

Doors open: 2:00 p.m.

Dinner: 4:00 p.m.

Place: 1964 West 162nd Street

Gardena, California

R.S.V.P.: by May 25, 1985

(213) 320-9218 Wayne or Jeraldine (parents)

(213) 532-1091 Fred or Rose Jarrett (grandparents)

The origin of the luau is a celebration of the first year of a child's life. Even after the influence of modern medicine in Hawaii, Native Hawaiian children had a high probability of dying in their first year. Every child that made it through was a blessing that demanded as big a celebration as the family could afford. At the same time, Native Hawaiians adopted Western traditions like the Sweet 16 party. (Courtesy of the Tanemura family.)

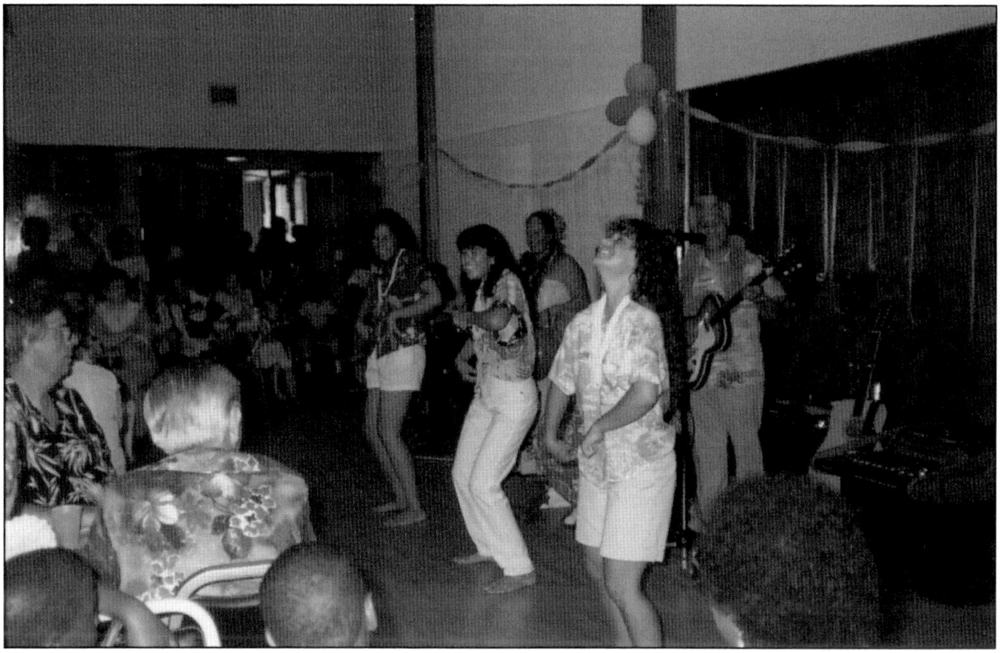

The first luau is filled with music, dancing, and food. Pictured above is the informal hula that characterizes Hawaiian parties. Unlike hired studios, the hula done at Hawaiian parties is filled with joy and spontaneity rather than precision and performance. The Tanemura luau was a huge occasion that took place at the Gardena VFW hall and was attended by the Tanemura's extended ohana, which included members of various hula halau (hula schools), civic clubs, family, and friends. (Both, courtesy of the Tanemura family.)

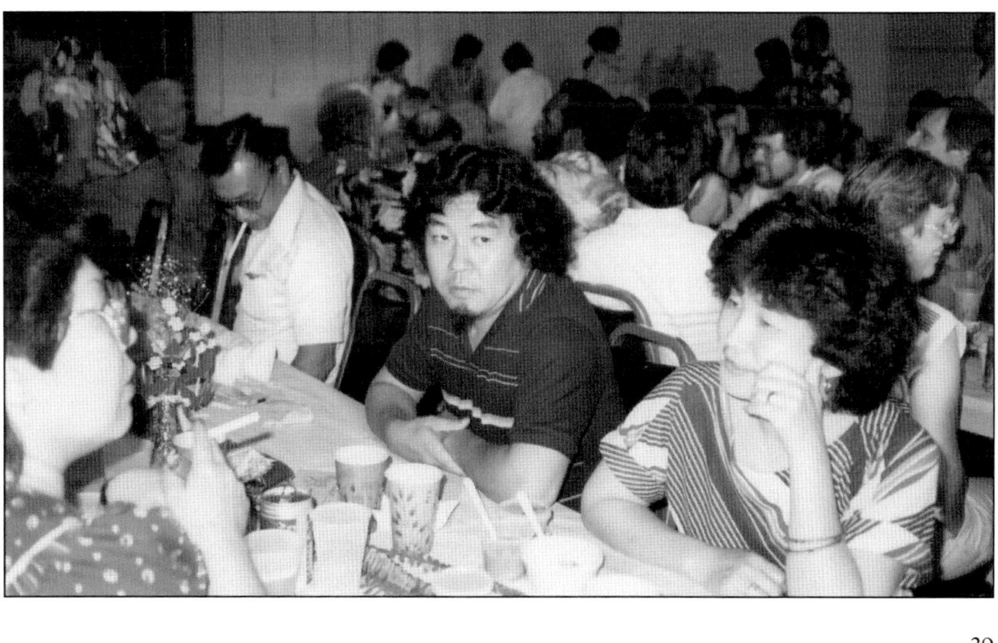

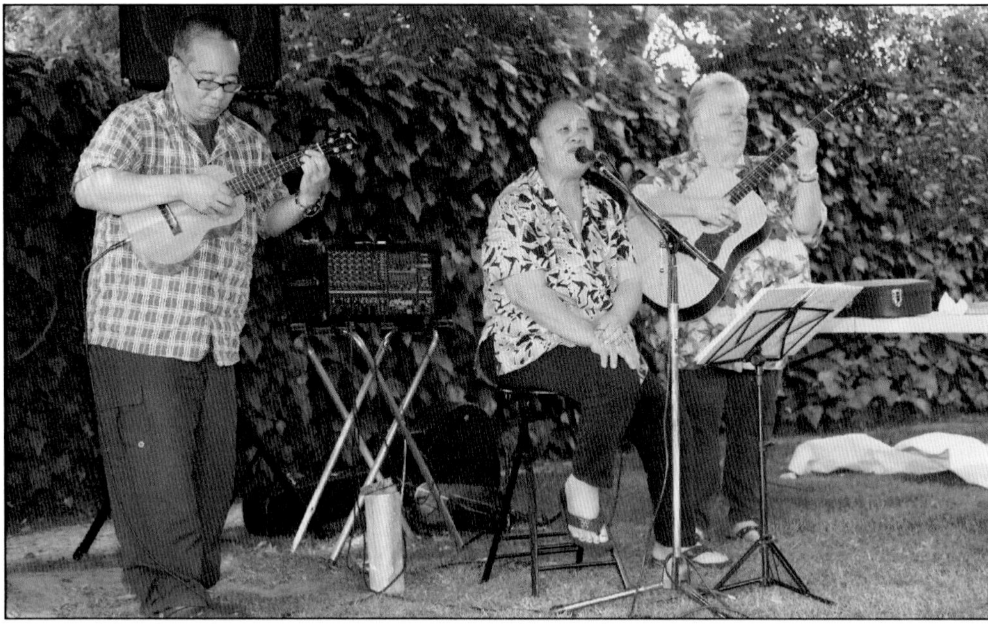

Luau and family gatherings are moments where the family entertains each other through *mele* (songs) that have significance to the family history. Pictured here is Geraldine Puanani Kuhia (center), who, while growing up in San Pedro and the Long Beach area, performed with her parents in shows and fundraisers for organizations like the International Longshore and Warehouse Union. Pictured with her are Rick Jitchaku (left) and Carole White (right). Kuhia dropped out of high school to pursue a career in country singing in Texas. Later, she returned to her family and roots in Los Angeles. In 2006, she received her high school diploma and started studying songs in her native language. Currently, she is the lead singer for the Mehana band (pictured), highlighting Hawaiian songs and ukulele music. She has made several albums and performed in both Los Angeles and Hawaii. (Both, courtesy of the Nihipali family.)

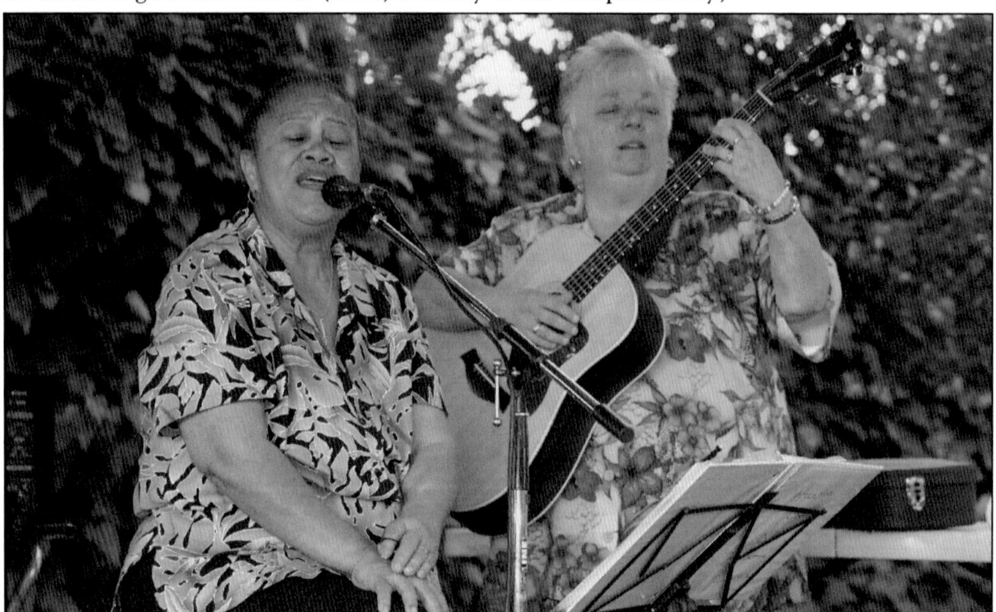

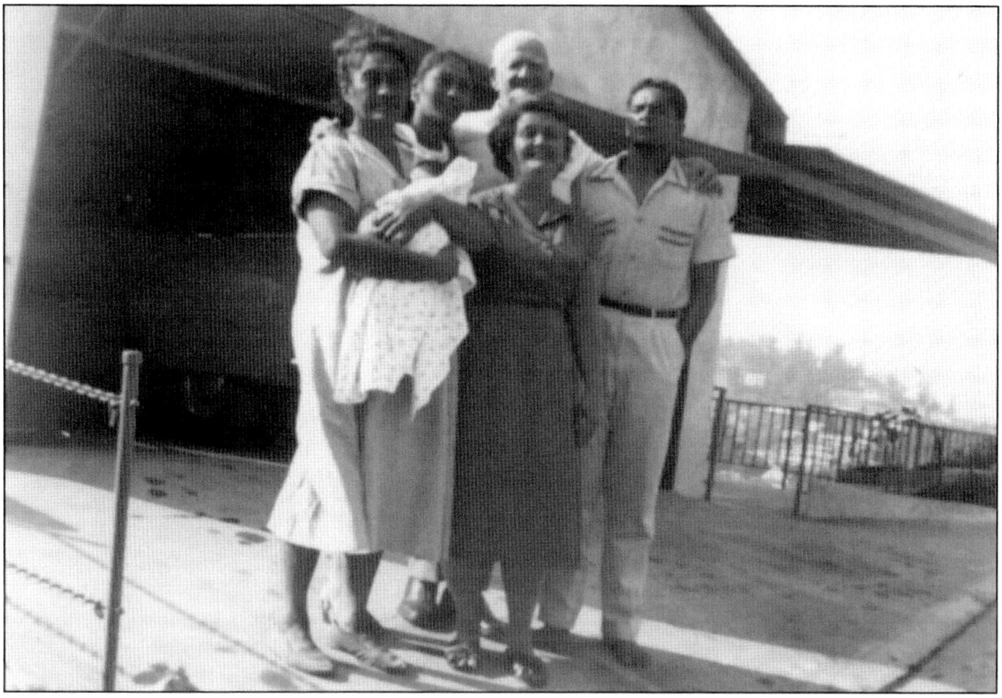

Sometimes the aloha that grandparents, parents, aunts, uncles, brothers, and sisters in Hawaii feel for the diasporic Hawaiians in Los Angeles is not enough to make a permanent jump from the most isolated point in the Pacific Ocean to the continent. In Hawaiian culture, ohana, both immediate and extended, is so important that the practice of *hanai* (multiple families raising children) was common. The purpose of hanai is to bridge social, emotional, and biological gaps between families. In the c. 1955 photograph above, Rose Kalei Pelayo holds her new grandson upon her arrival from Hawaii. Also pictured above are John and Louise Chave, Alice Richmond, and Alvin Pelayo in Silverwood around 1955. Below are Ipolani Vaughn, her daughter, and Maka Pelayo Crabbe (who were all visiting from Hawaii) with Mary Pelayo. (Above, courtesy of the Pelayo family; below, courtesy of the Letuli family.)

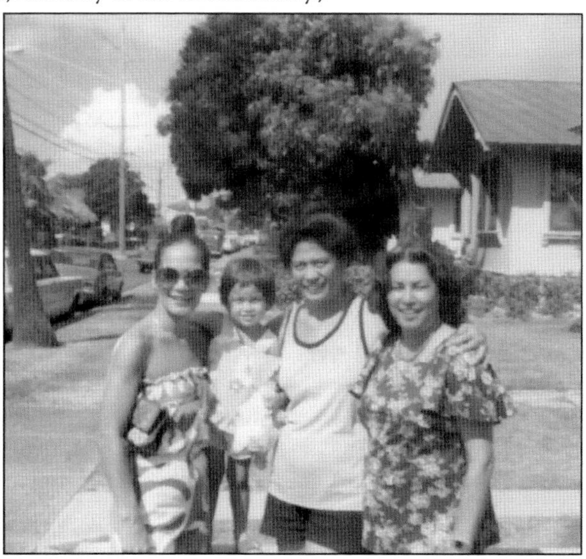

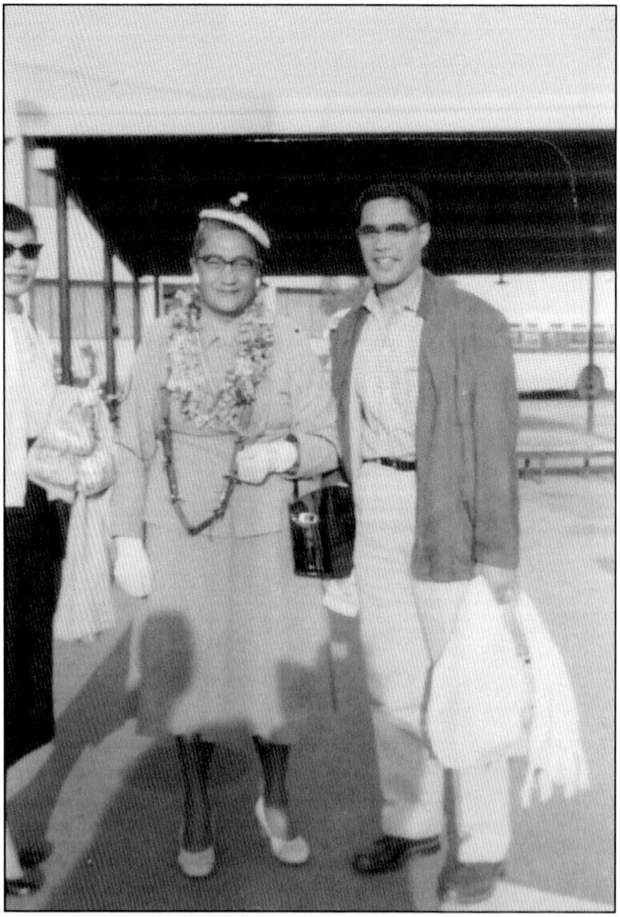

Visiting from Hawaii is a balancing act between joy and sorrow. The plane ride, in the absence of jet propulsion, could take as long as 12 hours on a smoky plane filled with the loud buzz of propellers. Shown on the left is Rose Kalei Pelayo visiting her children in Los Angeles. These visits, at the same time, allowed ohana to express aloha. *Aloha* means "hello," "goodbye," "I love you," and much more. Aloha is generosity and hospitality. Shown below are Alcario "Sonny" Pelayo and his nephew Eric Miller. For Native Hawaiians, everyone is a cousin, aunt, or uncle, depending on their age, and it is not unheard of for nieces and nephews to spend as much time with their uncles and aunts as they do with their parents. (Both, courtesy of the Pelayo family.)

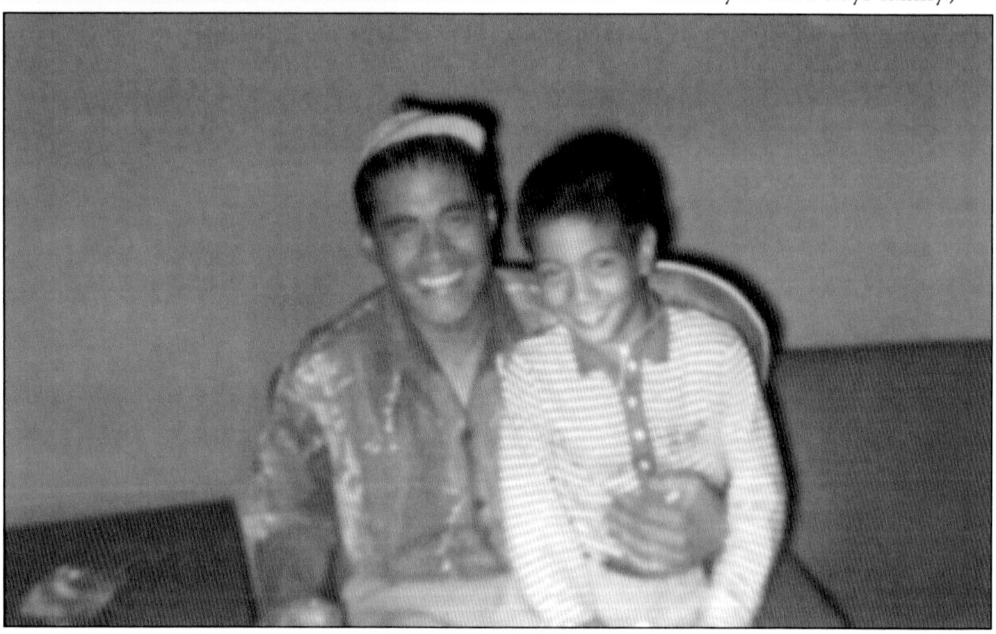

Two

Okage Sama De

Locals on the Continent

Okage sama de is Japanese for "I am who I am because of you." Island life leaves an indelible imprint on those that live in Hawaii. This imprint is structured around the concept of malama 'aina (take care of the land) by finding potential and using it. Unlike the early 20th-century racial tensions felt in America, the non-Western cultures in Hawaii chose to ignore physical difference. Instead, they focused on places where cultures intersected and common grounds like work, family, and life. So when the sugar plantations needed workers from Japan, Philippines, China, and Portugal, the kanaka did what the island always told them to do: take the good things and ignore the bad. By accepting traditional differences, the people of Hawaii started to recognize that the blending of cultures made people better. The key ingredient to Hawaiian culture was the Native Hawaiian's ability to incorporate differing perspectives into one perspective, one culture. In the end, Hawaiian culture in Los Angeles would look entirely different if it were not for local culture. Locals influence every aspect of Hawaiian culture, starting with a shared history working on the plantations and continuing through intermarriage. Local influence can be seen from King's Hawaiian® sweet bread, which was inspired by Portuguese sweet bread, to Hawaiian Creole Pidgin, which is English mixed with Hawaiian and words picked up from the cultures that reside in the islands. Hawaiian culture, from the outside, is the melting pot America has strived for, but the mixing of culture is a public and personal business. Hawaiian culture has become the catchall for the various people that inhabit Hawaii. Distinctly Hawaiian traits are the ability to travel from culture to culture with respect and ease, to *kokua* (help) even when it is not necessary, and to turn the potential into the actual. In the following chapter, the reader will see moments where the flavors of Hawaii, created by the locals, immigrate with the locals. The reader will also see the kuleana that was shown to one of America's heroes and one of Hawaii's lost sons.

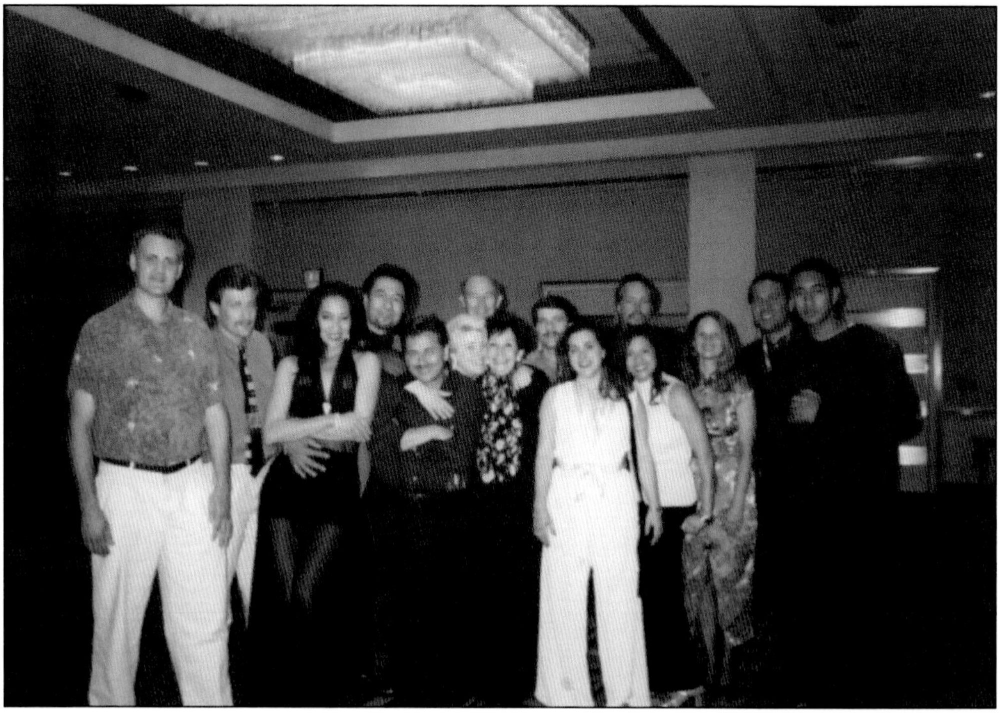

Whether local or native, being Hawaiian means having a mixed culture where friends and family celebrate various traditions, either through bloodlines or just association. The Richmond family (above) is Native Hawaiian but as the family's ohana expands, one can see Chinese, Filipino, Samoan, Fijian, Caucasian, and Hispanic in the people surrounding them. To drive this point home, the children (below) are at the Richmond house in Tarzana enjoying the pool. The kids are so racially mixed that it is hard to tell which ones are related. (Both, courtesy of the Letuli family.)

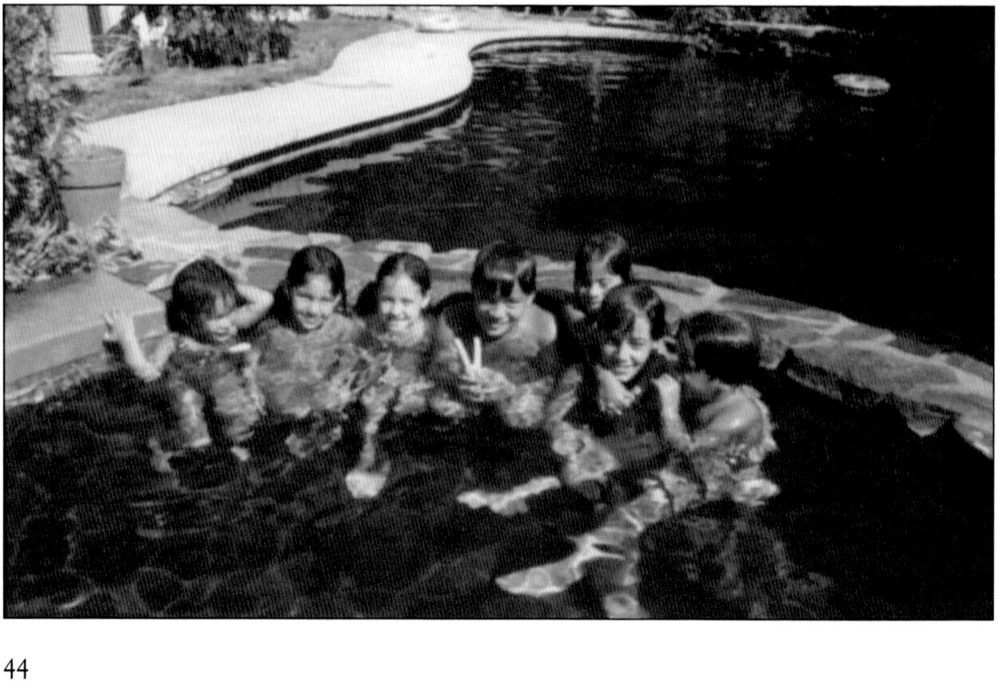

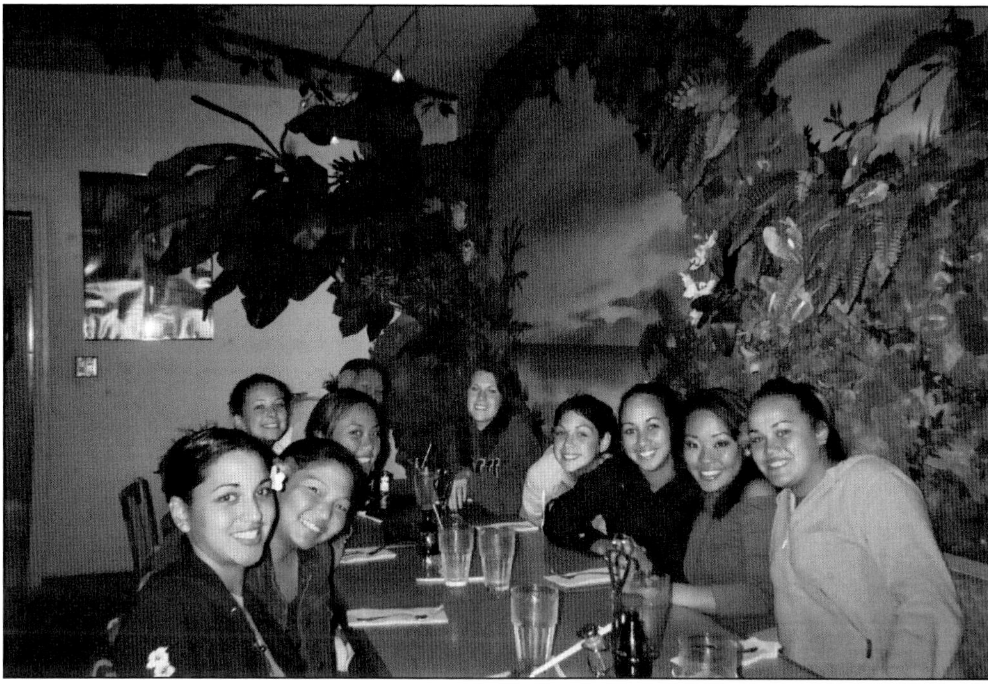

Migrations of Native Hawaiians and locals continue to the continent for the same reasons as those who migrated in our earlier chapter. Today, creating those bonds comes early and often, as universities, such as Loyola Marymount University (LMU), group students together by their original geographical location, sports played, and many other factors. These students get the chance to bond together through school, life, and extracurricular activities such as intramural sports and clubs like the Hawaii club. The first photograph is a group of LMU students, mostly originally from Hawaii, enjoying dinner at Back Home in Lahaina in Manhattan Beach. The second photograph shows the 2003–2004 LMU Intramural Boys Hawaii Softball Team, comprised of LMU students originally from Hawaii. (Both, courtesy of Mahina Cumpston Sayin.)

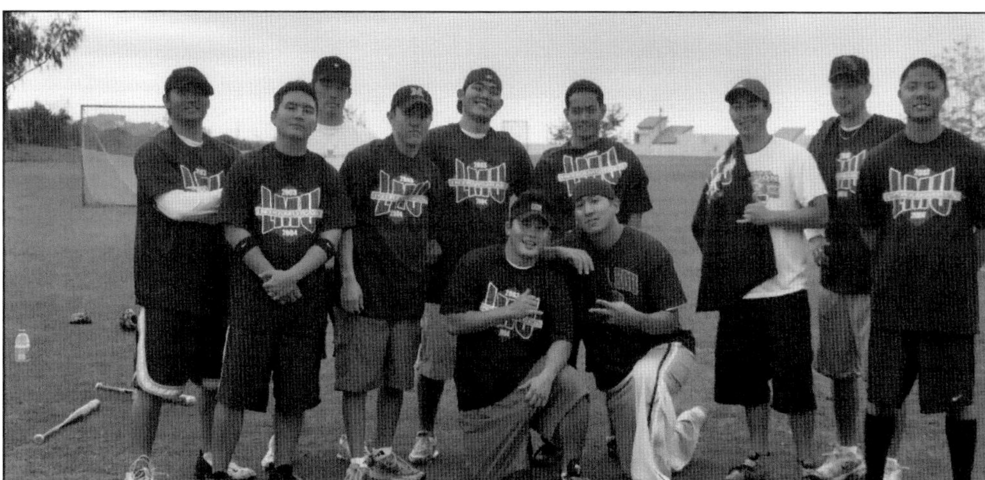

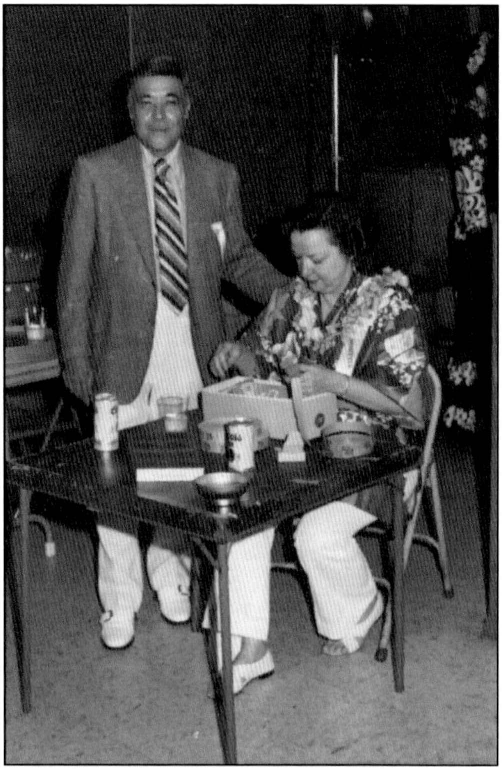

Upon arrival, even locals strive to re-create the close-knit Hawaiian communities they left. To that end, many Hawaiians started businesses and sponsored Hawaiian-themed contests. Shown here are Gary and Peggy Spears working behind the scenes of the Voice of Hawaii beauty pageant. Spears owned Little Hawaii, a nightclub on 8th and Alvarado Streets in Los Angeles that featured Hawaiian entertainers and was a gathering place for those who missed their *ohana* (family) and *hale* (home). (Courtesy of Charmaine Kuni Keoho.)

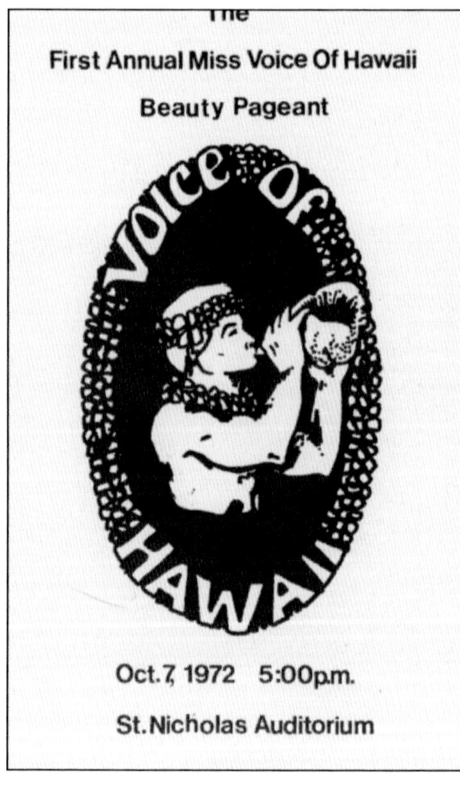

The Voice of Hawaii beauty pageant was a celebration of the Hawaiian community on the continent. The contestants had to be part Native Hawaiian but more importantly had to have a desire to create a community for Hawaiians, both native and local, on the continent. The contest coincided with the cultural renaissance happening back home. (Courtesy of Charmaine Kuni Keoho.)

While locals and Native Hawaiians came here with the goal of making a successful life, it also gave them the ability to start over. Harriet Hatsue Bittenbender, a nisei (second-generation Japanese immigrant), was born in Waipahu in 1918 and raised in Aiea. After her first husband, Norbert Kahalehili Keolanui, passed away from cancer, she remarried a Navy man, Robert Bittenbender, and they moved to California in 1954 with her two sons, Gus and Norby. (Courtesy of Gus Keolanui.)

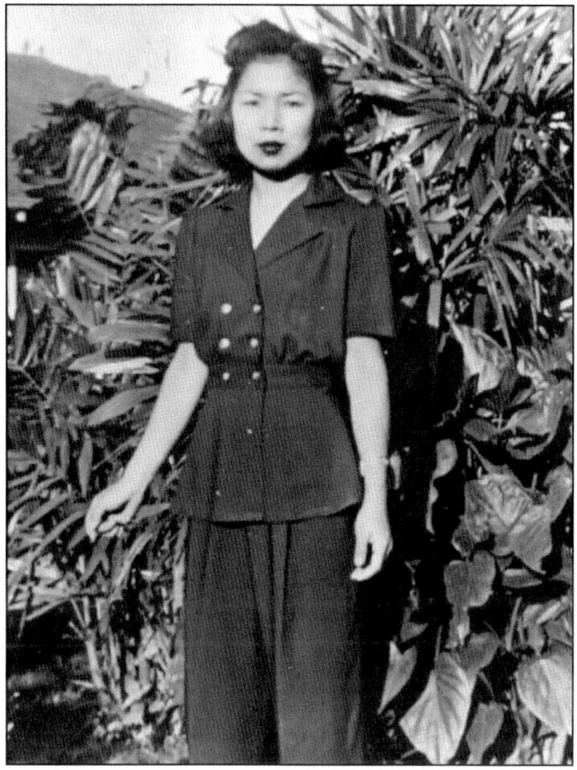

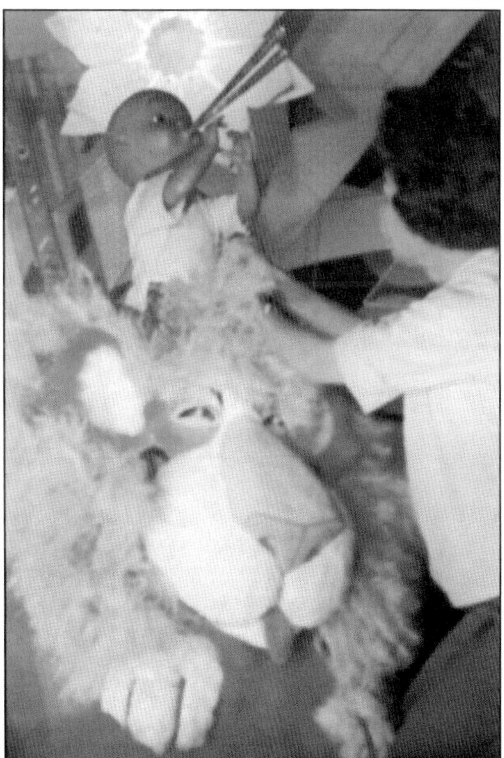

Harriet got a job as a costume designer at Disneyland when it opened in 1955. In this photograph, she is working on one of the dolls at the "It's a Small World" set. The distinction between locals and Native Hawaiians is at times confusing. Harriet, born in Hawaii, is of Japanese descent whereas her sons, Gus and Norby, share Native Hawaiian blood; however, all of them share innovative minds and entrepreneurial spirits. (Courtesy of Gus Keolanui.)

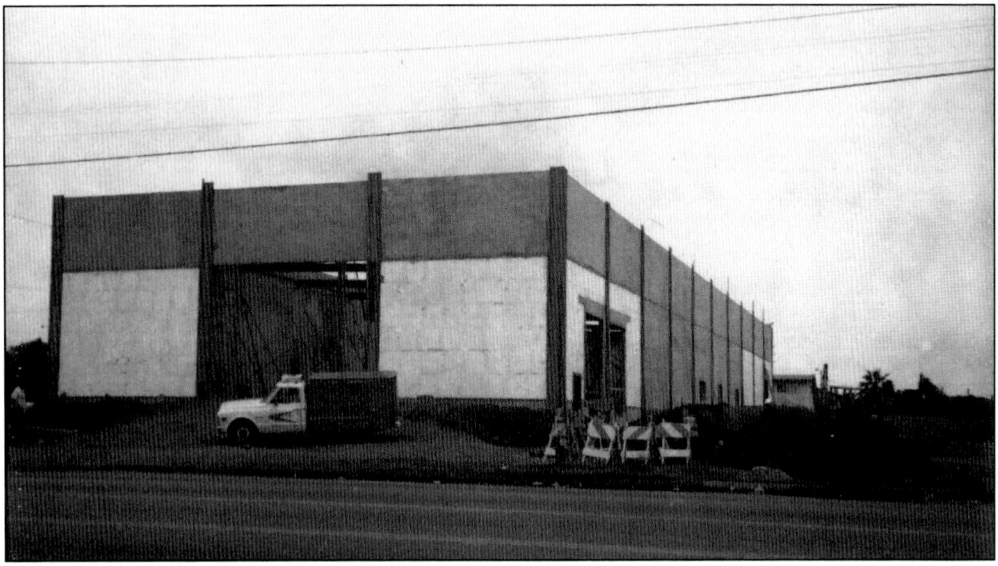

An ethnic mix of various cuisines and flavors found in the islands, Hawaiian food is an integral part of the culture. Many Hawaiians founded famous eateries in the island that are still considered landmarks today. In the 1950s, Hawaii-born Robert R. Taira, the son of Japanese immigrants, opened his first bakery, Robert's Bakery, in Hilo, Hawaii, where the Original Hawaiian Sweet Bread, inspired by a Portuguese bread, was born. In 1963, Robert moved his bakery to King Street in Honolulu, Oahu, where the bakery received a new name, King's Bakery. During this time, his Original Hawaiian Sweet Bread was shipped all over by locals and tourists as gifts to family and friends living on the mainland. By 1977, Robert was ready to expand and move his business to the continent, building a commercial bakery (pictured above) in Torrance, California and honoring his business's island heritage by changing the name to King's Hawaiian® Bakery. Below, Robert R. Taira breaks ground on the Torrance factory. (Both, courtesy of King's Hawaiian® Bakery.)

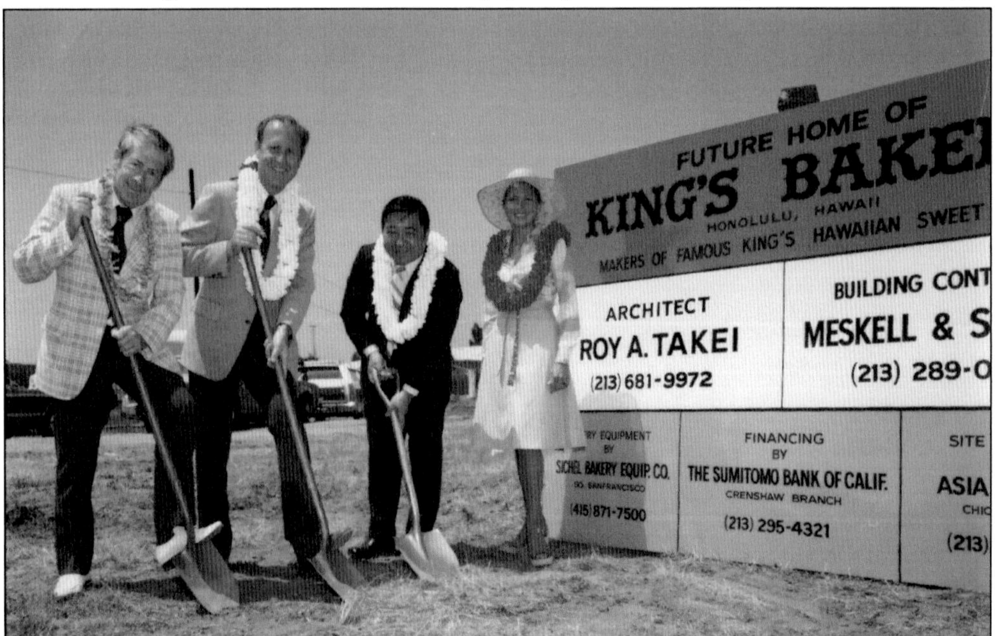

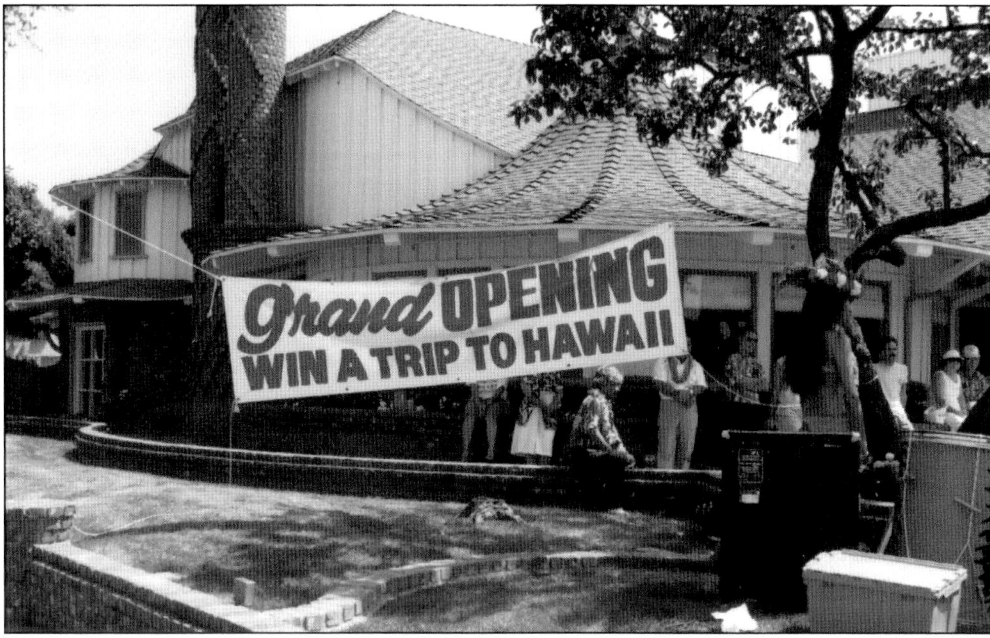

Robert R. Taira opened King's Hawaiian® Bakery & Restaurant in Torrance in 1988. Pictured above, King's Hawaiian® supports the community by hosting regular fundraisers for local clubs, sports, and other groups. The Local Place Bakery & Café, which opened in 2002, in Torrance, next to the Western bakery, is a casual meeting place for Hawaiians in the South Bay. Robert R. Taira's commitment to the highest quality Hawaiian food continues on the continent as his family continues to spread the aloha spirit beyond the South Bay, and to the entire United States with King's Hawaiian® bread products based on their original recipe. Pictured below are Robert R. Taira and Janice Hahn breaking ground on the Western Bakery in Torrance, California. (Both, courtesy of King's Hawaiian® Bakery.)

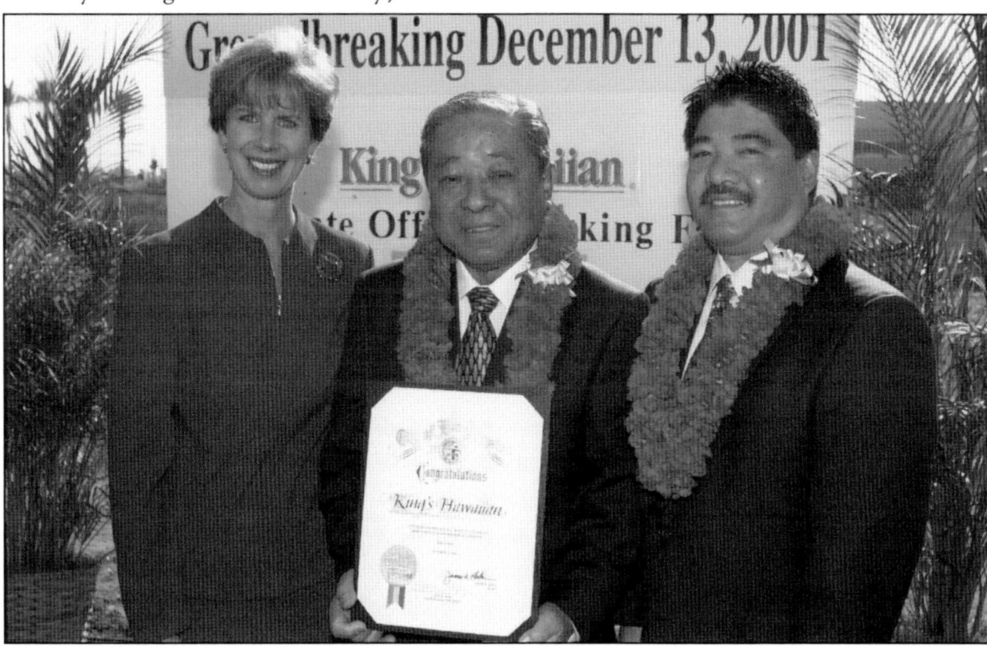

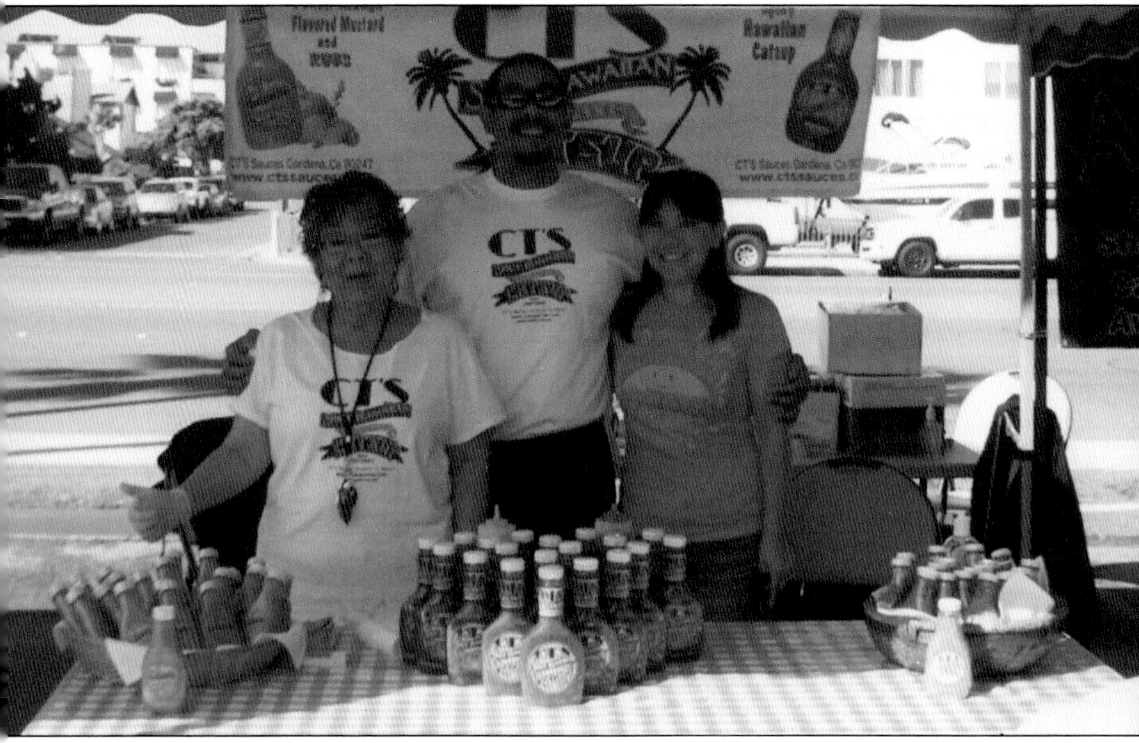

While King's Hawaiian® Bakery might be the model of local food on the continent, it only scratches the surface of the Hawaiian-influenced food and restaurants available in Los Angeles. Cynthia Wong Tinson, born May 2, 1943, in Wahiawa, Oahu, came to California in 1963 and lived in Gardena. She owned and operated two restaurants: Kreole Kitchen in Long Beach and Gramma's Kitchen in Gardena. Both restaurants have since closed, but both of them celebrated traditional and multicultural foods influenced by Hawaii. After her two restaurants closed down, Cynthia (pictured far left with her son Shawn and daughter Jodi Abercrombie) was encouraged by her family to sell her sauces. She developed and bottled Peach-Mango Mustard and Spicy Hawaiian Ketchup. Her first bottle was sold at the Farmer's Market at Peter's Landing in Huntington Beach. (Courtesy of Cynthia Tinson.)

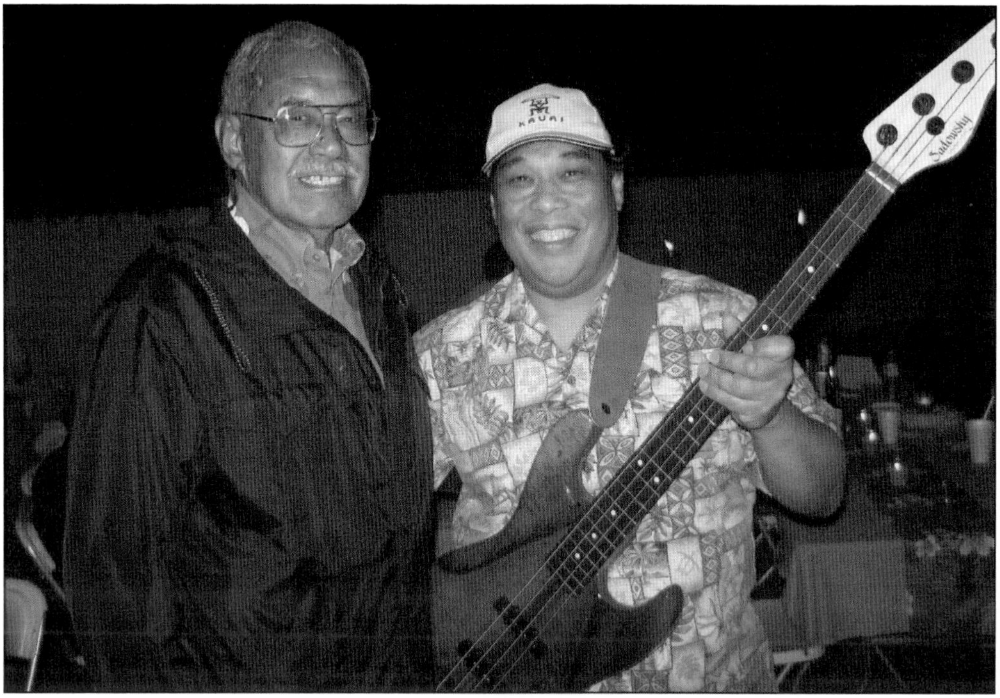

Sometimes, Los Angeles called locals to the continent for their ingenuity. Pictured above with Alcario "Sonny" Pelayo is Jack Balauro (right) who was recruited by Hughes Aircraft Company while attending the University of Hawaii. They paid for a one-way airplane ticket plus handled moving costs. Today, Jack works for Raytheon in El Segundo and plays Hawaiian music on the weekends. (Courtesy of Jack Balauro.)

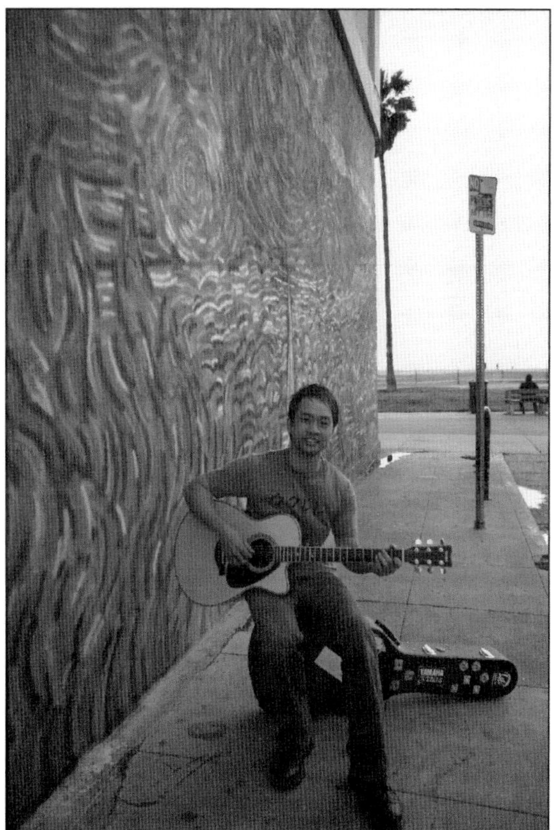

Others come attracted to the entertainment industry. Daniel Ho is an accomplished musician, singer, and songwriter born and raised on Oahu. He moved to the continent after high school to attend the Grove School of Music in Los Angeles. In 1990, he formed the jazz group, Kilauea. By 1997, this group had released six chart topping albums with two hitting the top 10 on Billboard's jazz charts. (Courtesy of Daniel Ho.)

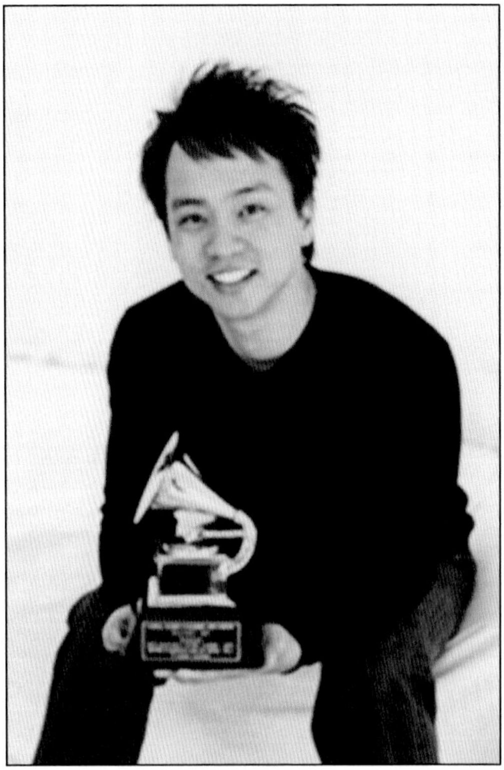

In 1998, Ho created Daniel Ho Creations, an independent record label that would allow him the freedom to collaborate and make unconventional musical decisions as well as incorporate his talents in photography and graphic design. Ho has received numerous awards and accolades from the music industry, including 3 Na Hoku Hanohano awards, 15 Hawaii Music Awards, and 6 Grammy Awards. (Courtesy of Daniel Ho.)

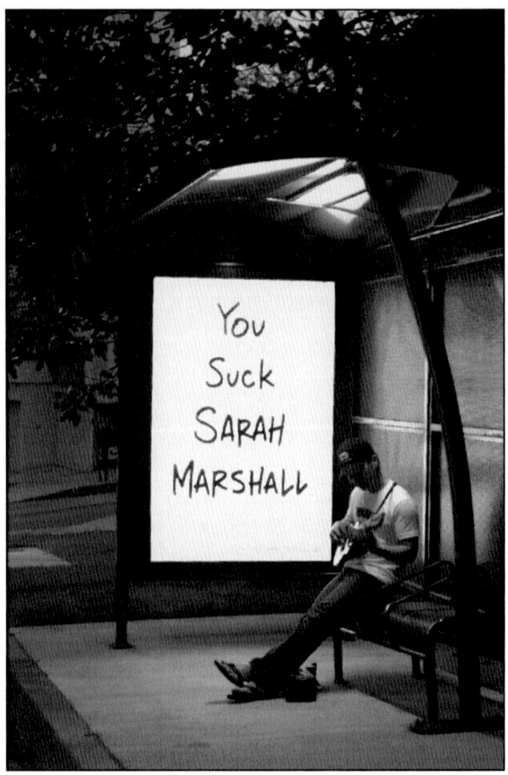

Daniel Ho is pictured here at a bus stop located on Beverly Glen Boulevard in Westwood, California. In 2008, Ho appeared in and recorded several tracks for the film *Forgetting Sarah Marshall* under the pseudonym the Coconutz. (Courtesy of Daniel Ho.)

Adriano F. Abatayo III moved to Southern California 36 years ago to pursue opportunities not readily available in Hawaii. These opportunities have culminated in his work being acquired by the likes of Steven Spielberg, Coretta Scott King, Edward James Olmos, and Pres. Bill Clinton. (Courtesy of Adriano Abatayo III.)

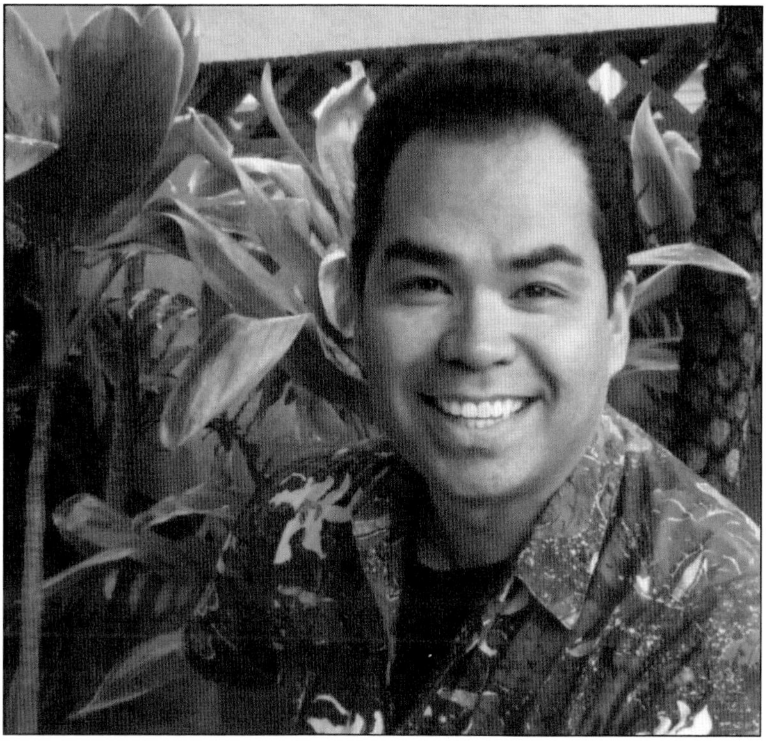

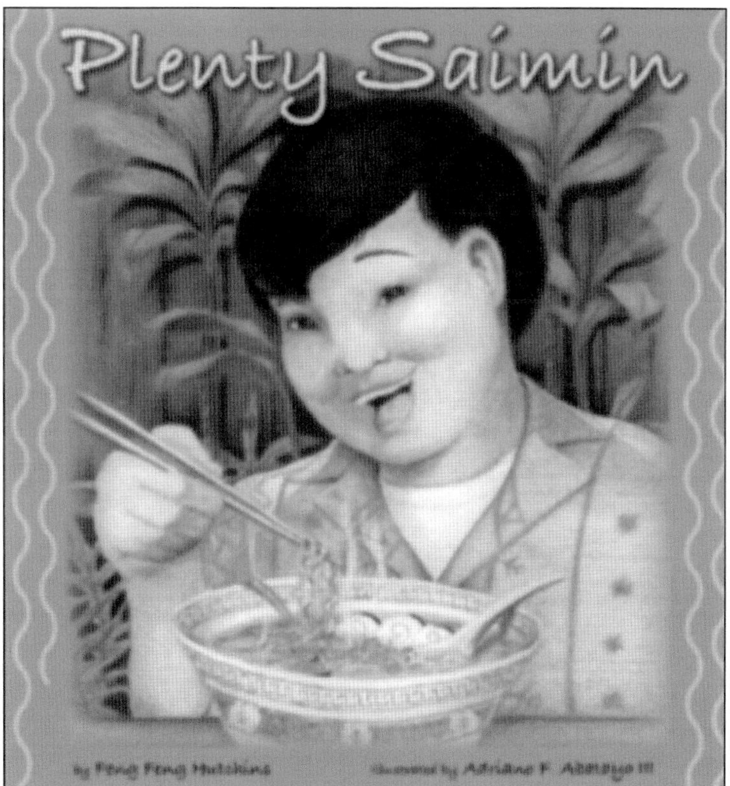

Adriano F. Abatayo's work was also featured in the children's picture book *Plenty Saimin* (Island Paradise Publishing), which highlights the Hawaiian values of *ohana* (family) and *aloha* (sharing and generosity) in 1950s rural Hawaii. It won the Ka Palapala Po'okela Award for "Excellence in Children's Literature." He is currently working on the story and illustrations for his own book, tentatively titled *My Poi Dog King*. (Courtesy of Adriano Abatayo III.)

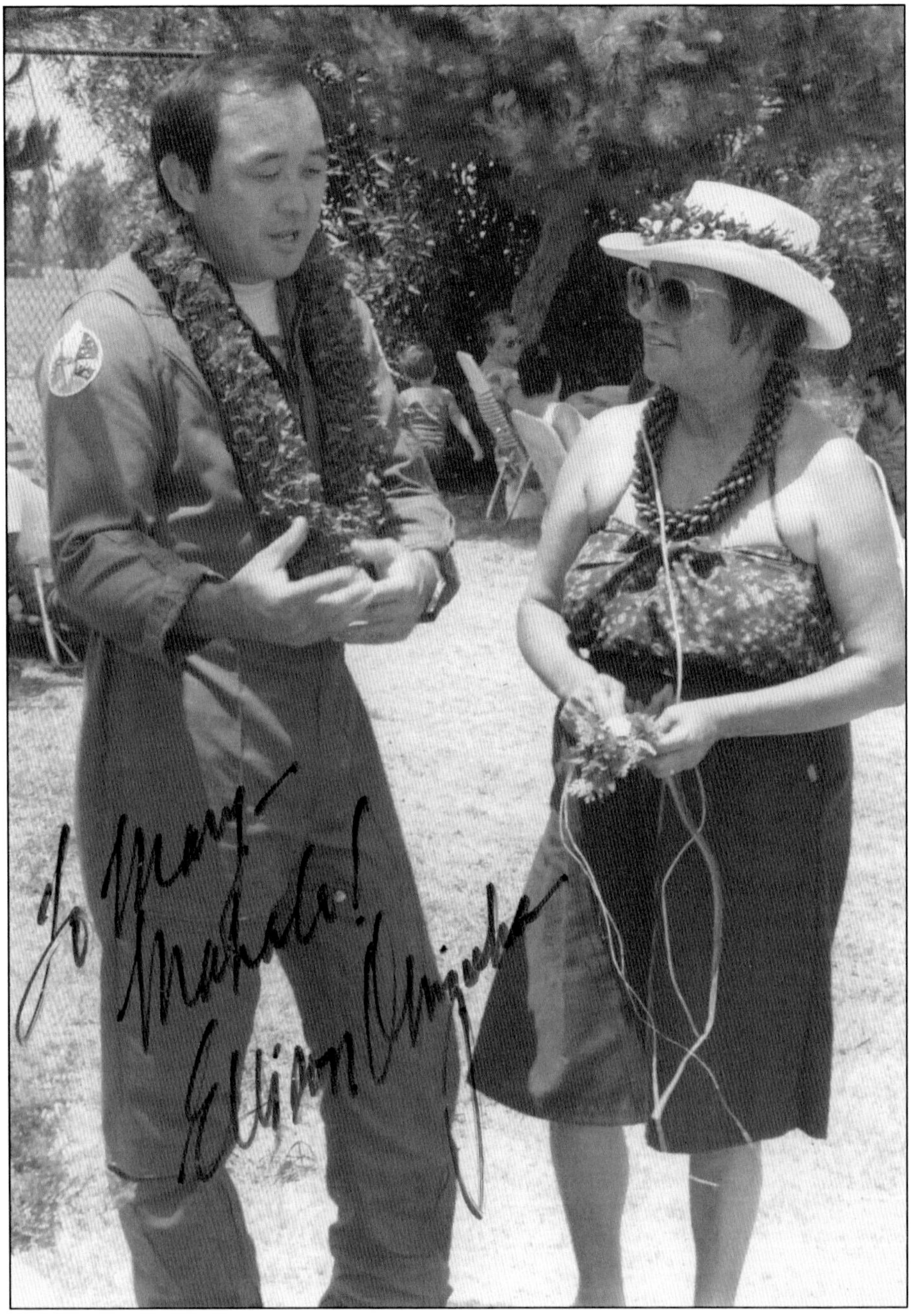

One of the highest peaks that demonstrate Hawaiian innovation is lieutenant colonel and NASA astronaut Ellison Onizuka. Ellison was born in Kealakekua, Kona, to nisei parents and was the pride of Hawaiians working in the aerospace industry. Ellison (left) is pictured with Mary Pelayo, taking part as grand marshal at the Alondra Park Ho'olaule'a. Many of the Hawaiian Civic Clubs supported him through his career. Ellison's life also shows how the Hawaiian community honors their own. In 1986, the *Challenger*, with Ellison on board, exploded. His life was celebrated by Hawaiians in Hawaii and Southern California. (Courtesy of the Pelayo family.)

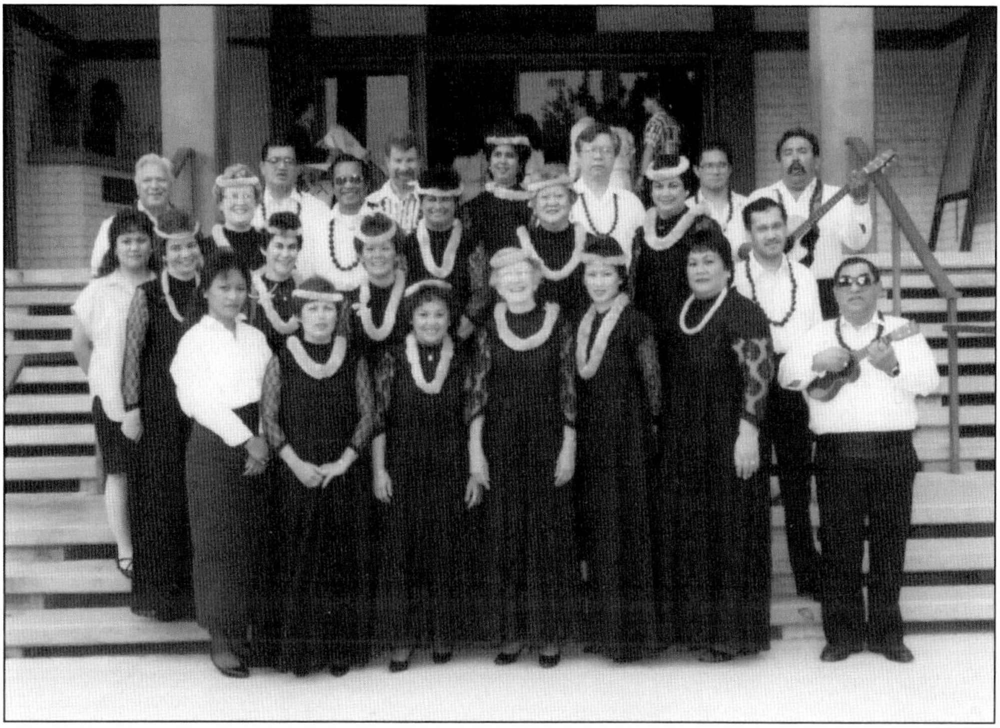

In memory of Ellison Onizuka's sacrifice for the country and science, the Hawaiian community in Los Angeles helped sponsor a memorial. As with any Hawaiian gathering, the deep emotions of the event, in this case of loss and respect, are augmented by song and dance. Pictured above are members of the Ahahui o Liliuokalani choir that performed at the ceremony. Pictured below is a Maori dance performed in honor of the fallen astronaut. (Both, courtesy of the Pelayo family.)

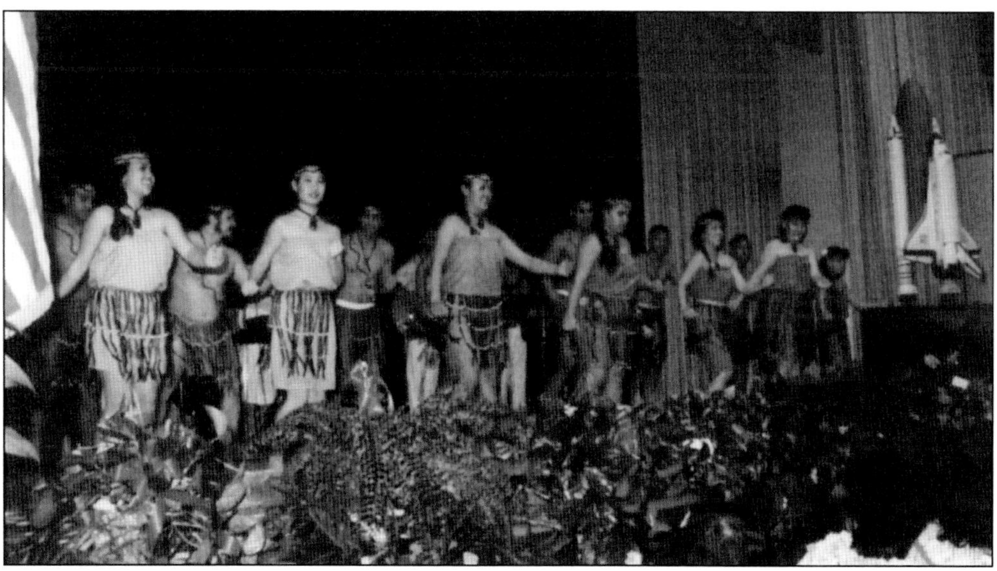

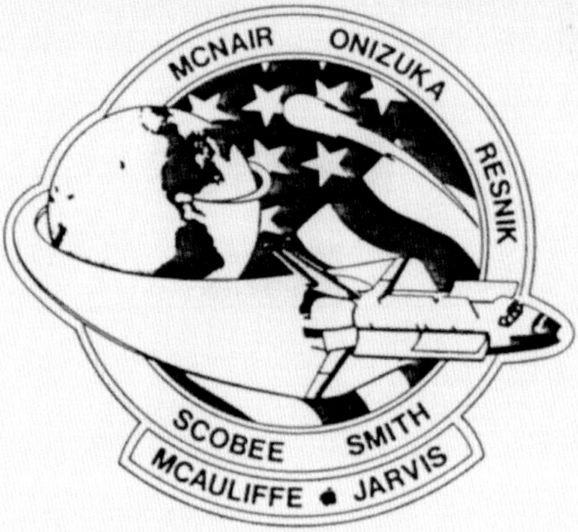

My daughters and I would like to sincerely thank you for your thoughtful support and encouragement these past several months. We are touched by your sincerity and will cherish always, your expressions of warm Aloha.

El was indeed fortunate for the ability and opportunities to pursue a career he so loved. You honored him with your gracious support throughout his quest for realizing his greatest dreams. Thank you for sharing your friendship and thoughtfulness with me and my daughters.

With love and Mahalo,

Lorna L. Onizuka

This is a thank-you letter to the Hawaiian Civic Clubs from the Onizuka family. (Courtesy of the Pelayo family.)

Three

As 'Aina Grows

The Following Generations and Their Culture

The keiki of the first-generation Hawaiian-Angelenos thrived under the California sun, which is surprising considering the extra burden of malama 'aina thrust upon them. Unlike the other residents of Los Angeles, the children of Hawaiians were asked to succeed in the East (when seen through the eyes of a Pacific immigrant) while maintaining a cultural identity that is misunderstood by society at large. However, this burden is as natural to Southern California as it is to the Hawaiian Islands.

Like the reality of Hawaii's misrepresentation hidden by a sunny image, California's entertainment industry and racial diversity leaves most with the impression that there is a vast history of Mexican rule. In reality, Mexican rule was only for a handful of decades, and California's history, filled with its own indigenous groups, is left largely unrecognized. It is almost as if the fault lines under our feet are the land's way of showing the difference between where Los Angeles Hawaiians think they are and what the land actually is. If the faults are the distance between the real and the image, the Hawaiians of Los Angeles have done a good job living with a foot on both sides.

Raised in a land with values greatly different from their own, Hawaiians adapted to new kinds of knowledge and found success in high school and college. While strengthening Hawaiian traditions, they adapted to the traditions around them and attempted to make new ones. They became as part of the fabric of Los Angeles as any other group. One can see the second-generation Hawaiians excel in entertainment, cuisine, and sports, all the while maintaining ties with the land they come from and hope to return to.

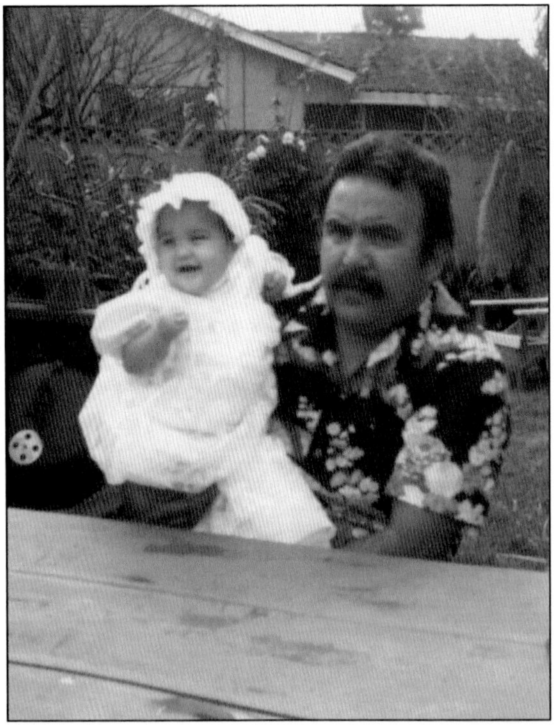

Equal to Hawaii's racial diversity is its religious diversity. Unlike the image of Hawaii seen through luau and hula, many religions are represented in the islands. When Hawaiians came to Southern California, they made sure to reinforce all the beliefs they held back home, which includes faith. Lessa Kanani'opua Pelayo is pictured on the left in her Catholic baptism gown. Holding her is Sam Rosero, who through various civic clubs helped perpetuate Hawaiian culture in Los Angeles. Pictured below are Michael and Mitchell Kekauoha with their father, Hosea, after their Mormon Baptism. (Above, courtesy of the Pelayo family; below, courtesy of the Kekauoha family.)

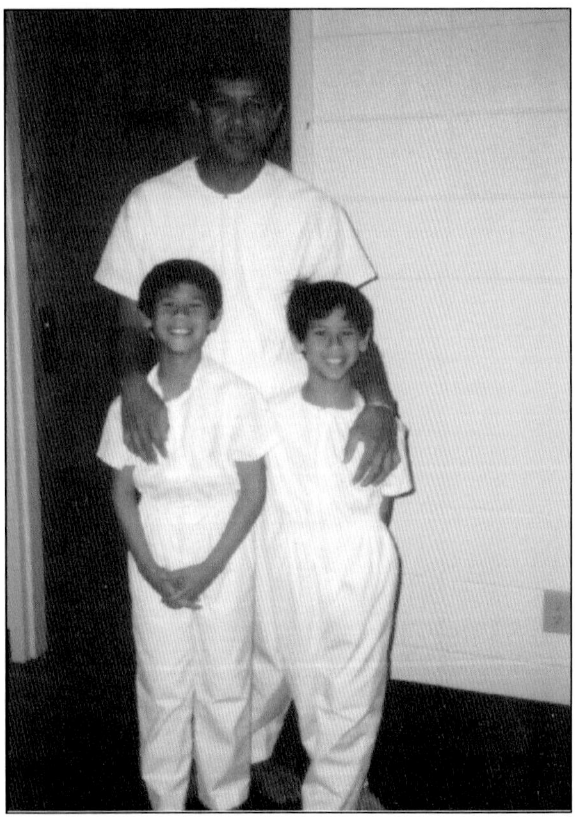

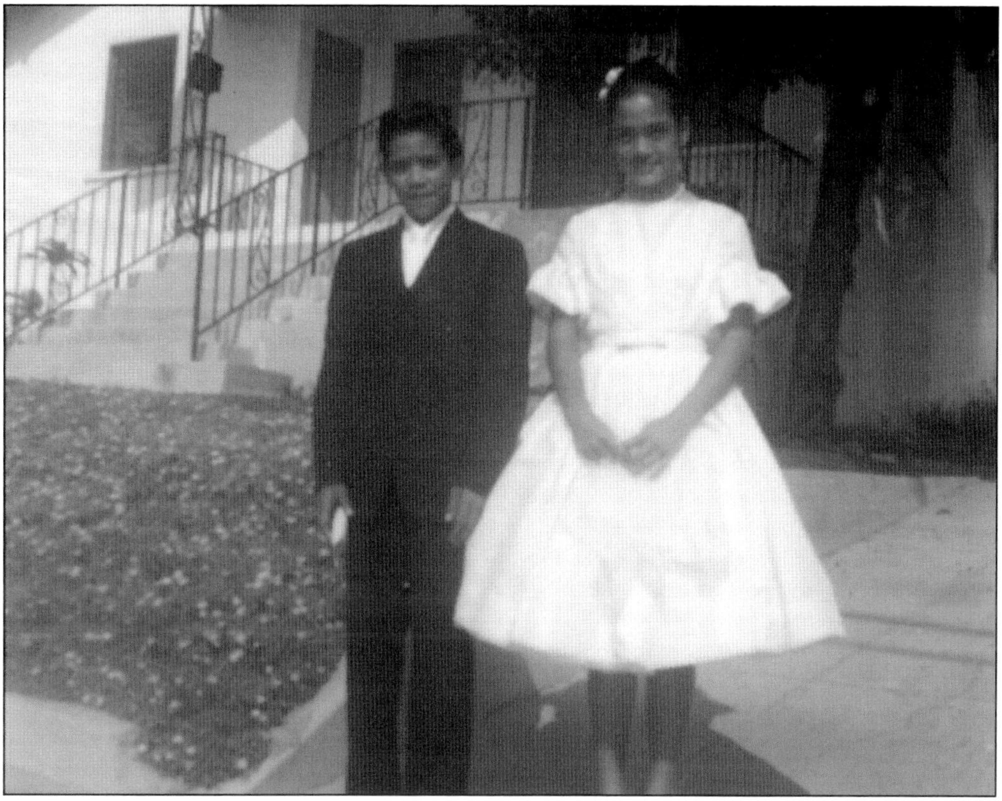

Western religion's influence on Hawaiians is American influence. The first long-term and permanent residents to Hawaii were American missionaries who brought the printed word and education. Shown above are Ipolani Vaughn (left) and her friend dressed up for their First Communion. Shown below is Mitchell Kekauoha celebrating Easter. (Above, courtesy of the Pelayo family; below, courtesy of the Kekauoha family.)

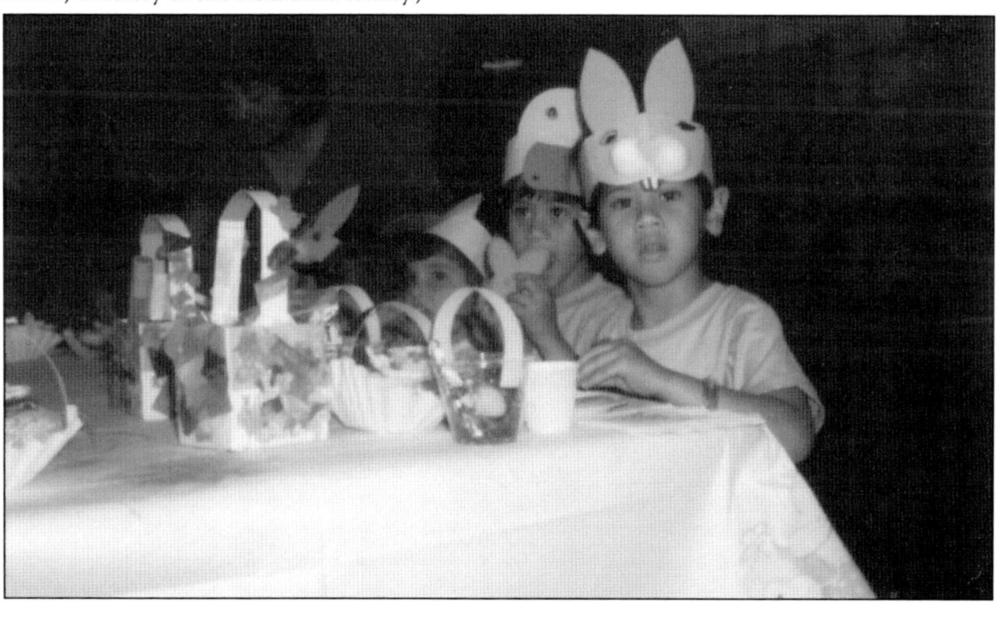

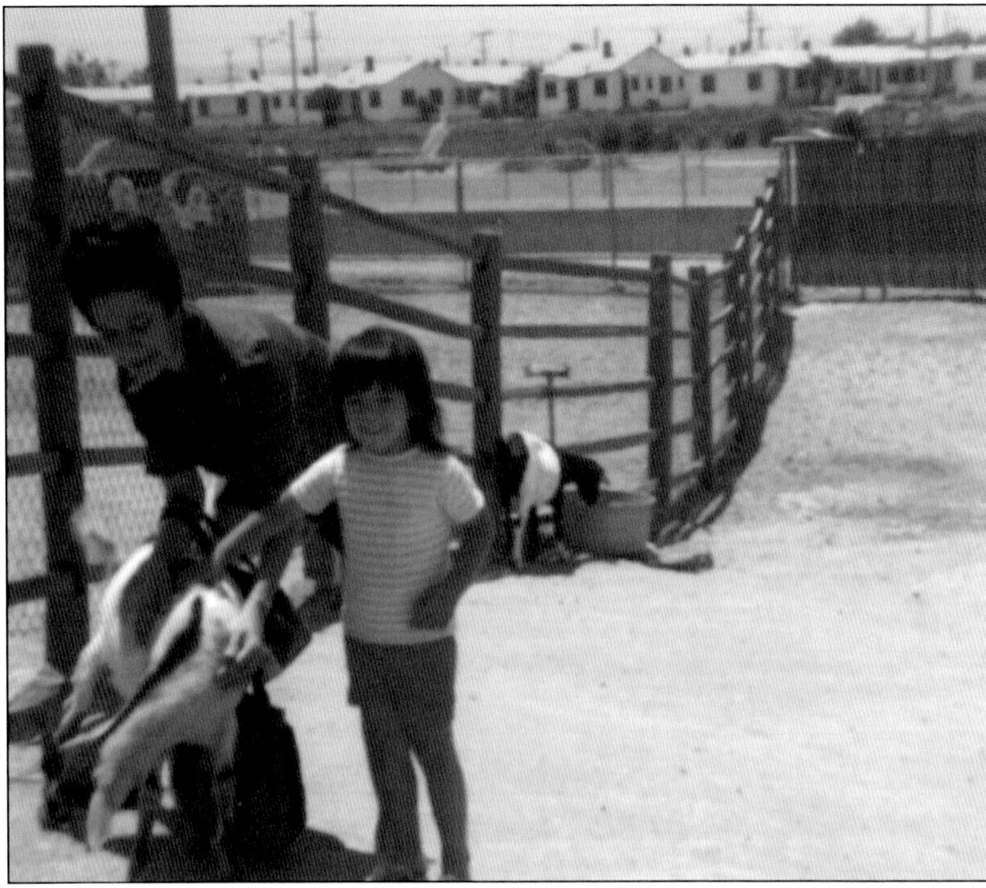

When the Hawaiians had children, they were left without the support structure that they would have had in Hawaii. That support structure, normally extended ohana, would help teach the children Hawaiian values like kokua, kuleana, and malama. An example of this is Rose Jarrett showing her granddaughter Lehuanani Tanemura the proper way to treat animals in Los Angeles. Without that support structure, the Hawaiians turned to more American sources of community like the Boy Scouts of America. Pictured below is Dexter Kekauoha (second from left) as a Boy Scout, creating a community on the continent. (Above, courtesy of the Tanemura family; below, courtesy of the Kekauoha family.)

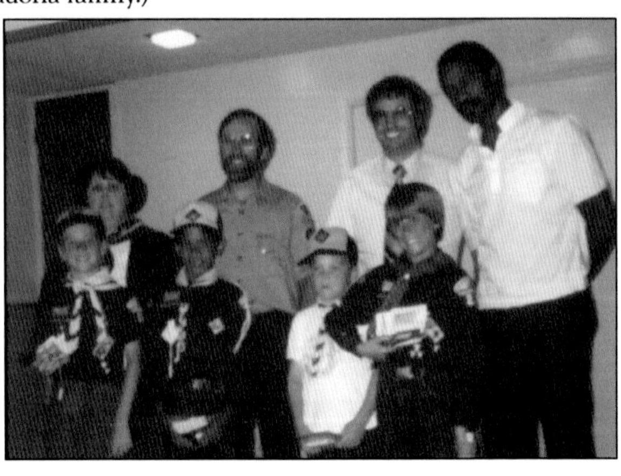

One of the main responsibilities that Hawaiians brought with them was to malama 'aina (to take care of the land), and when the Hawaiians had children, they worked hard to instill a love for nature into their children. While this might sound like hard work, it is as easy as immersing them in nature. In the image on the right are Lehuanani Tanemura (right) with her cousins Roxy (foreground) and Darin (left) enjoying Seaside Lagoon in Redondo Beach. The photograph below shows Bryce Ranck (left) and Alec Pelayo (right) enjoying barbeque at an 'Ahahui o Liliuokalani Hawaiian Civic Club campout at Camp Pendleton Beach. (Above, courtesy of the Tanemura family; below, courtesy of the Rosero family.)

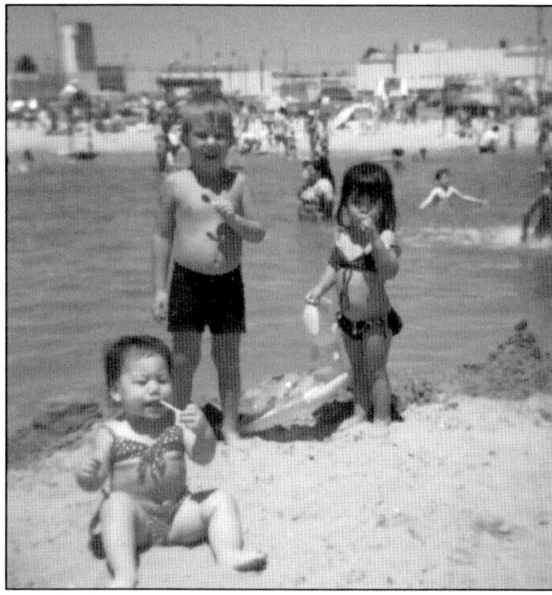

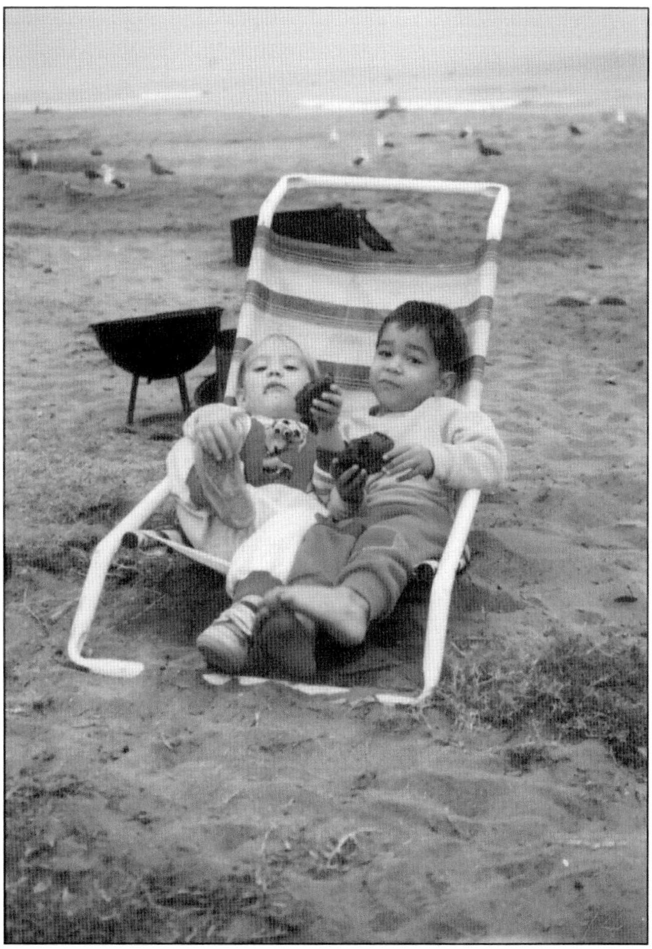

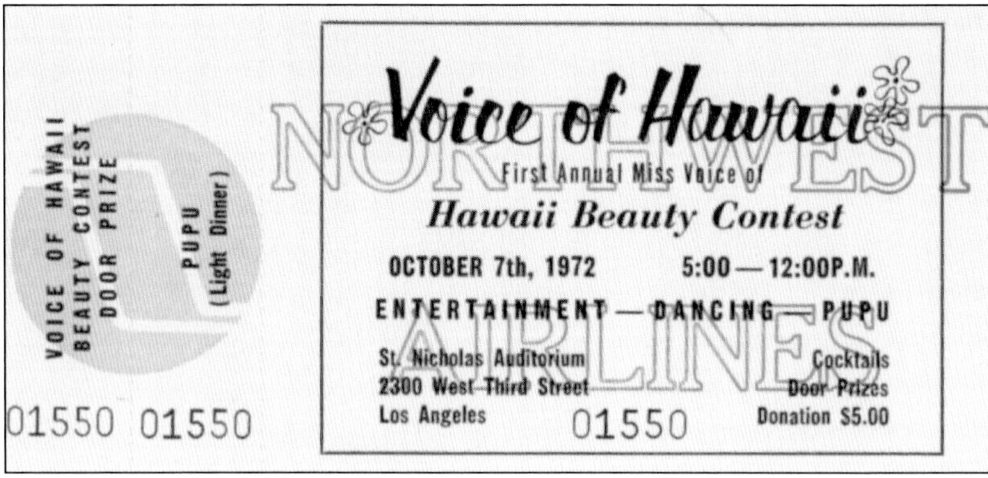

To celebrate the Hawaiian community in Los Angeles, the *Voice of Hawaii* newspaper created the Voice of Hawaii pageant. *Voice of Hawaii* was a news outlet that kept diasporic Hawaiians connected. Pictured here are Bobby Chun (far left) and the judges of the pageant. Contestants were asked to write letters describing the value of news outlets like *Voice of Hawaii*. A common thread in those letters showed the consistent need for attempts to keep the Hawaiian community connected, which the *Voice of Hawaii* helped with. (Both, courtesy of Charmaine Kuni Keoho.)

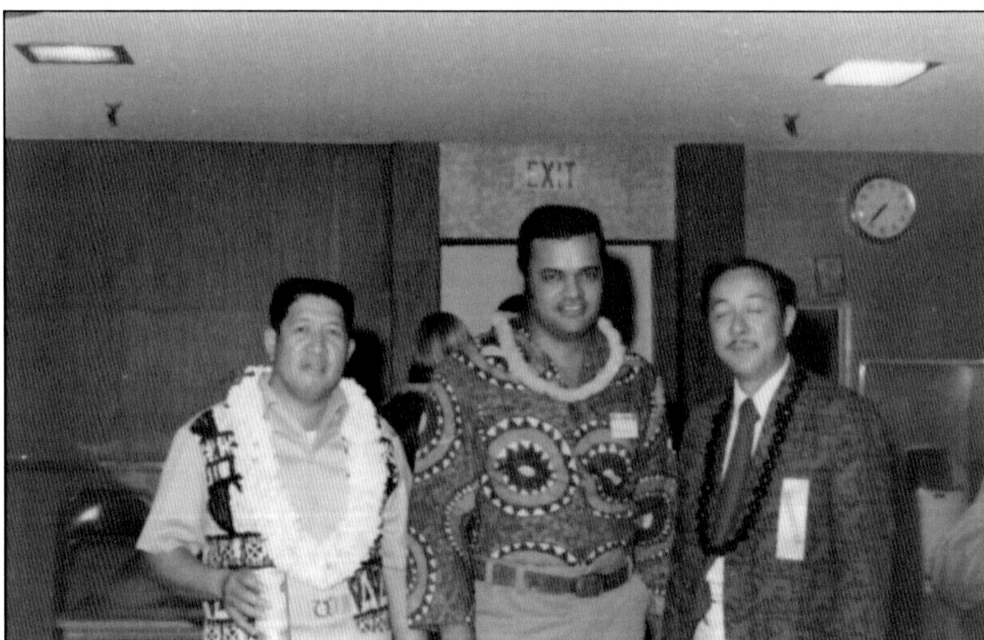

Luana Kuni (right) became the first Miss Voice of Hawaii, and for a year, she helped advertise for Hawaiian-centered businesses. Miss Voice of Hawaii's promotion of Hawaiian business was a good move for organizers like Gary Spears, Bobby Chun, and Joe Keawe because it kept Hawaiian money circulating between Hawaiians, which created a stronger and more successful community. The Voice of Hawaii pageant was a ripple from the rebirth of Hawaiian culture in Hawaii. The children of the second-generation Hawaiians were taken up in the wave. Below, Roland "Tuffy" Chang, Moana Chang, and Randy Chang play while women dance at a plaza opening in Gardena. (Above, courtesy of Charmaine Kuni Keoho; below, courtesy of Randy Kaulana Chang.)

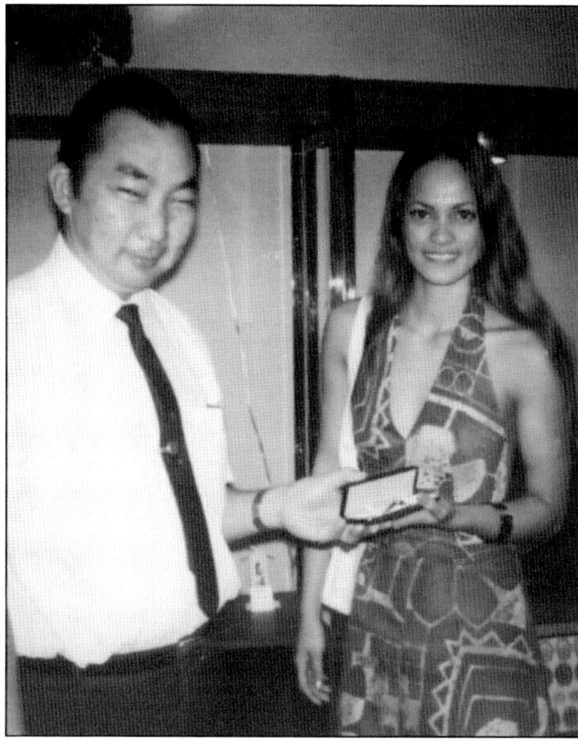

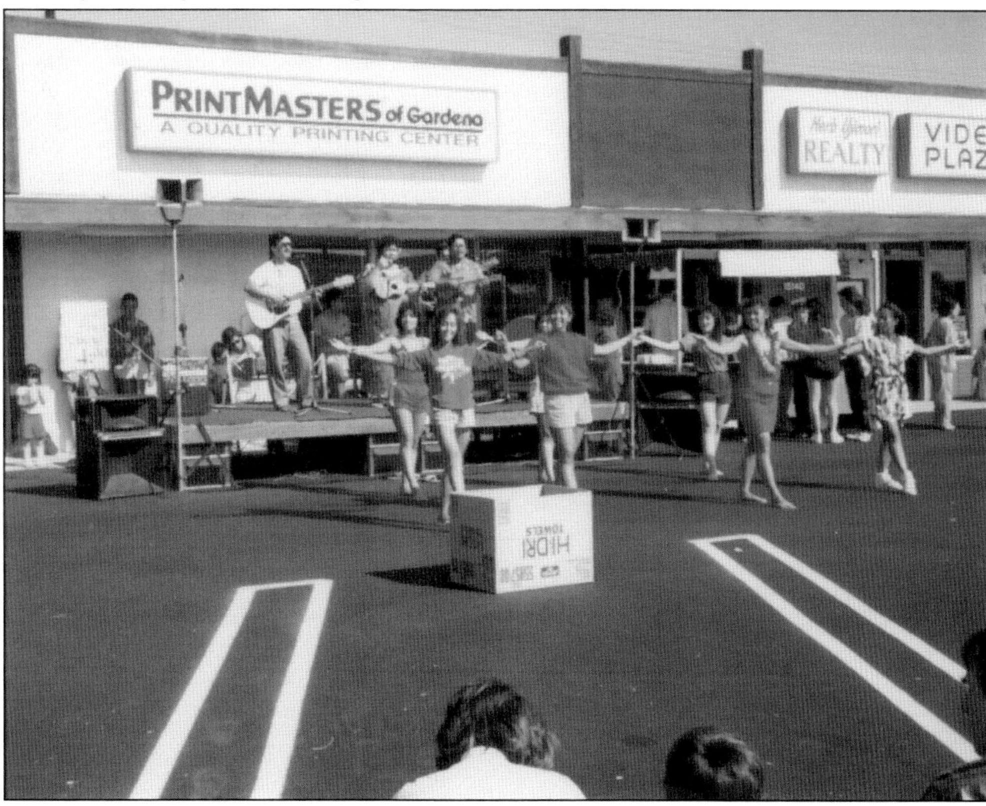

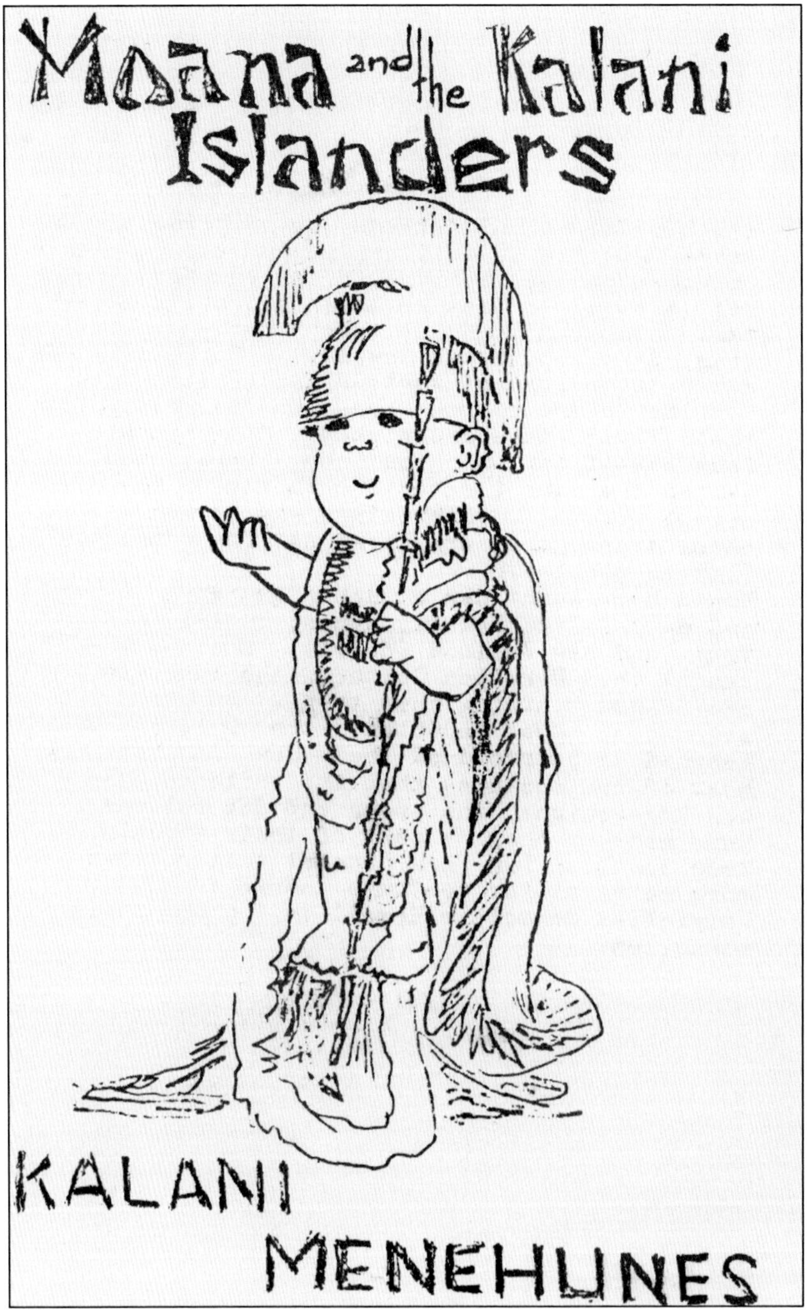

With the growth of the Hawaiian community in Los Angeles came a growing need for cultural education. Moana Chang gathered the children of Native Hawaiians each weekend, created a hula halau called the Kalani Islanders, and taught them Hawaiian culture. What made the Kalani Islanders unique was its broad definition of Hawaiian culture. Not only did the children learn to dance and sing, they learned etiquette, how to play instruments, make their costumes, and respect all cultures. To do this, Chang would spend Sundays taking the children to every church their respective families were part of, so they would be exposed to multiple faiths. (Courtesy of Randy Kaulana Chang.)

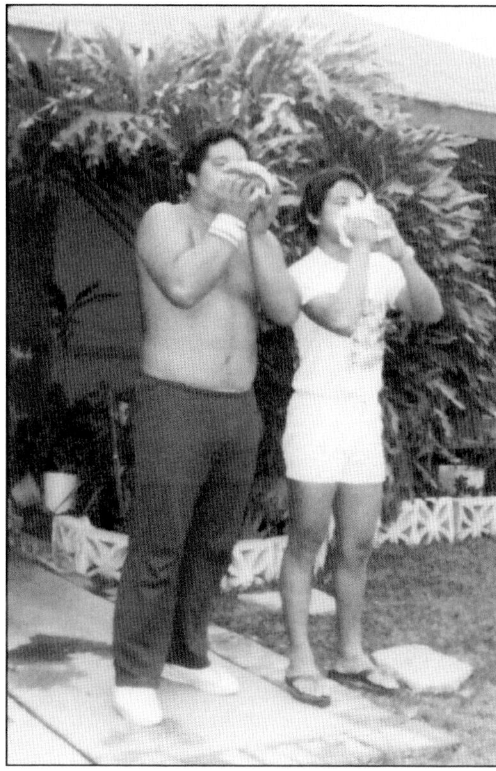

The Chang home in Carson became the center for all aspects of hula, from the conch shell signaling the start of gatherings to dancing and playing music. Pictured on the right are Lono Makanui and Roland "Tuffy" Chang playing the conch shell. Below are Kalani Islanders practicing. (Both, courtesy of Randy Kaulana Chang.)

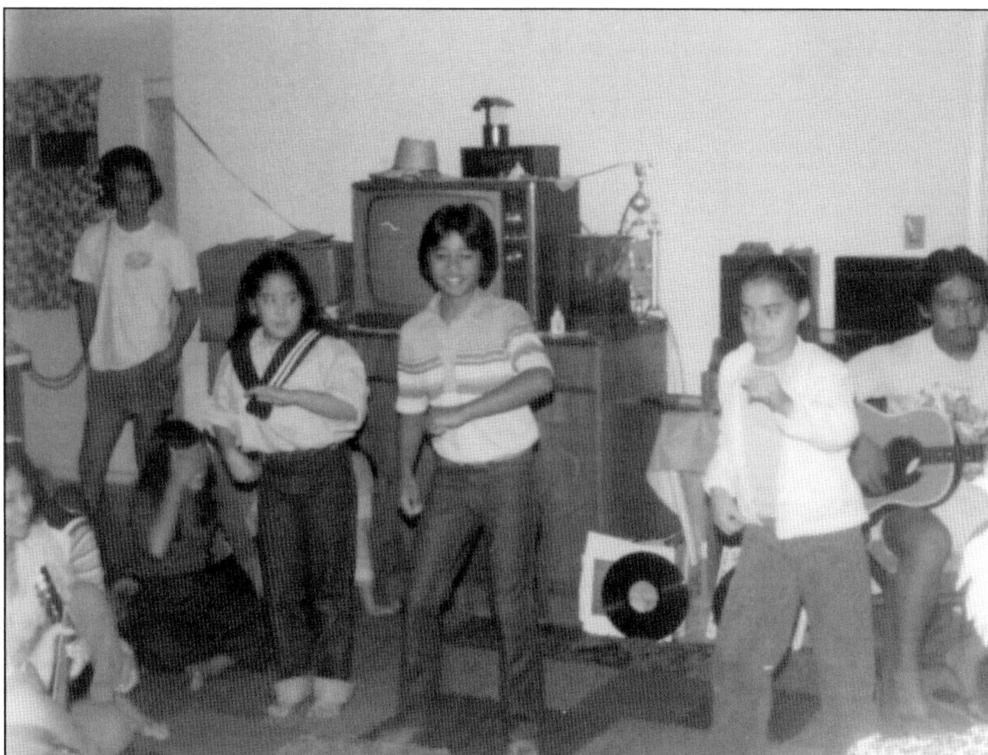

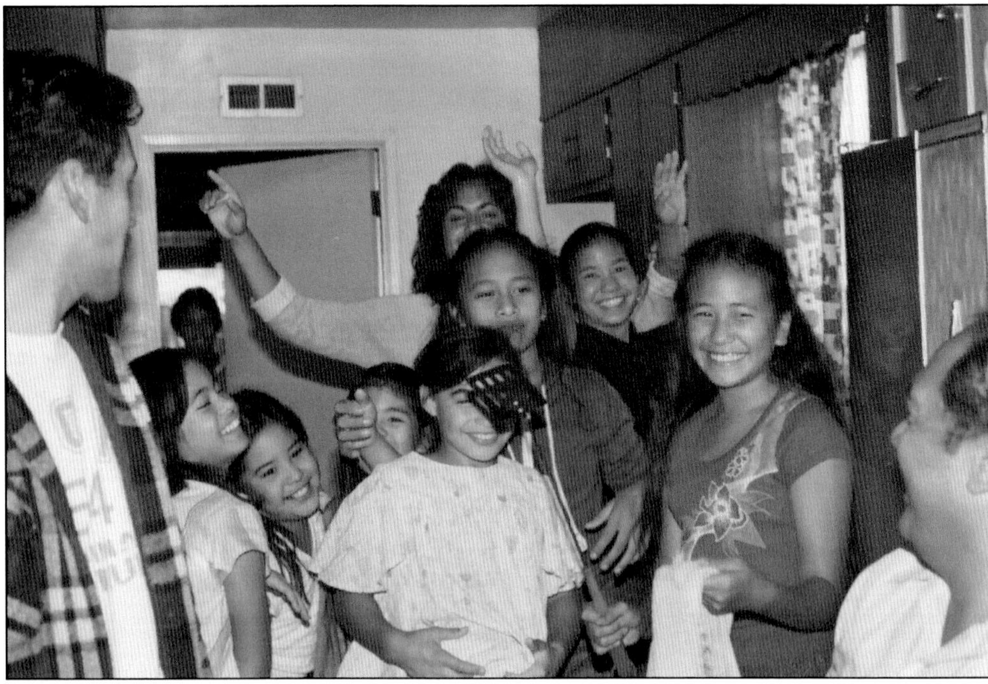

Perhaps more important than hula, Moana Chang taught the children how to be part of a larger community, which meant more than just dancing. It meant having fun and working together. (Both, courtesy of Randy Kaulana Chang.)

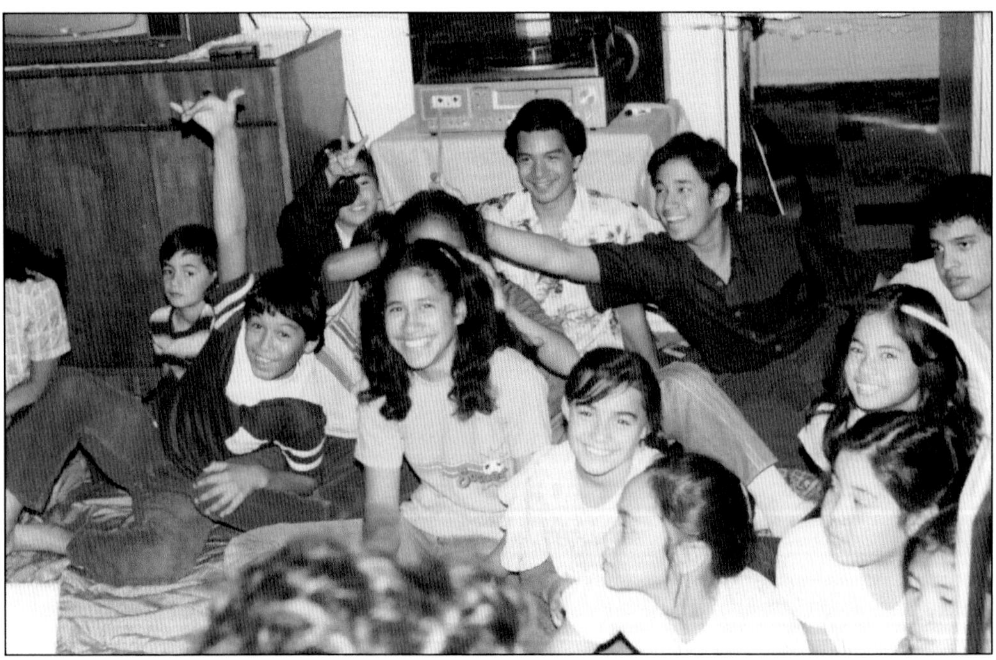

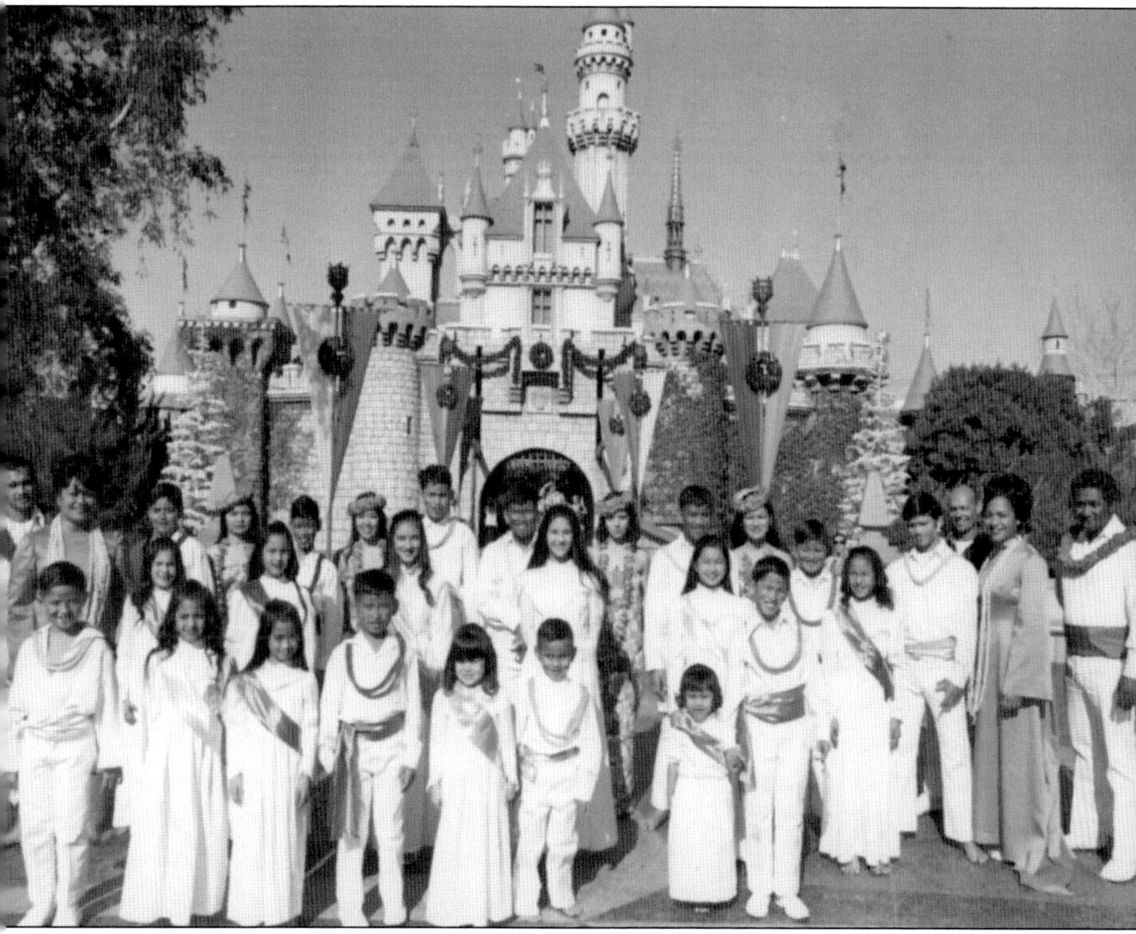

Overall, the Kalani Islanders, and hula halau in general, had a resounding affect on the Hawaiians in Los Angeles. Many culturally enriching traditions unique to Los Angeles, like the Ho'olaule'a (Hawaiian festival) in Alondra Park, Northridge, Cerritos, and Long Beach were started as venues for halau to raise money for competitions, costumes, and trips home to Hawaii. Pictured above are the Kalani Islanders at Disneyland, where they performed at the Carnation Plaza. (Courtesy of Randy Kaulana Chang.)

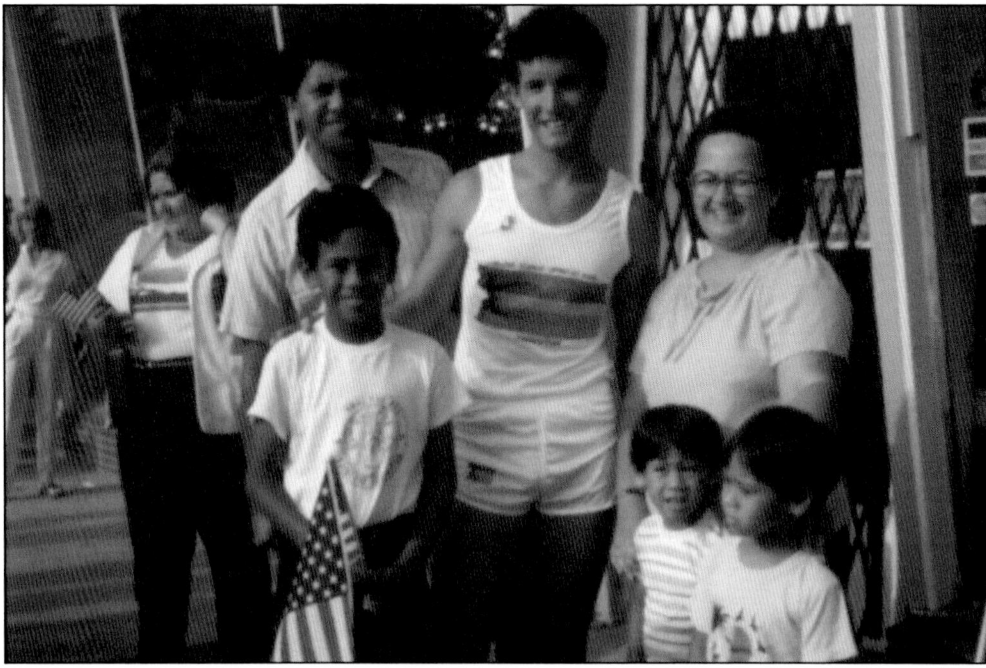

Being part of a community means that the big events in the area are big for everybody, whether it is something common like Christmas or the Olympics. The Kekauoha family (above) celebrates the arrival of the 1984 Olympic torch. Below, Eric Miller explains Christmas to his daughter Leilani. (Above, courtesy of the Kekauoha family; below, courtesy of the Pelayo family.)

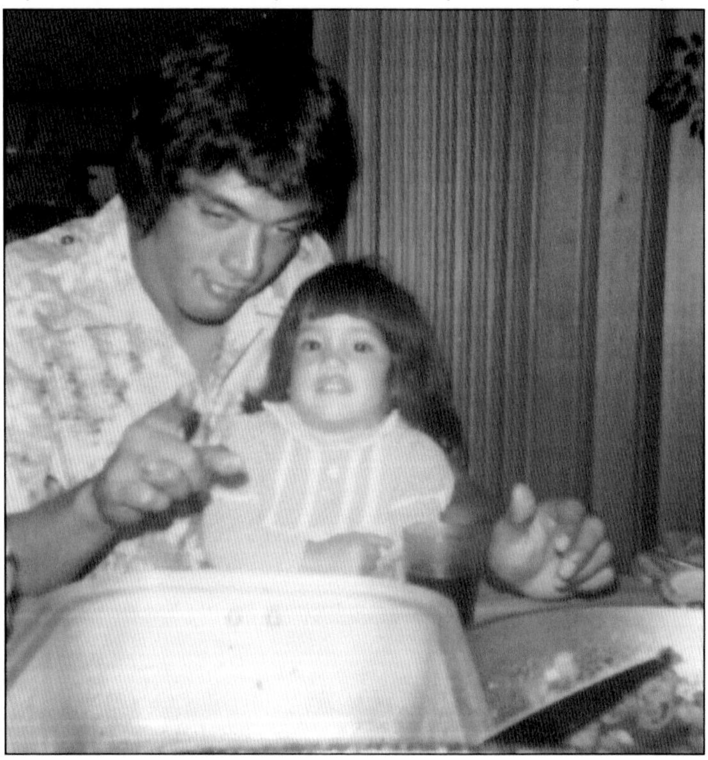

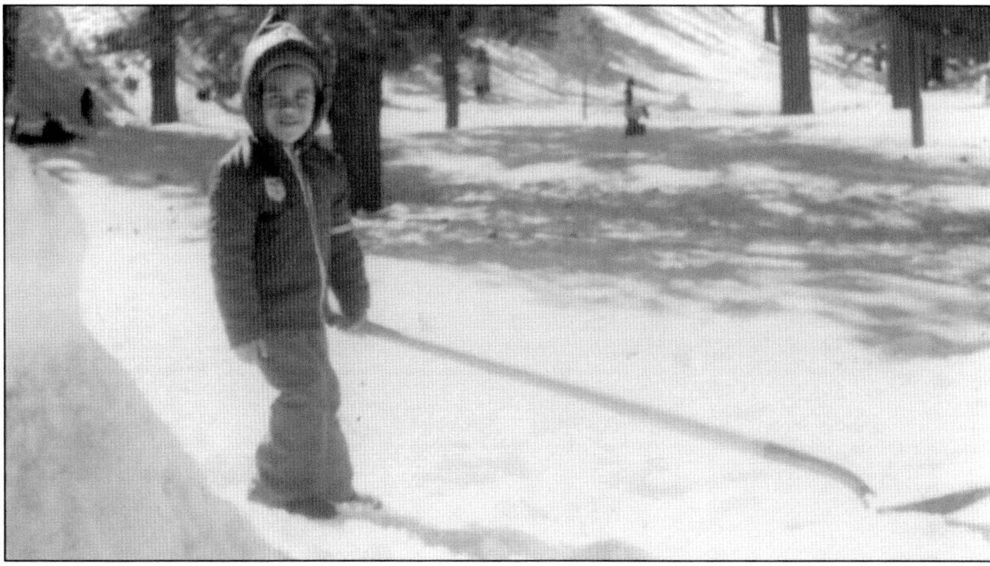

Conservation of nature and tradition was not restricted to purely Hawaiian-themed lands and traditions. Dexter Kekauoha (above) is shown enjoying the slopes in Wrightwood in 1979. Living on the continent means that Hawaiians are exposed to hobbies and events that do not occur in Hawaii. One such event that happens across the continental United States but not in Hawaii is the Renaissance Pleasure Faire. Shown below are Alden Lono Pelayo and his wife, Laurie Pooler Pelayo, who began visiting the Renaissance Pleasure Faires in Agoura Hills in the late 1970s. They continue to visit the place today at its current location in Santa Fe Dam as participants in St. Michael's Guild. (Above, courtesy of the Kekauoha family; below, courtesy of the Pelayo family.)

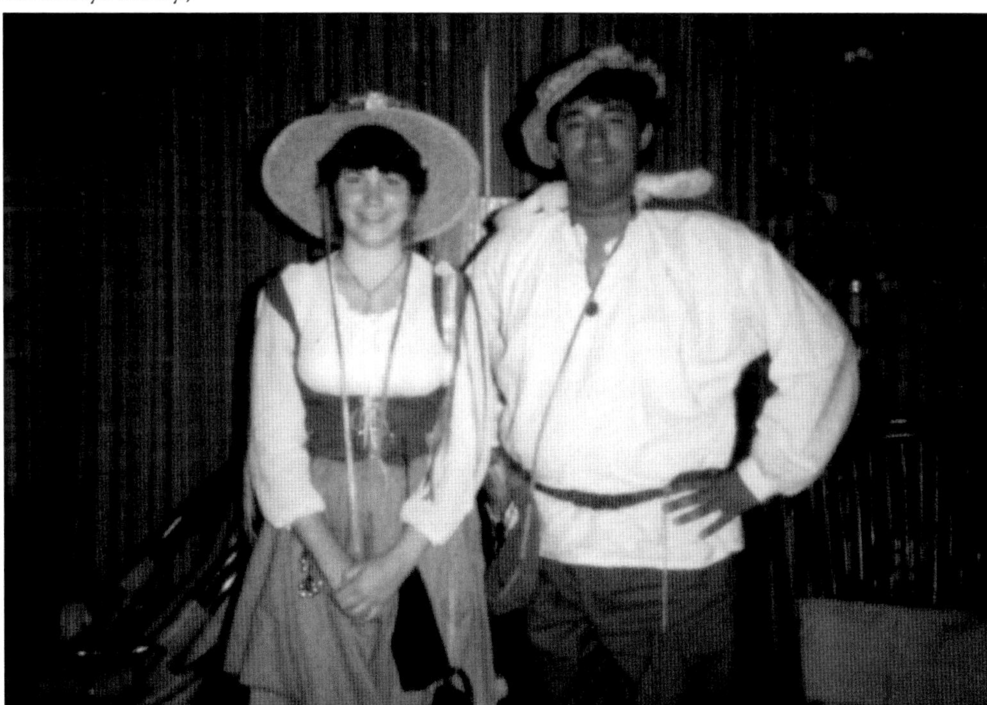

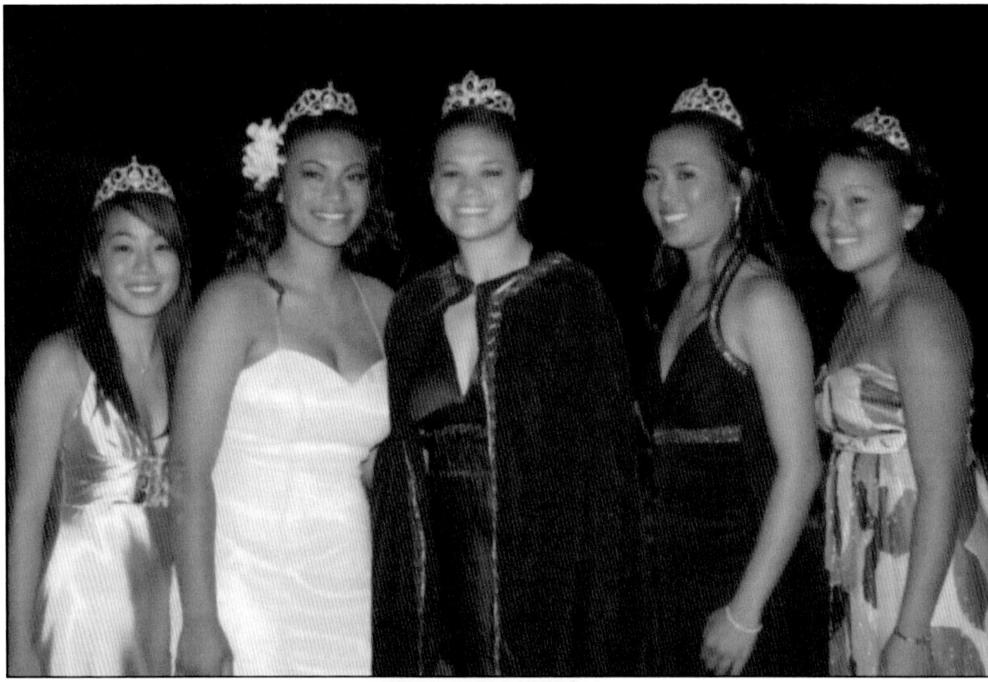

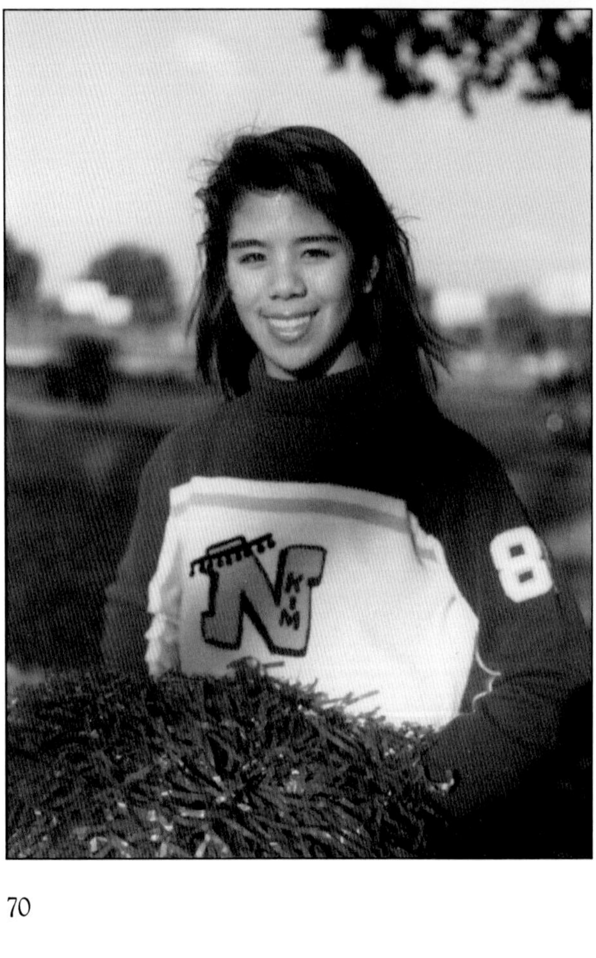

There are common threads through life in America, and high school is one of them. While the experience may not exactly be the same for everyone, there are events that happen year in and year out, such as homecomings, proms, football games, and student body elections. Pictured above is Anuhea Letuli (second from the left) as a homecoming princess for North High School. Lehuanani Tanemura is pictured below in her Narbonne High School cheerleading outfit. (Above, courtesy of the Letuli family; below, courtesy of the Tanemura family.)

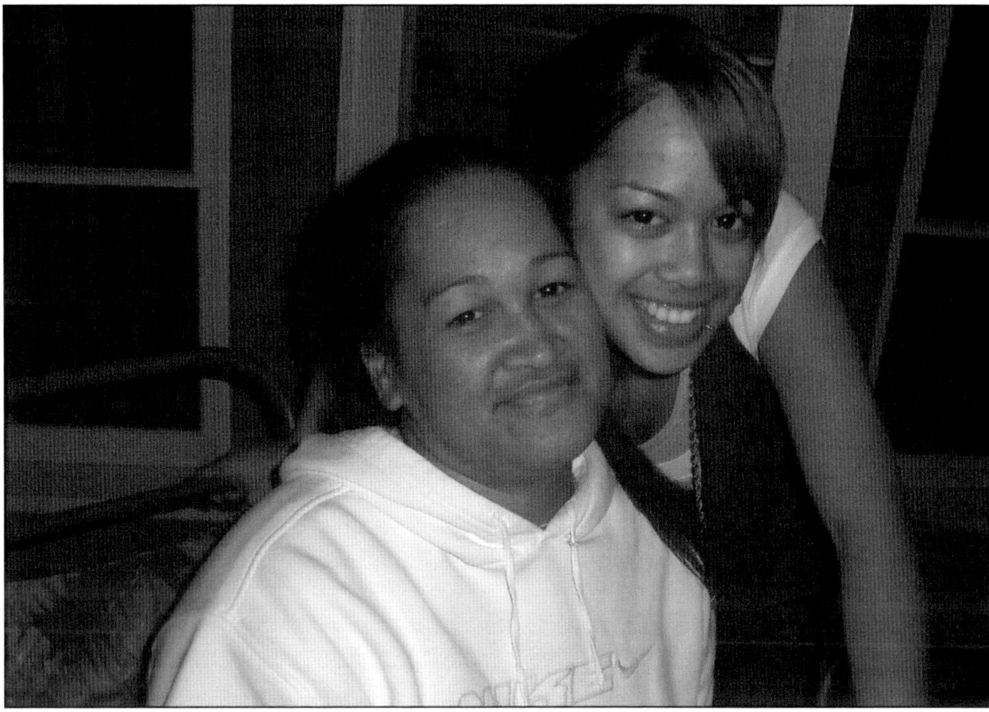

Hawaiians suffer from an emotional toll that comes with a culture defined by its connection to the land that it does not own. Many Native Hawaiians suffer from socioeconomic shortcomings. Shown above with her daughter Precious, Mana Nihipali's life is an example of Native Hawaiian struggle and perseverance. She grew up in Carson, experienced difficulties at Carson High School, and left to pursue her GED. She got married and found peace as a stay-at-home mom. The struggle for education has been a part of and continues to be part of the Hawaiian experience. Pictured below is David Mickey Kuhia with 30 of his great-grandchildren. All are pursuing their education in public or private schools and various colleges and universities, such as Long Beach Community College, California State University, Long Beach, and California State University, Dominguez Hills. (Both, courtesy of Elizabeth "Nani" Nihipali.)

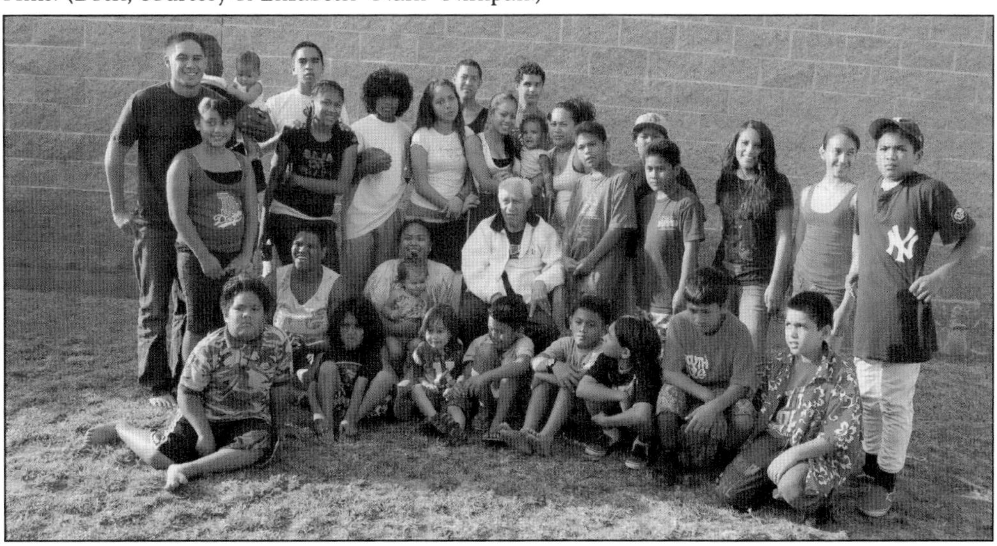

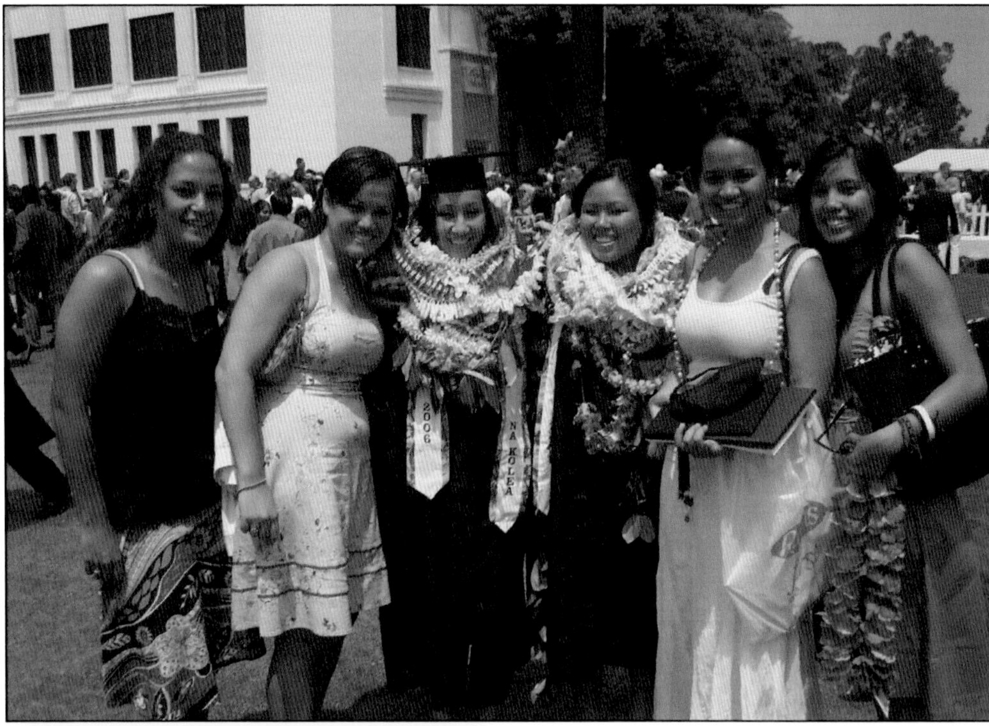

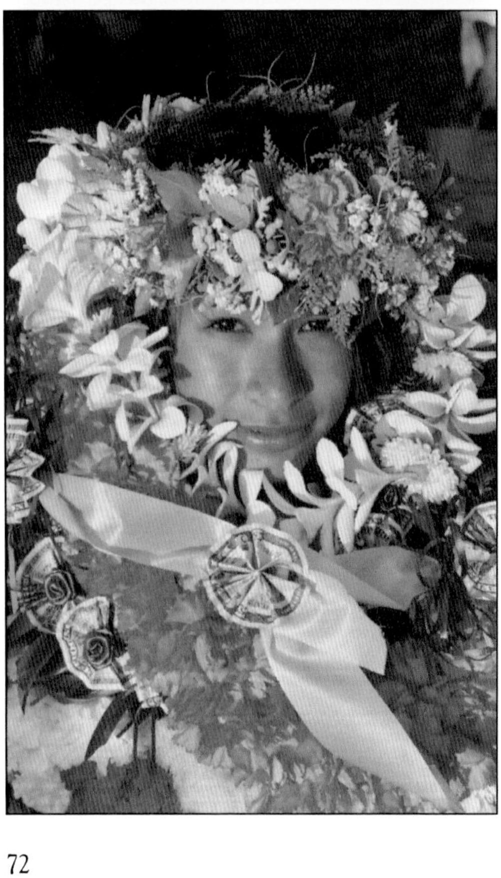

One of the main reasons for coming to the continent was for opportunities that were less available in Hawaii, such as quality education, and California continues to attract the best from the islands. Graduation from anything is an important achievement for Native Hawaiians and their families, a group that suffers from low education rates. Taimane Letuli (left) is adorned with so many leis that they no longer fit on her head after her graduation from North High School. Also shown above (left to right) are Elizabeth Kalama, Mahina Cumpston Sayin, Brandi Jean Nalani Balutski, Courtney Conching, Billie Gomes, and Malia Rodrigues Bayless, who graduated from Loyola Marymount University. The majority of girls graduated high school from Kamehameha School, Kapalama Campus, a private school reserved for Native Hawaiians, in 2003, and Malia graduated from Baldwin High School on Maui. (Above, courtesy of Mahina Cumpston Sayin; left, courtesy of the Letuli family.)

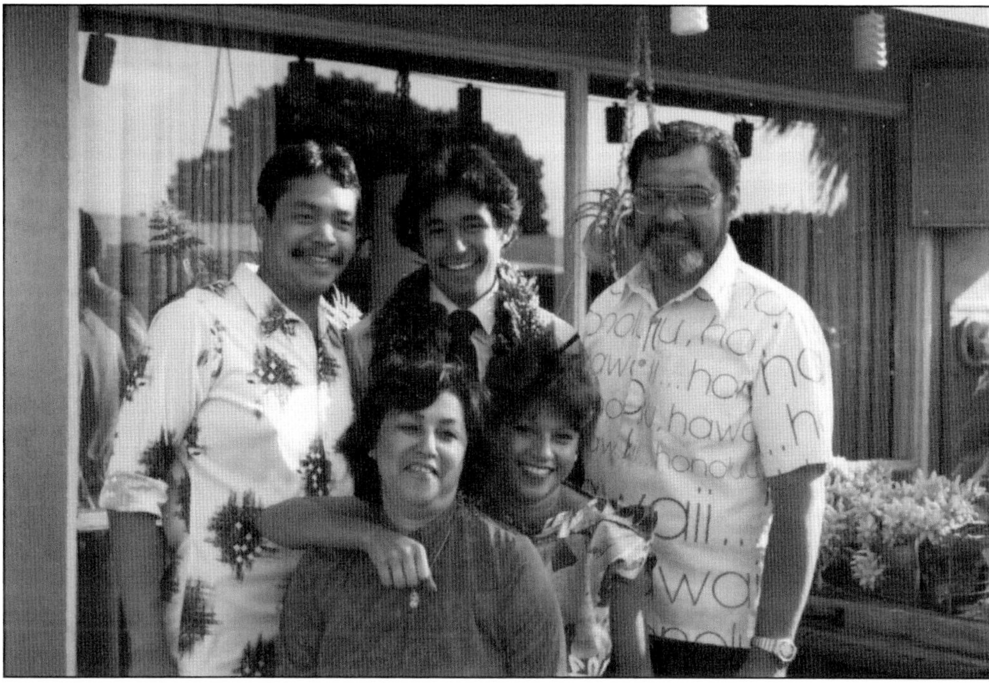

As with any Hawaiian celebration, there is a big luau honoring the graduate. The photographs displayed here are from Alden Lono Pelayo's 1982 Bishop Montgomery High School graduation party at the Pelayo home in Torrance. The above shows the proud family, Allen (North High School graduate), Alden Lono, Alcario "Sonny," Mary, and Maile Pelayo (Bishop Montgomery High School graduate). As with any luau, the honoree must make a speech and demonstrate his skills. At right, Alden Lono dances his favorite dance, Rocking Chair Hula, with his hula brother from the Kalani Islanders, Randy Kaulana Chang. (Both, courtesy of the Pelayo family.)

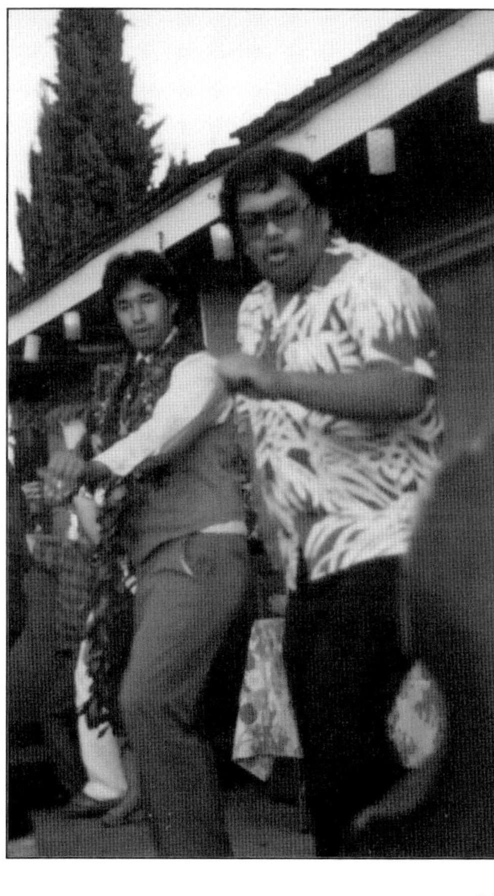

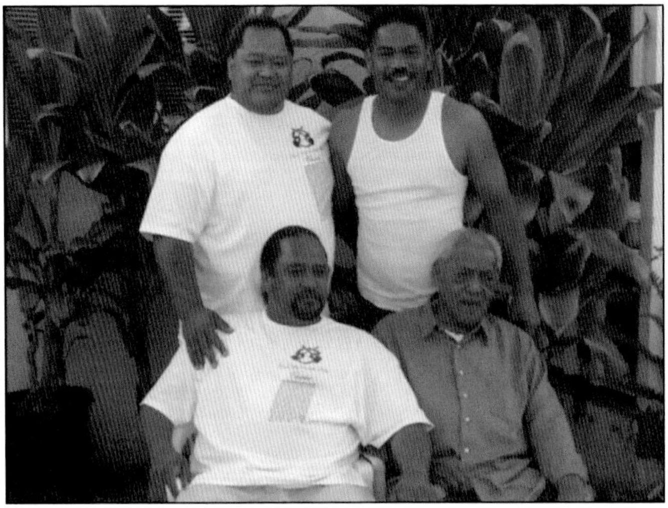

Like their father, Paul Nihipali (bottom right), Michael, Paul (top row), and Thomas (bottom left) are committed to supporting their families in occupations ranging from glaziers for housing projects and high rises in Los Angeles to aerospace employees at Boeing in Long Beach. (Courtesy of the Nihipali family.)

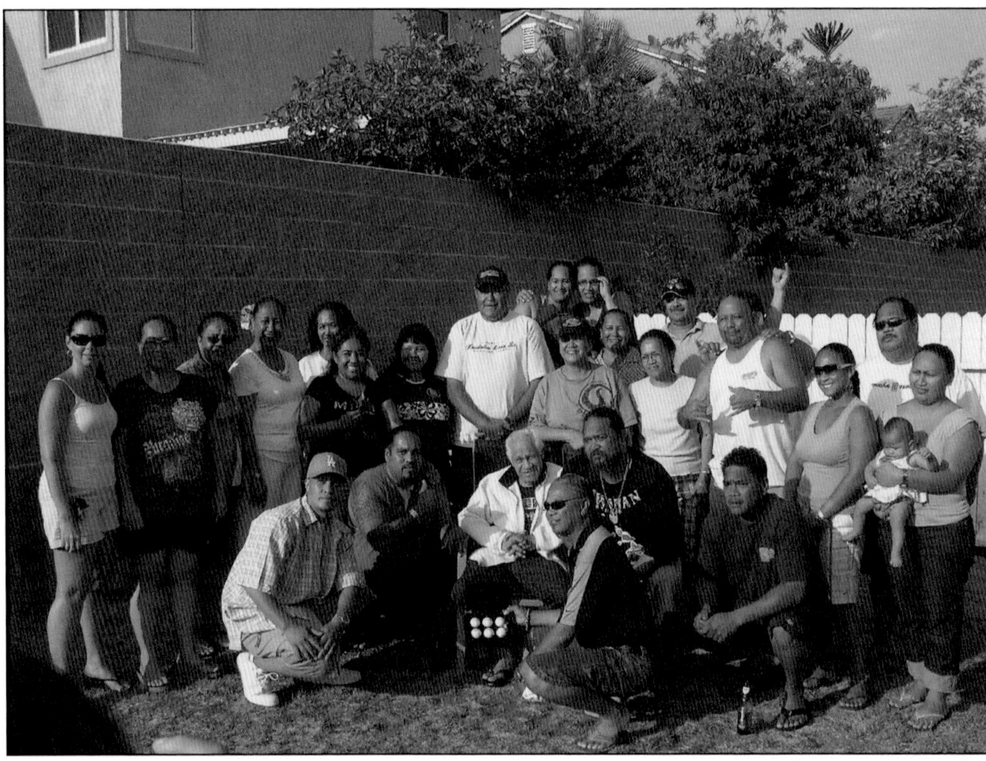

The Nihipali boys took their parents' culture and drive and passed it onto the generations that followed. The second, third, and fourth-generation Hawaiians in Los Angeles continue the traditions of ohana where everyone crams together under one roof to celebrate togetherness. These get-togethers reflect respect for elders and cultivation of multigenerational and multicultural connections of Hawaiian culture. (Courtesy of the Nihipali family.)

Ohana learns from ohana. In Los Angeles, the entertainment industry offers so many different forms of employment. There is always a need for acting, but there is also always a need for people in production and, perhaps more importantly, people who can make the action look real. Eric Miller (on the right) was a stuntman in Hollywood for many years with his brother Branscombe Richmond, pictured below. (Both, courtesy of the Pelayo family.)

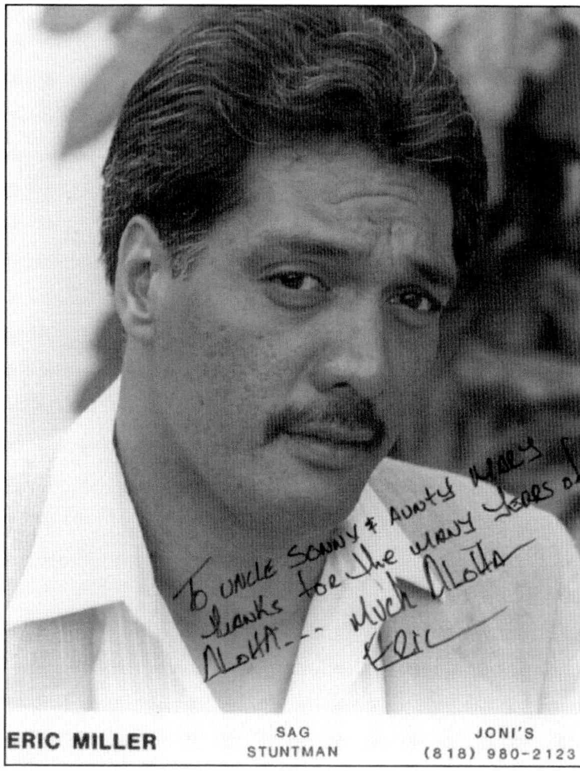

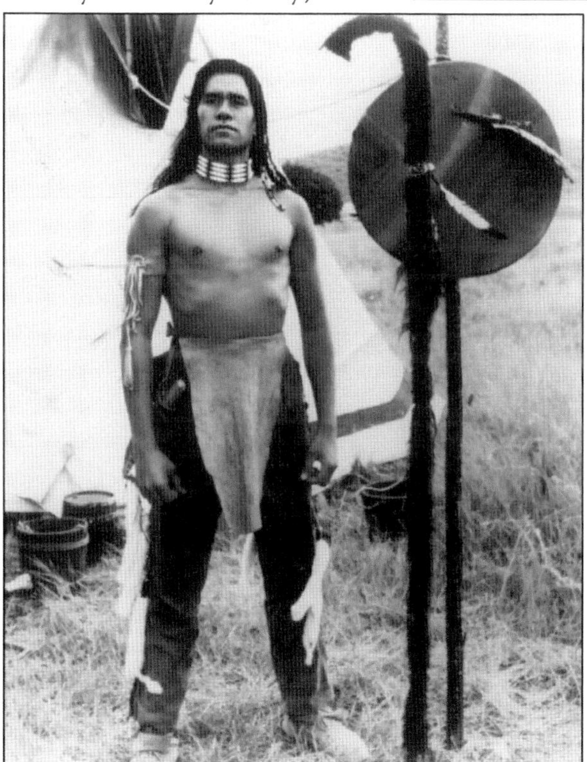

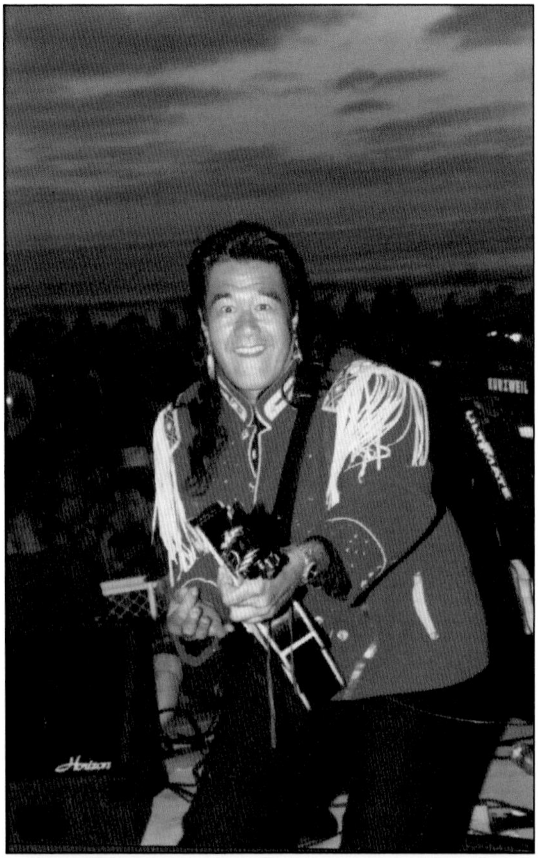

Combining his mixed-race features with Hawaiian ingenuity, Branscombe Richmond expanded his acting career to other forms of entertainment. His role on the television show *Renegade* with Lorenzo Lamas led to his place as spokesman for Indian Motorcycle. His love for music allows him to travel around the world with his band. Now living on homestead land on Maui with his wife, former Miss Hawaii Lei Ma'a Richmond, Branscombe has also started entertainment-based news shows for the local television station. (Both, courtesy of the Letuli family.)

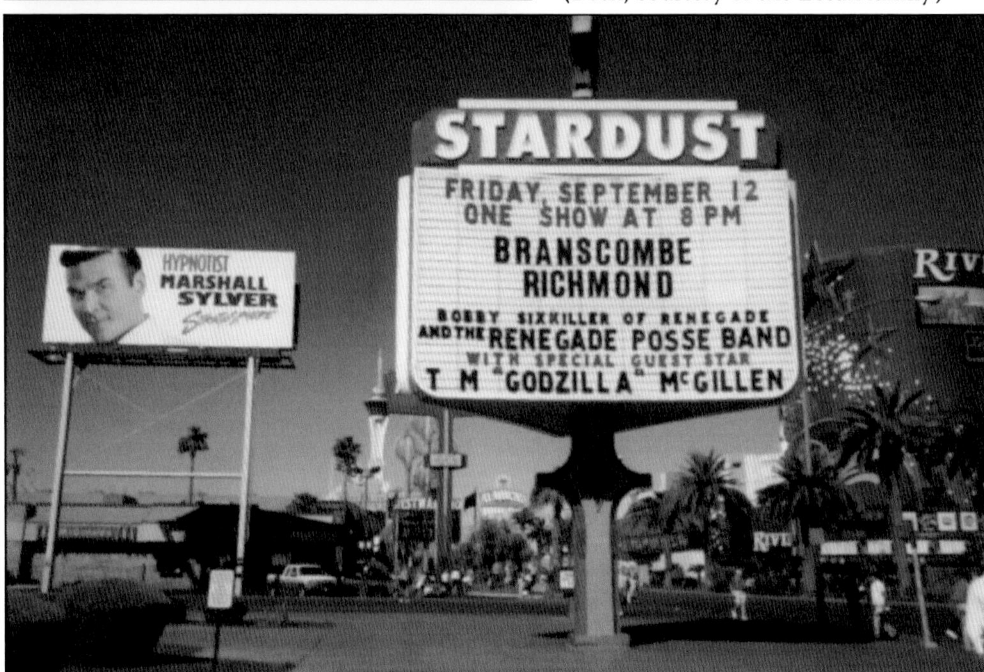

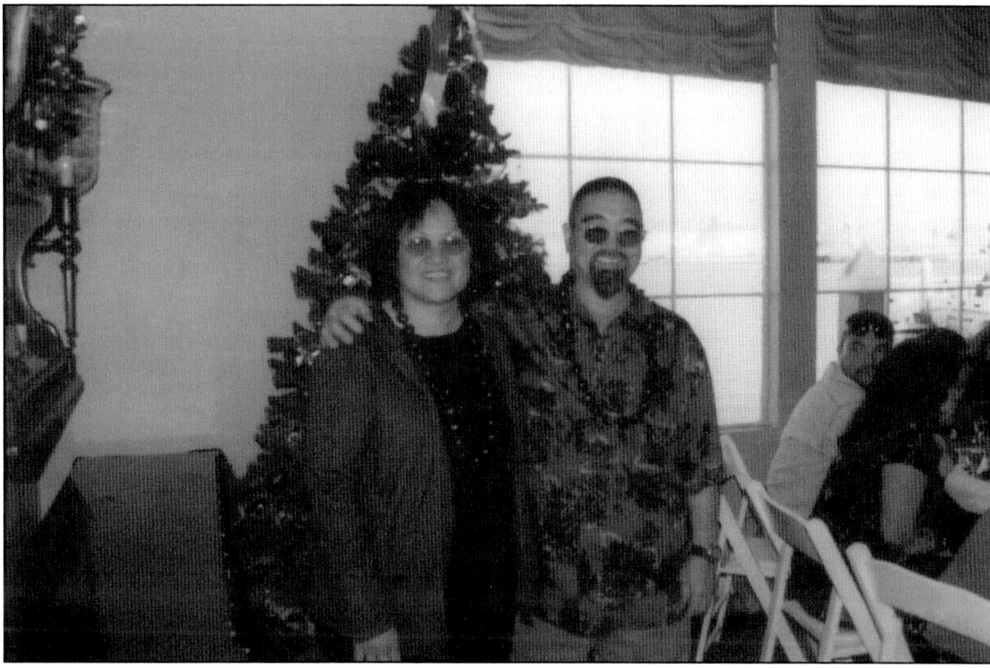

Just as much as others used their mixed-race skin as a commodity, other Hawaiians used their mixed-race culture. Diane and Wally Wachi were born and raised on Oahu but did not meet each other until they moved to California during the 1960s. They met at the Chico Military base. They got married and later moved to Carson, California. Diane has had a long career working with the city of Carson in the Public Safety Department. (Courtesy of Ron Wachi.)

Ron Wachi, president of Back Home, Inc., always wanted to be a restaurateur. In 2001, he opened Back Home in Lahaina in Manhattan Beach, California, with the goal of providing high end Asian Fusion food with a restaurant ambiance that encompasses "Ohana with the Aloha Spirit." The demographics and the close proximity to the ocean were perfect for this location. In 2003, he opened his second restaurant with the same name, in Carson. (Courtesy of Ron Wachi.)

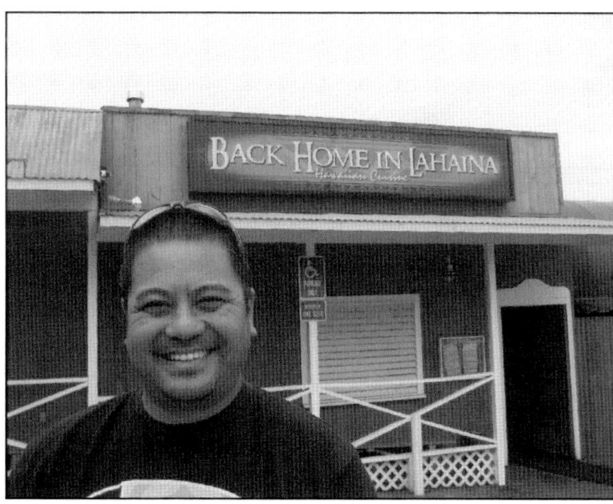

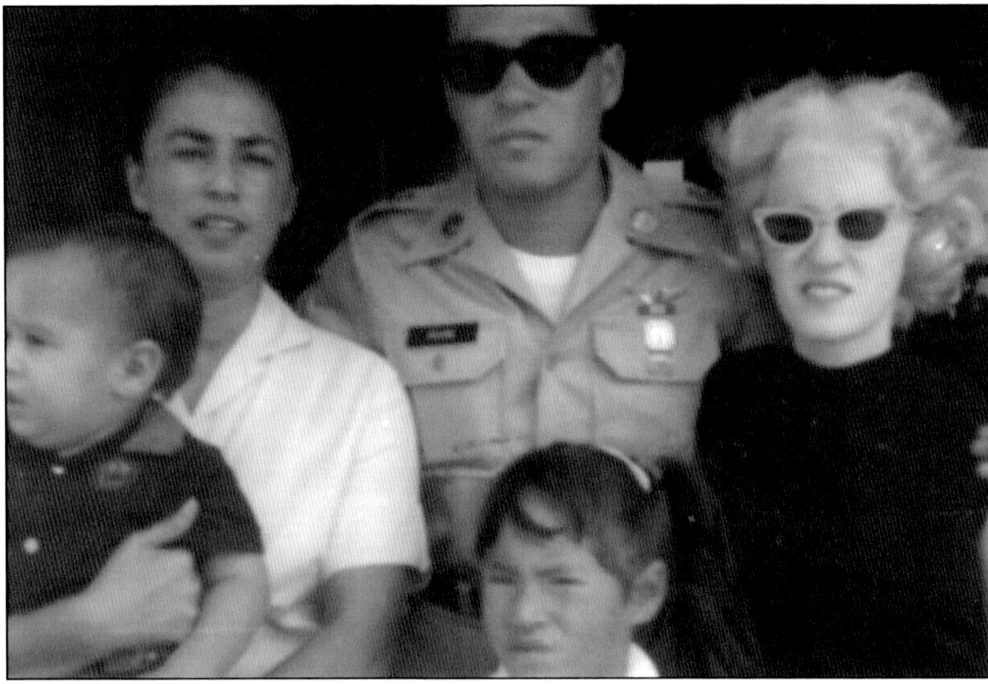

Carrying on the traditions of their parents, many second-generation Hawaiians followed their parents into service defending their country. Above, Dickey Irvine is seen with his mother, Mary Pelayo (holding her grandson Biggie Irvine), his older sister Lorraine Irvine, and his youngest sister Maile Pelayo before he leaves for Vietnam in 1967. The photograph below is of Dickey's younger brother Allen Pelayo returning home from the Gulf War with his daughter Rose Kalei Pelayo and his wife, Suzanne Pelayo. (Both, courtesy of the Pelayo family.)

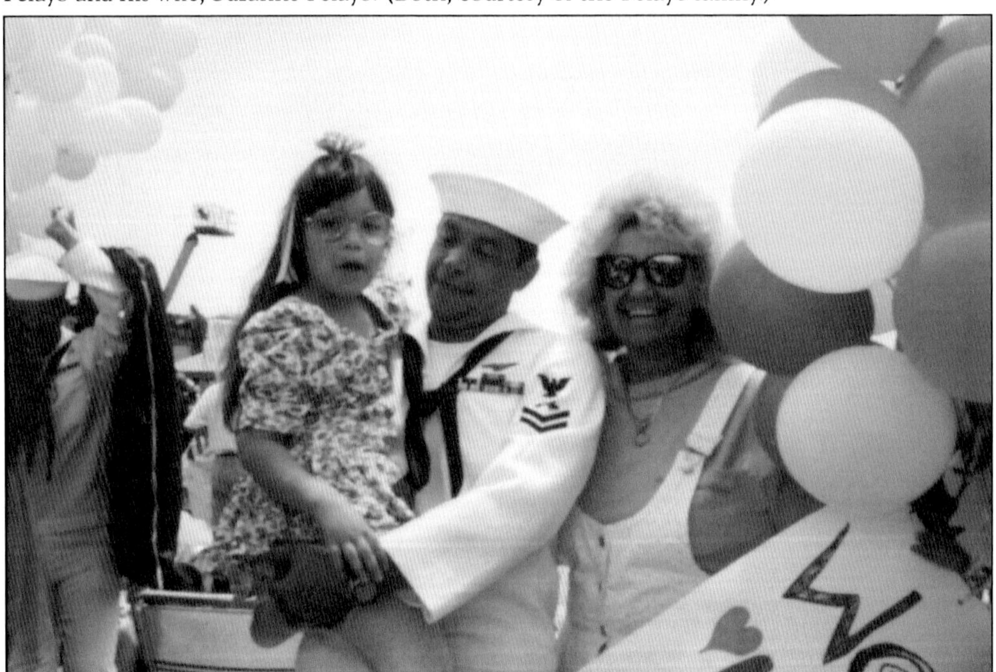

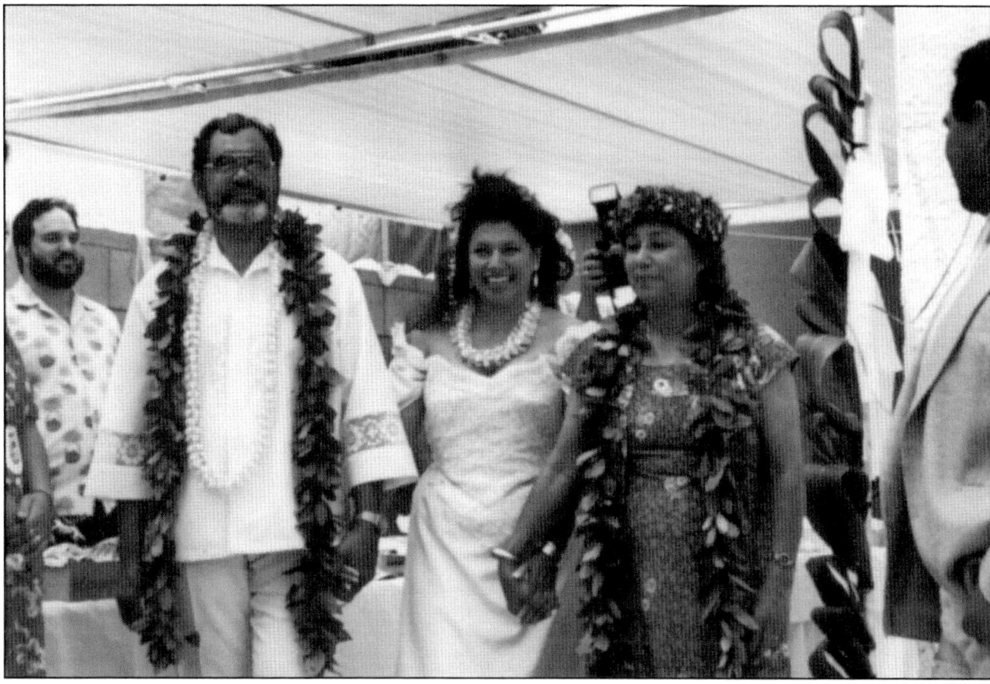

With Western education and successes influenced by Hawaiian culture and traditions, Hawaiians found a way to merge both worlds into one world. Weddings are a special occasion for any family, and for Hawaiians living on the continent, incorporating elements from the islands is important to any ceremony. Shown here is the wedding of Tui Letuli to Maile Pelayo. Maile walked down the aisle supported by both of her parents, Alcario "Sonny" and Mary Pelayo, both wearing the traditional ceremonial maile lei. The photograph below shows Maile and Tui together listening to the words of the pastor just before they exchange their own maile leis, followed by the Western wedding ring. (Both, courtesy of the Pelayo family.)

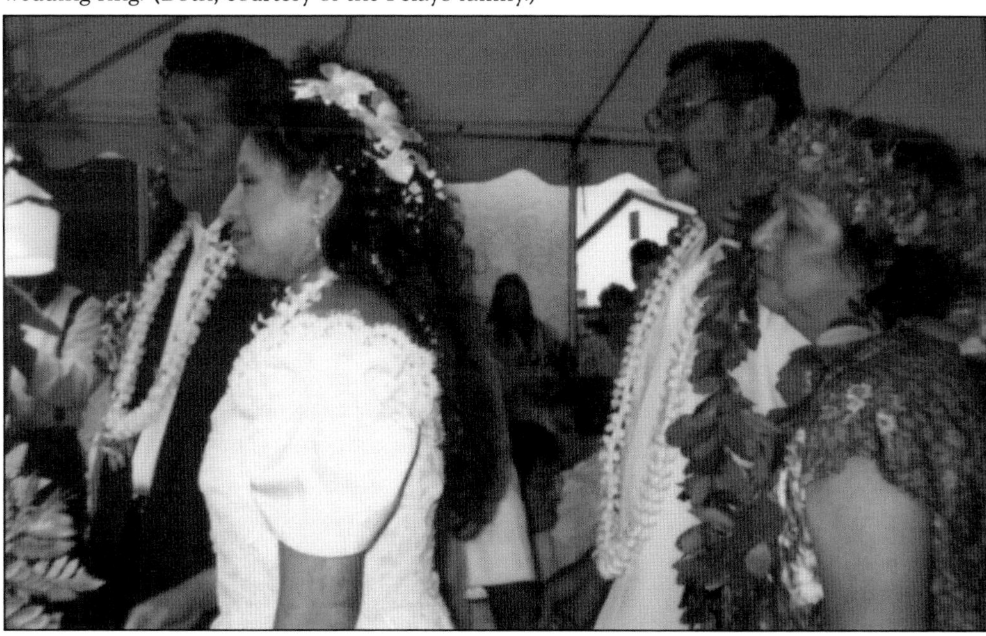

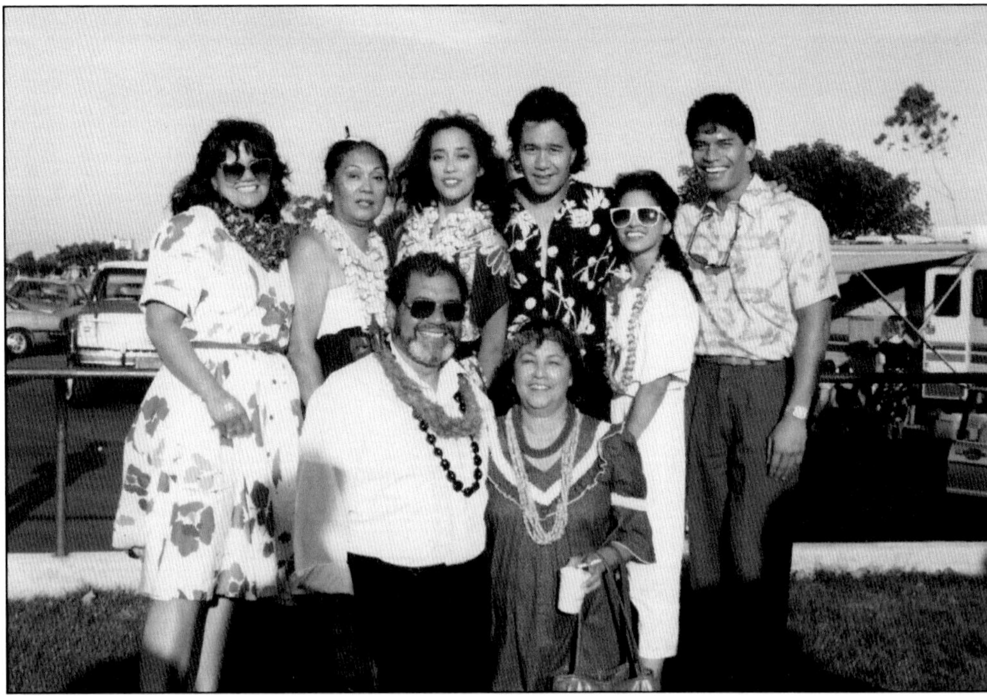

Keeping the culture alive is important to Native Hawaiians living in Los Angeles, and so is supporting those who help perpetuate the culture. Pictured from left to right are Gretta Sarkissian, Alice Richmond, Lei Ma'a Richmond, Branscombe Richmond, Maile Pelayo Letuli, Michael Crabbe, Alcario "Sonny" Pelayo, and Mary Pelayo came together to help support the first concert of Hula Halau Na Meakanu, run by Rolanda Reese of Ke Po'okela Foundation, who moved to Los Angeles in the 1980s. (Courtesy of the Pelayo family.)

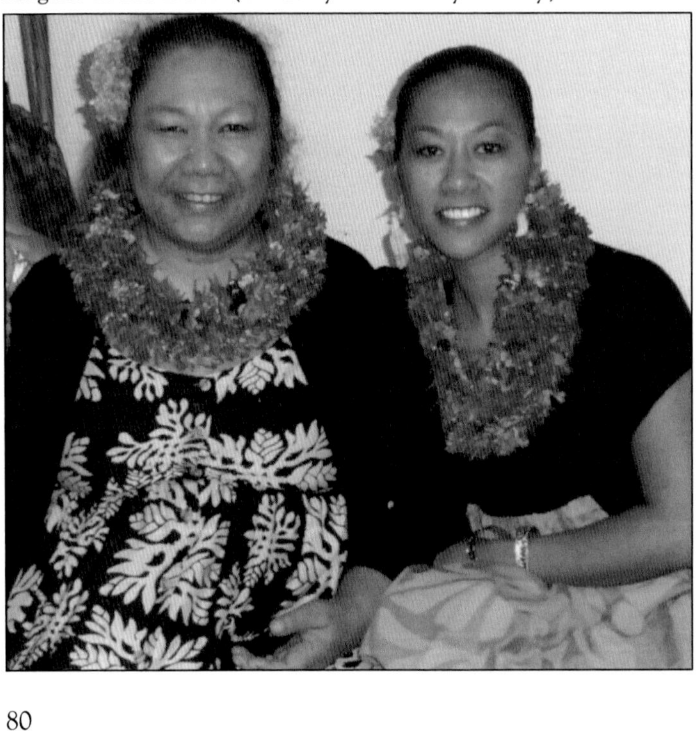

Annette Kaio McCormack, born in San Pedro in 1974, is the firstborn daughter of Lincoln and Sissy Kaio and was given to her grandparents to be raised in traditional Hawaiian ways. At the age of 16, Annette began teaching hula. In April 2011, she became a *kumu* (teacher) of Hula Halau O' Lilinoe. (Courtesy of the Nihipali family.)

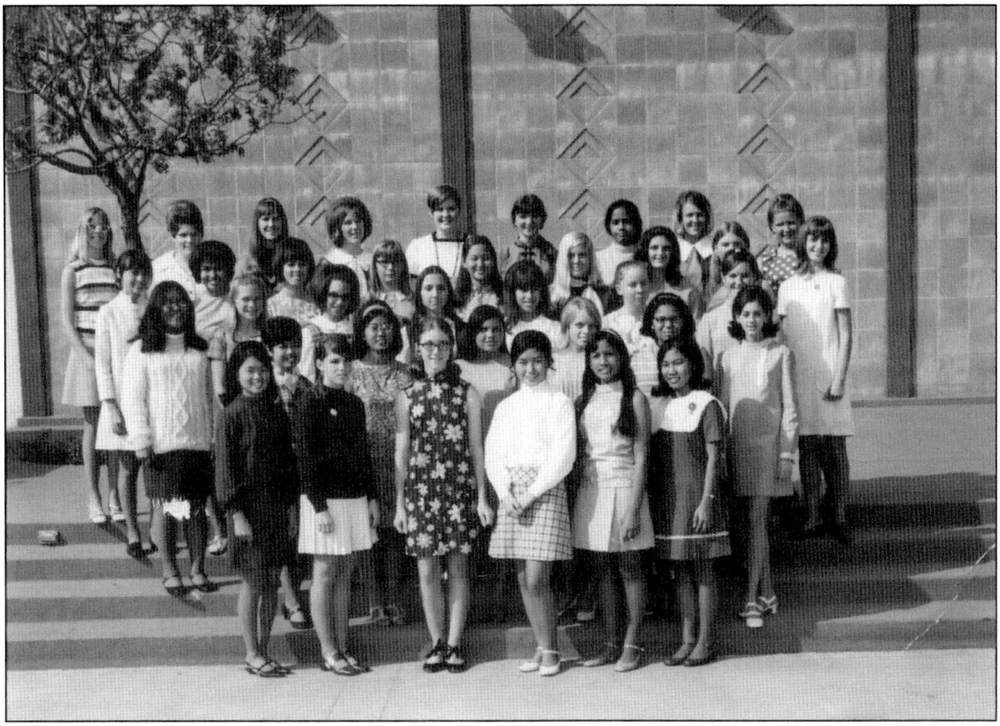

Pictured on the right is April "Sissy" Lilinoe Aguon Kaio at 27 years old, when she became a kumu. Her lineage is stemmed from Hawaiian priests, priestesses, kumu, chanters, and *kahuna*. Her family lines are descendants of Pele. It is through her study of ancient hula that she eventually understood her identity as a Hawaiian on the continent. She believes in ancestral knowledge and that the chanters guided her in the building of Halau. Above, Sissy (front row, far right) stands with her Carson High School leadership class. (Both, courtesy of Sissy Kaio.)

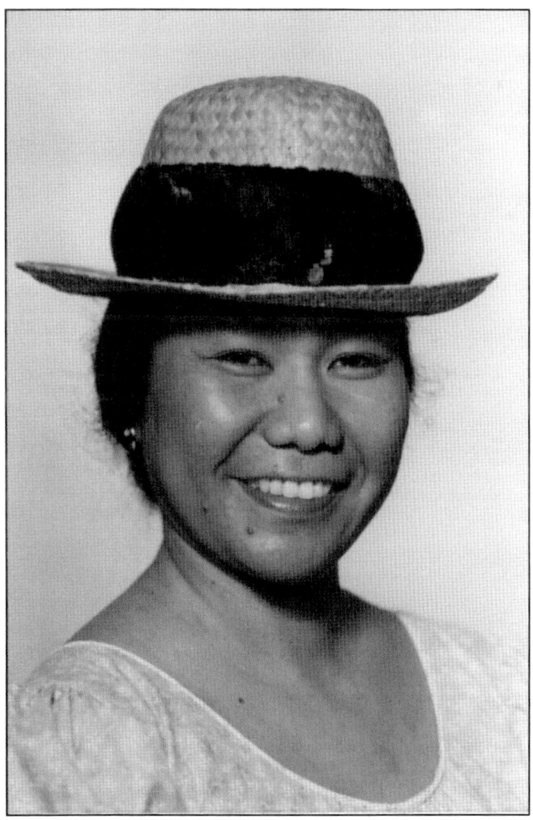

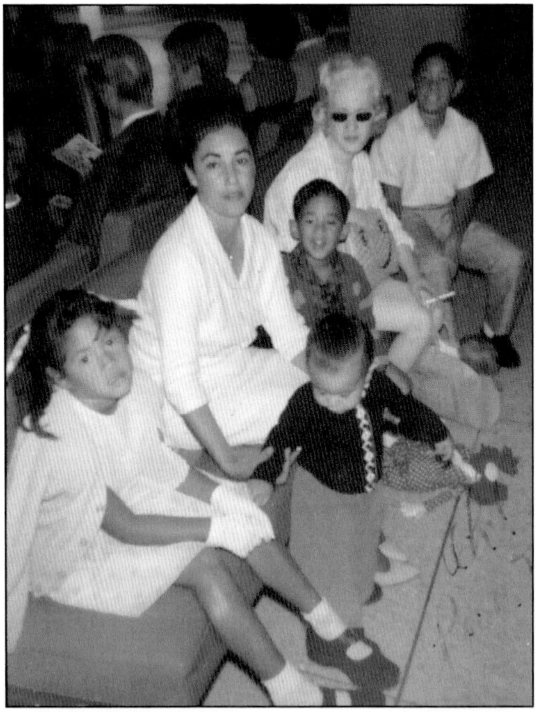

As noted in the first chapter of this book, it was important for family, especially grandmothers and siblings, to visit Los Angeles from Hawaii as diasporic Hawaiian families grew on the continent. Once the children of the first Hawaiians in Los Angeles were born, they were asked to keep their feet in Southern California but their heart in Hawaii. This responsibility can be seen in the scary trip the young ones have to make to Hawaii, many times without their parents. Above, in 1968 at Los Angeles International Airport, Mary Pelayo, her oldest daughter, Lorraine Irvine (with Lorraine's young son Biggie), and Mary's youngest son, Alden Lono Pelayo, send off Maile Pelayo Letuli and Allen Pelayo for their first solo trip to Hawaii to visit family. Below, Rose Jarrett and her mother wait with their mo'opuna Darin and Lehuanani for a flight. (Above, courtesy of the Pelayo family; below, courtesy of the Tanemura family.)

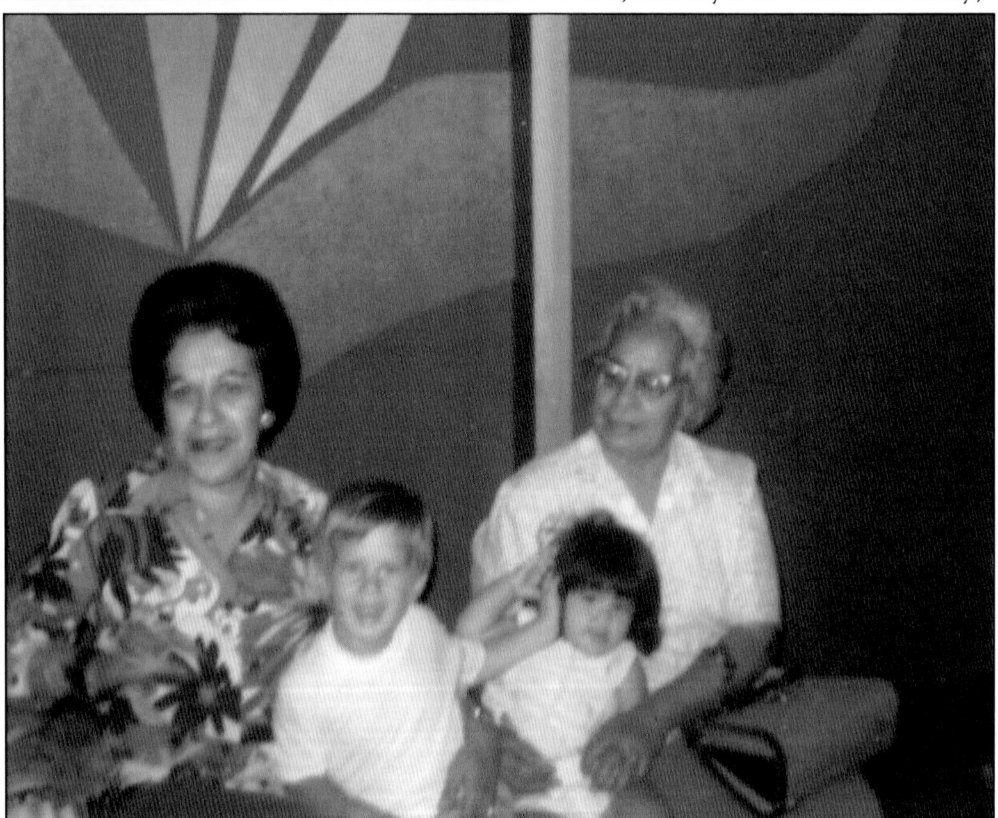

Four

Teaching Kokua

Civic Clubs

The core of Hawaiian culture is unified under the umbrella of aloha. Most people know that aloha means "hello," "goodbye," and "I love you," but it also means giving. Through aloha, Hawaiians are quick to offer *kokua* (aid) even when they do not have the resources to help, maybe especially when they do not have the resources to help. For much of Hawaii's modern history, these concepts were felt and lived but never vocalized, so Hawaiian families shared and loved on an individual and personal level.

In the 1970s, Hawaii witnessed a rebirth of tradition and culture during the Hawaiian Renaissance. In this time, scholars, kumu, and other Native Hawaiians reestablished the Hawaiian language, dances, and customs that were outlawed at various times since the overthrow of the monarchy. The Hawaiian Renaissance spread to the continent. In the spirit of the renaissance and kokua, the Hawaiians in Los Angeles started a movement to serve the communities they now lived in, culminating in the Ho'olaule'a, which first occurred in Northridge, then settled in Lawndale, and finally splintered into multiple events throughout the Southland.

As much as Ho'olaule'a is about the celebration of Hawaiian culture, the civic clubs of Hawaii also provide scholarships; teach Hawaiian arts like cooking, music, and lei making; and offer moments of bonding beyond Native Hawaiian ohana. Most importantly, they increased awareness of current issues, both Hawaiian and universal. If nothing else, the Hawaiian civic clubs created outlets for Hawaiian culture to thrive in the Southland desert.

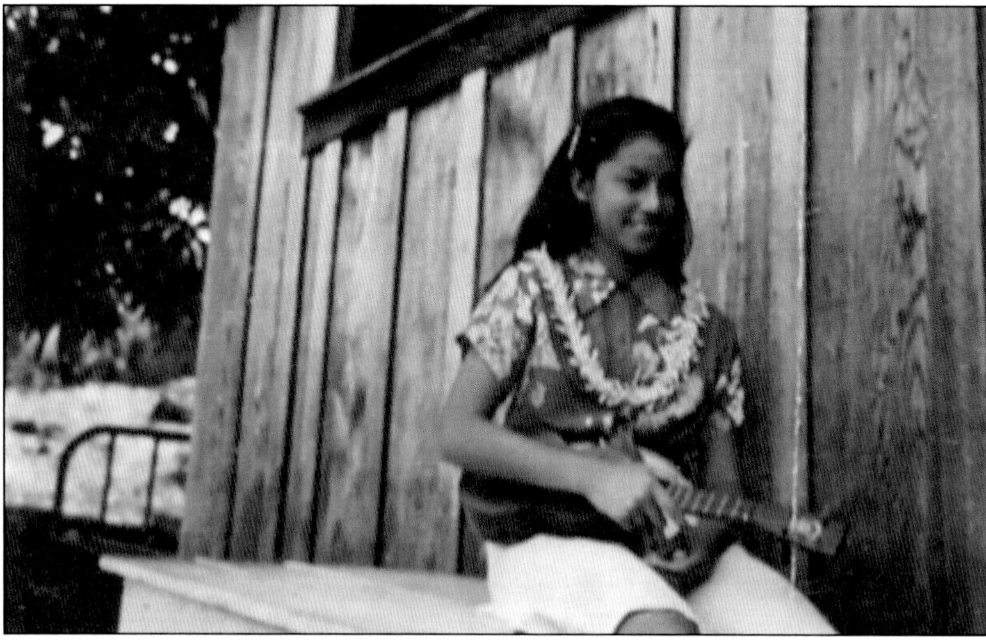

Civic clubs were necessary to help establish a Hawaiian community in Los Angeles because they allowed kanaka, locals, and the Hawaiians at heart to share their skills in various crafts. Mary Pelayo began playing ukulele at the age of 12 with the song "Five Foot Two," while she lived in Papakolea, Oahu. For Mary, the love of ukulele playing was so deep that she shared it with anyone who was willing to strum and listen. Mary Pelayo and her husband, Alcario "Sonny" Pelayo, were often the musical entertainment and hosts at their parties, along with their close friends the Roseros. In an effort to expand her love for music and to help fulfill their mission of perpetuating Hawaiian culture, Mary Pelayo began giving ukulele lessons to 'Ahahui o Liliuokalani Hawaiian Civic Club members. In this photograph are members of 'Ahahui playing their ukuleles and singing at Cerritos Mall. (Both, courtesy of the Pelayo family.)

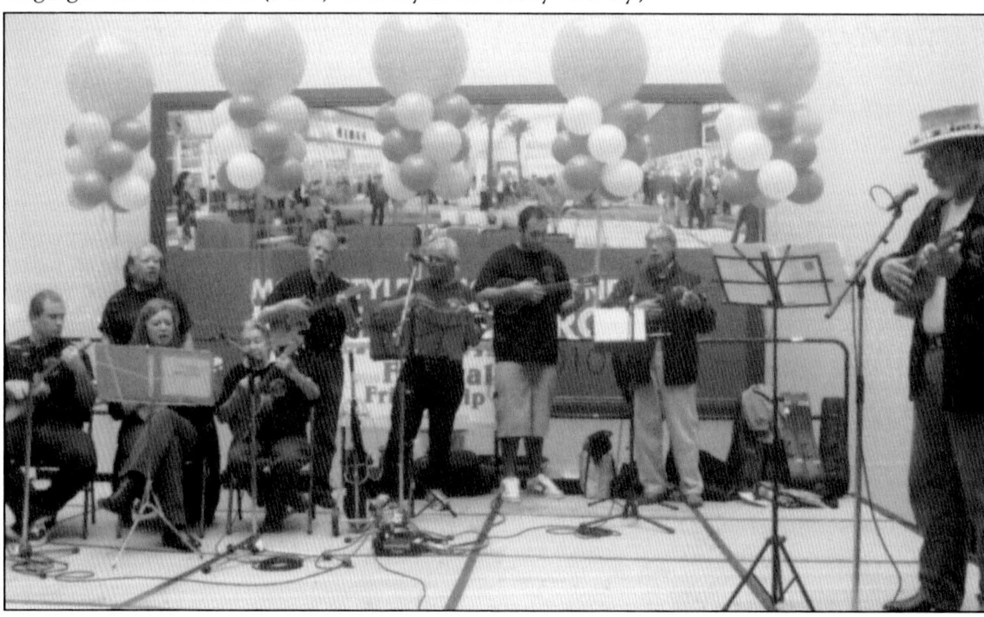

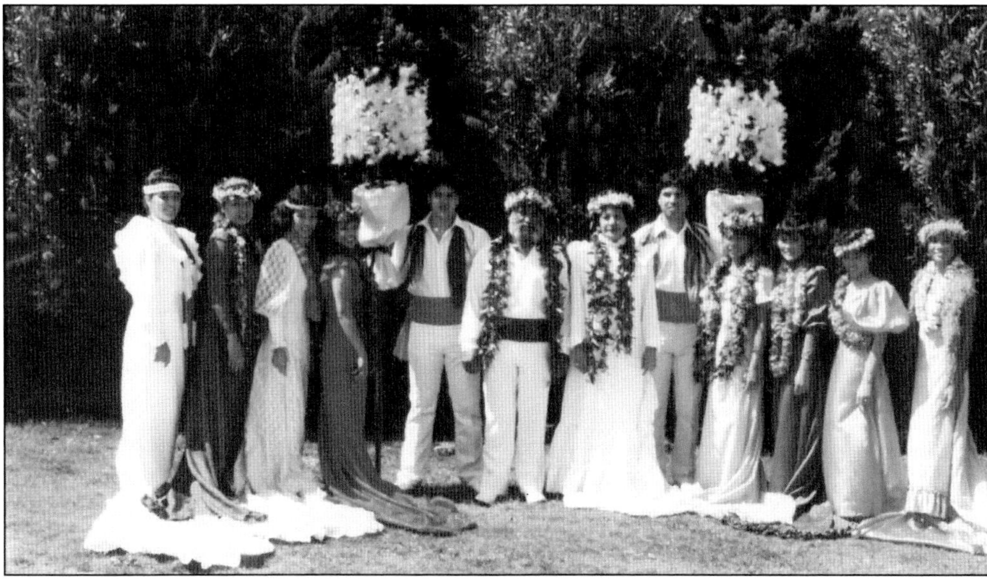

In Hawaii, and later on the continent, Hawaiians were able to celebrate their traditions once a year. May Day or Lei Day is a state holiday recognizing Hawaiian culture. The symbol of lei day, the lei, is (more than anything else) an accurate representation of Hawaiiana. The lei requires skillful hands to turn almost any plant, flower, or material into a gift. One event which ‘Ahahui o Liliuokalani Hawaiian Civic Club sponsored was a May Day celebration at Alondra Park. As discussed in chapter one, Lei Day usually includes a reenactment of the royal court. The image above shows the 1983 ‘Ahahui May Day court. Shown in the below photograph are some of the princesses of the 1984 May Day celebration. They are from left to right Rose Jarrett, Melanie Rosero, Carole Kahue, and Diana Hui. (Above, courtesy of the Rosero family; below, courtesy of the Pelayo family.)

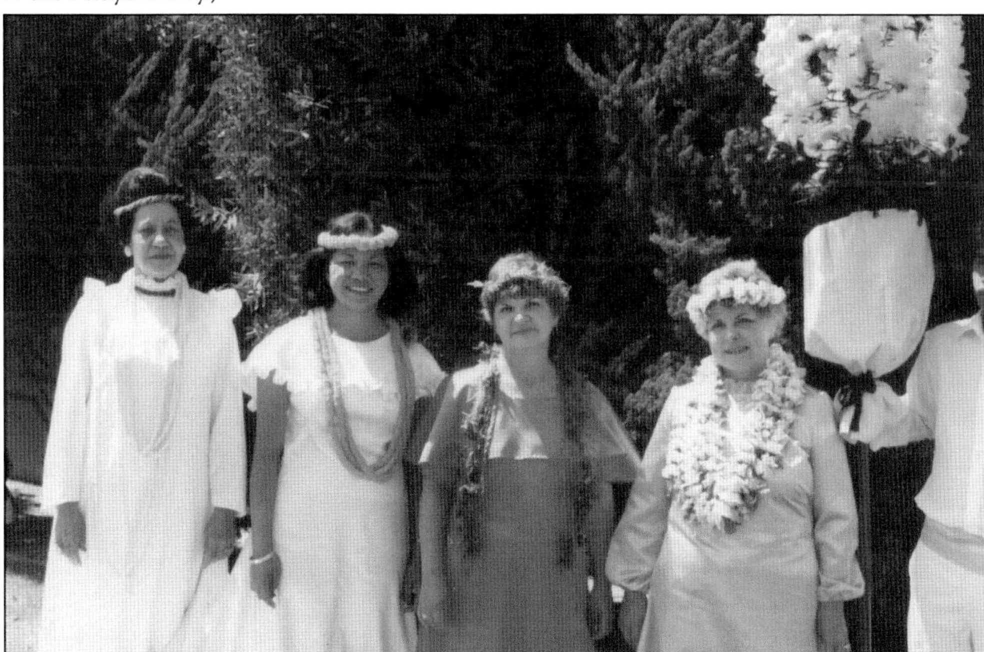

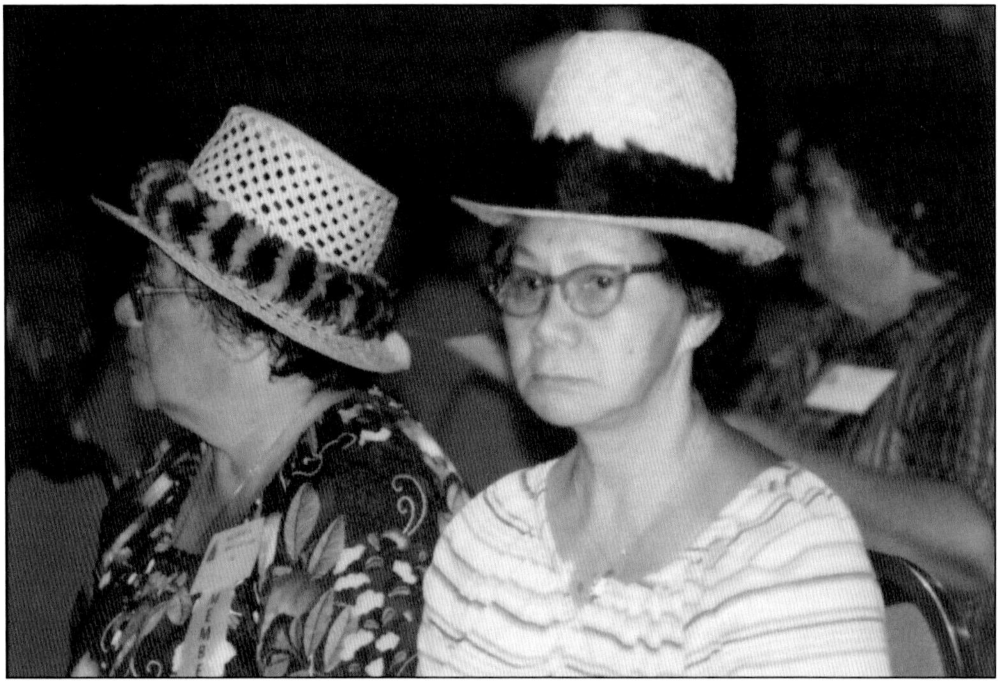

For civic clubs, Lei Day was a moment to show Hawaiian tradition and ingenuity, but to create that celebration, Hawaiians needed a foundation to teach ancient crafts. Lei Hulu of California was founded by Mary Kahihilani Duarte-Kovich in 1983. Lei Hulu perpetuates the art of ancient Hawaiian feather craft through workshops at events like the Polynesian Interclub Council (PICC) Pacific Islander Festival. (Courtesy of the Pelayo family.)

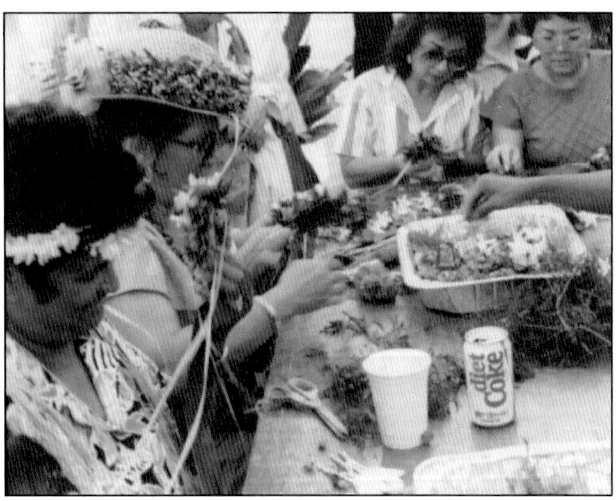

Perpetuating Hawaiian arts is important to all the civic clubs, and one of the most common symbols of Hawaiian culture is the lei. Naturally, most Hawaiian events with workshops, such as the Alondra Park Ho'olaule'a and PICC's Pacific Islander Festival include lei making workshops and, often, lei contests. Lei Jensen and other women are pictured here working on haku leis. (Courtesy of the Pelayo Family.)

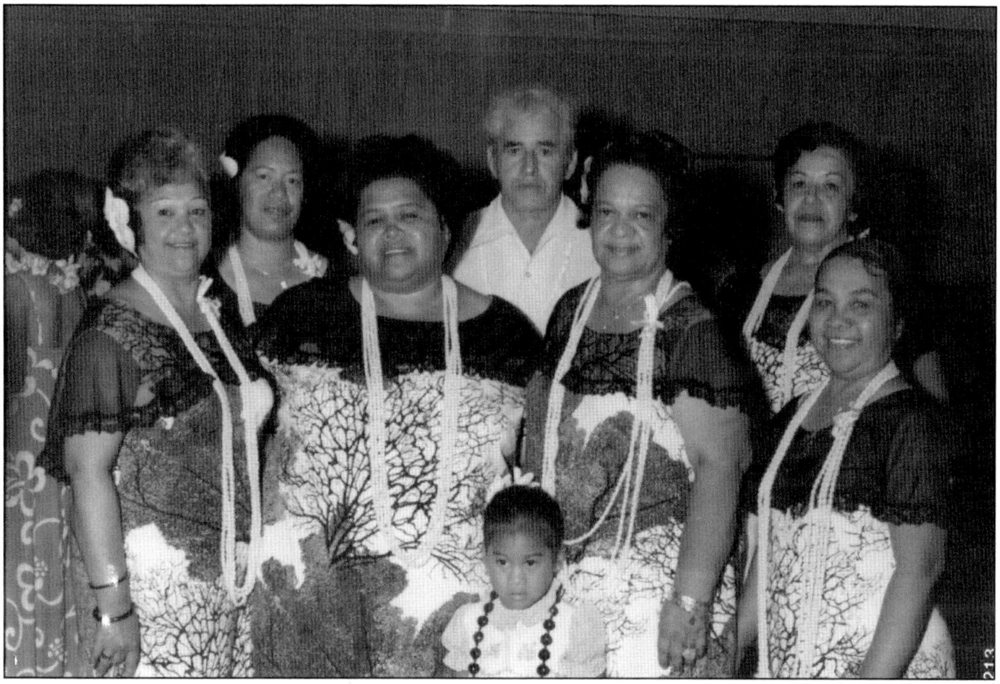

One aspect of Hawaiian culture lost on the West Coast was the power of women. Hawaii has a long history of female leaders who ruled with foresight and pragmatism. To represent that history, Hawaii's Daughters Guild of California (HDG) was incorporated in 1977 and was founded by Martha Hansen. HDG has a mission of perpetuating the arts and culture of Hawaii while also raising funds and awarding educational scholarships to young Polynesian women. Since 1970, HDG has awarded more than $150,000 in scholarships. They raise their money through food sales at festivals like the Alondra Park Ho'olaule'a and their annual Holoku Ball (shown below). Four of the founding members of the HDG are represented above. (Above, courtesy of Sissy and Lincoln Kaio; below, courtesy of and Hawaii's Daughters Guild of California.)

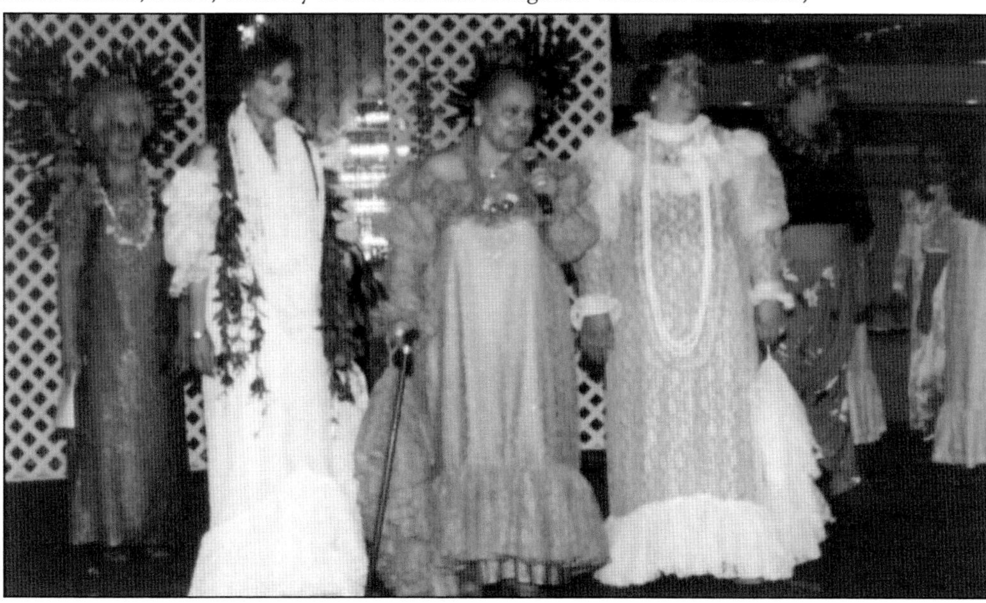

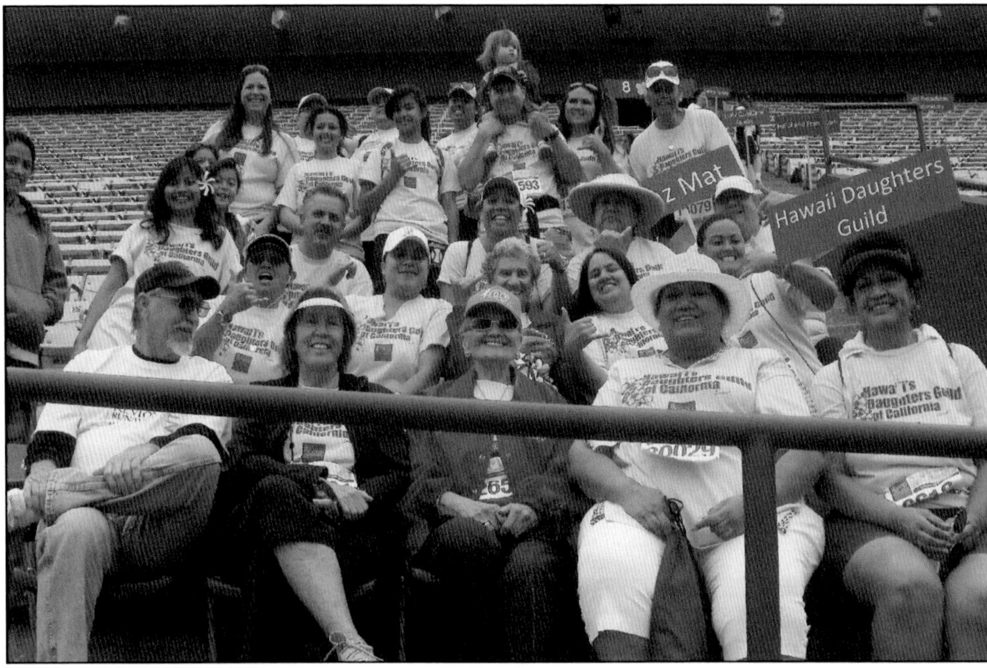

Kokua most often expands beyond immediate ohana. To that end, Hawaii's Daughters Guild of California supports more than just young Hawaiian and Polynesian women. They support women all across the world. This commitment to women can be seen in these photographs of HDG members participating in the Revlon Run/Walk in support of breast cancer research. The Revlon Run/Walk is an important event in the Los Angeles area with support from men and women of all walks of life. (Both, courtesy of Hawaii's Daughters Guild of California.)

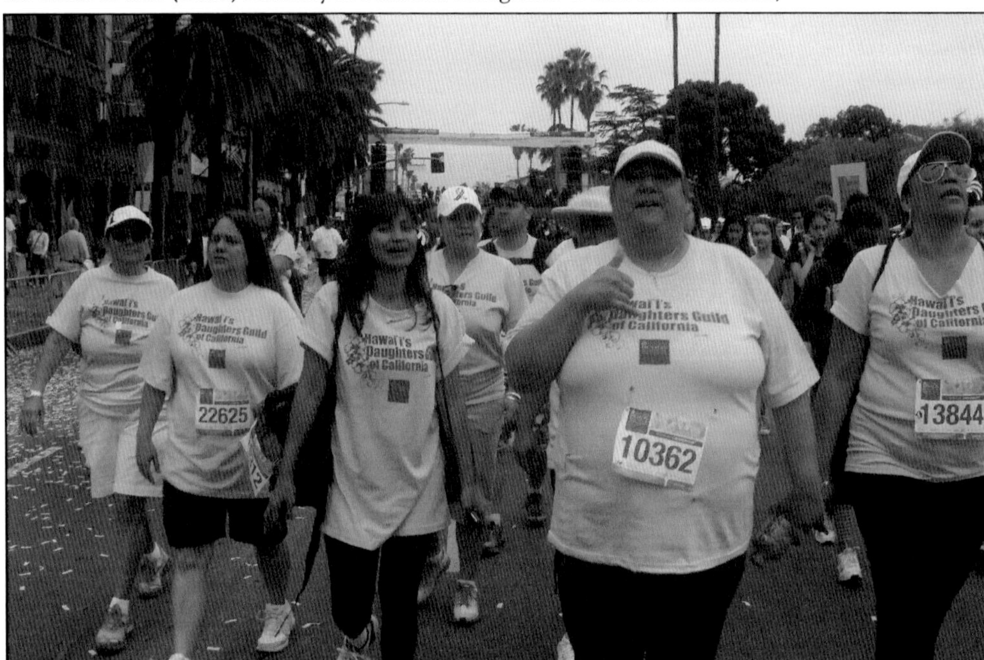

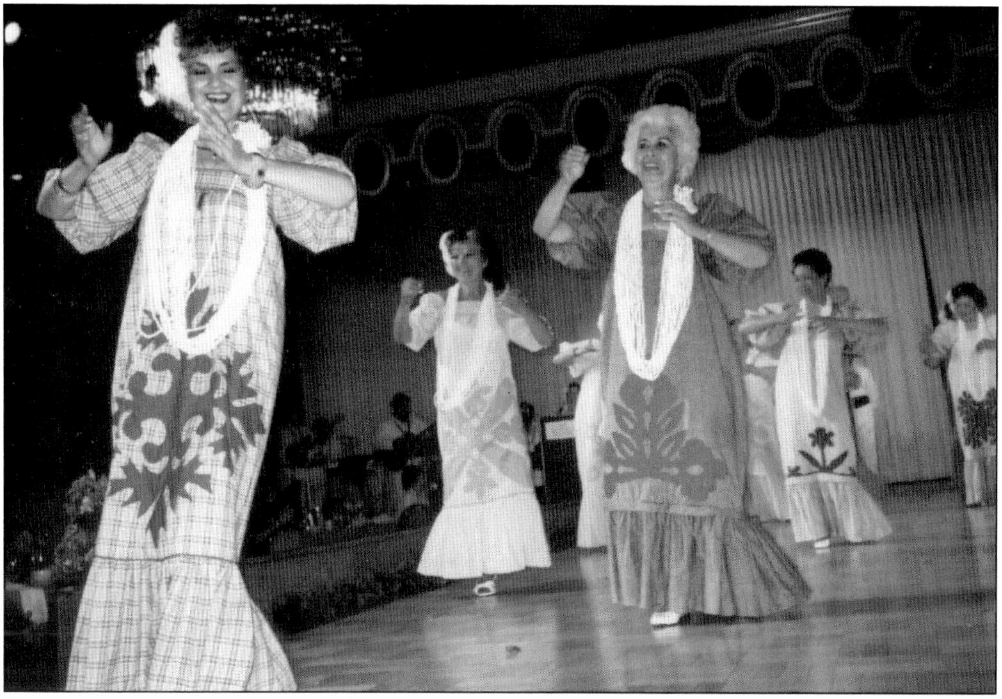

One way Hawaii's Daughters Guild of California raises money and maintains cultural traditions is through their annual Holoku Ball. In the 1800s, Hawaiian women were forced to dress in the Western fashion, and the holoku became the Hawaiian adaptation in the 1820s. Pictured above are American day gowns, which were the stepping stones for the current mu'umu'u. At one time, the holoku was for everyday wear, but today, the holoku is reserved for formal events, such as Holoku Balls or May Day. The Holoku Ball is a celebration of Hawaiian culture and shows the changes and adaptations of Hawaiian culture and the Western way of life. Amber Kanani Reed (right) participated in the 2004 Holoku Ball as a princess of Hawaii to help welcome guests at the event. (Above, courtesy of Hawaii's Daughters Guild of California; below, courtesy of Amber Kanani Reed.)

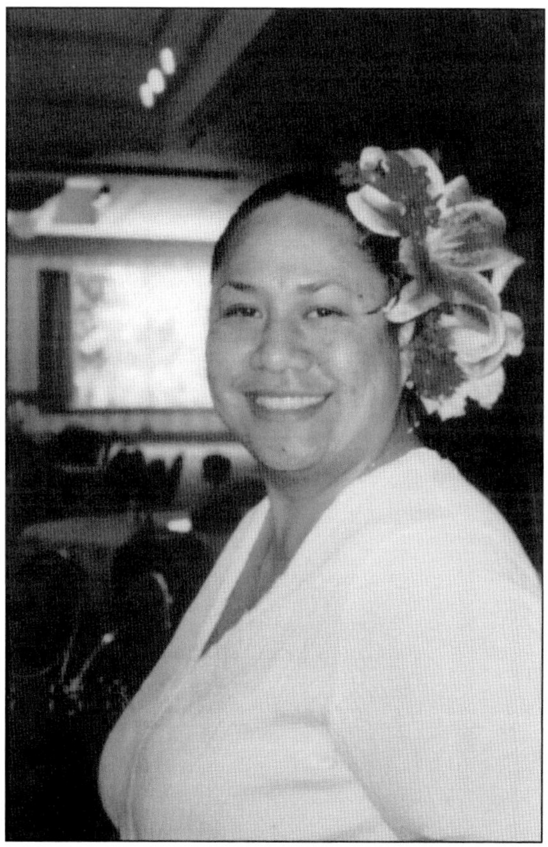

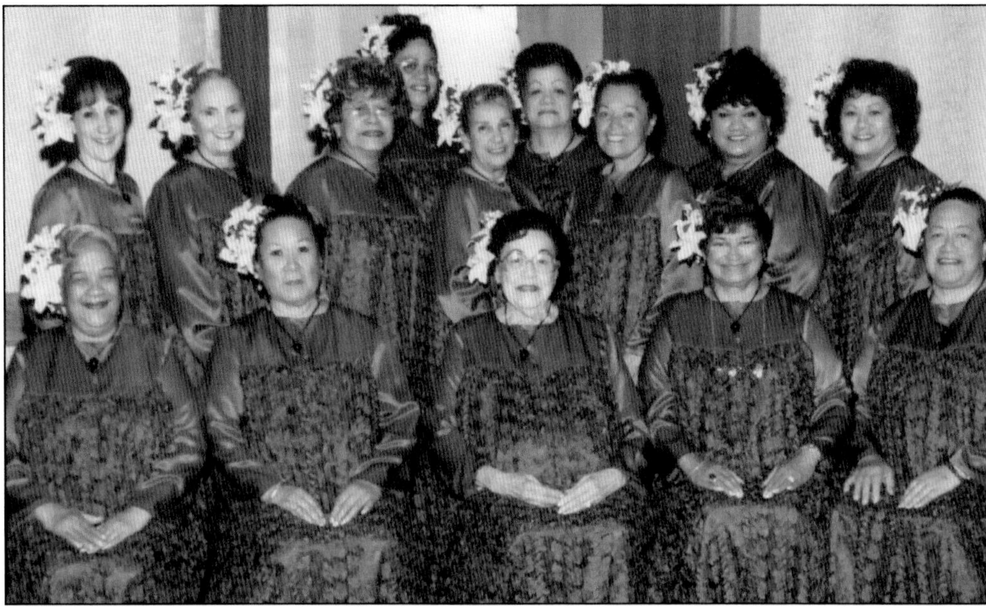

One of the goals of the civic clubs is to show that Hawaiian culture is alive and growing while recognizing its roots. In the image below, you can see the transformation of the holoku dress and, in many respects, the modernization and cultural changes of Hawaii. Like all women of the Western world, society asked Hawaiian women to abandon their wraps and skirts for fashions that covered everything from neck to toe. Over time, social norms became less strict and comfort took precedence over convention. The dress styles range from 19th-century styles that are closer to the original holoku to modern, sleeveless styles. In the image above, members of Hawaii's Daughters Guild of California pose for a formal group shot. (Both, courtesy of Hawaii's Daughters Guild of California.)

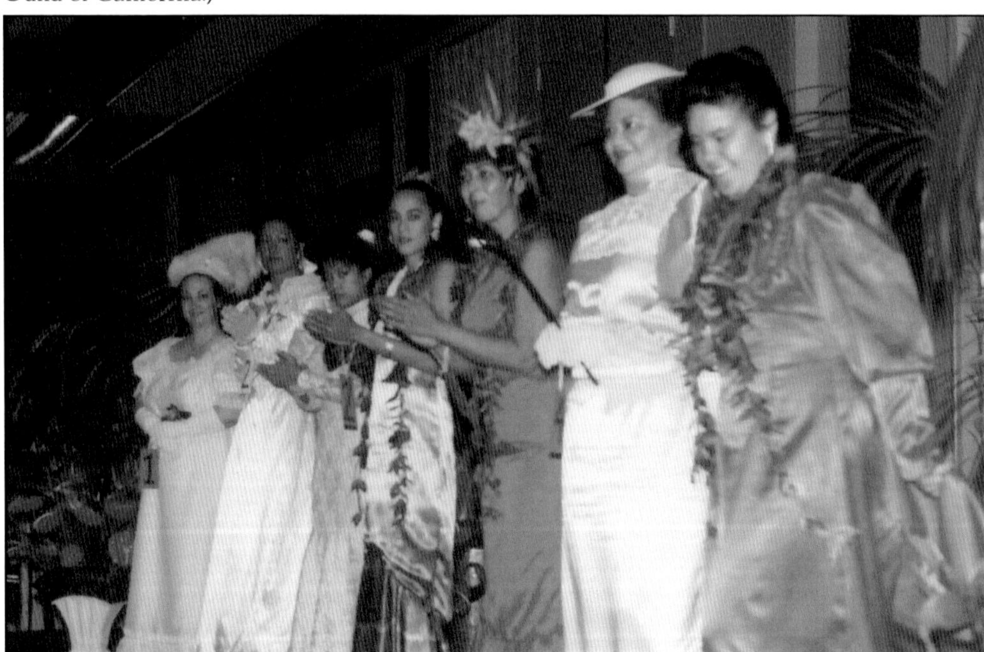

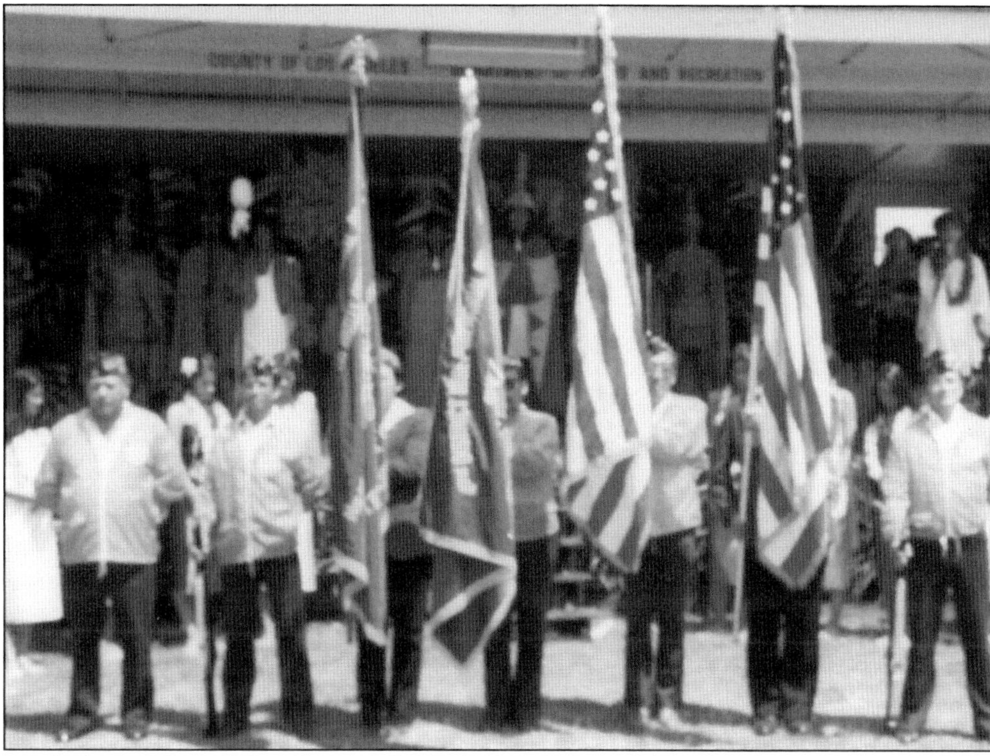

While the Holoku Ball demonstrates the changes in Hawaiian fashion, the inclusion of local civic clubs in Los Angeles shows the diversity of Hawaii and Hawaiian culture. Above, nisei present the color guard at the Alondra Park Ho'olaule'a in 1984. The connection between Japan and Hawaii goes back further than 1942. Before World War II, many Japanese immigrated to Hawaii during the sugar plantation days. During America's 20th-century wars, nisei served their country just as faithfully as Hawaiians, despite questions of loyalty. The nisei, part of Gardena's VFW Post 1961, maintain relationships with Native Hawaiians due to their shared status as Veterans of Foreign Wars (VFW). Pictured in the photograph below are, from left to right, Alcario "Sonny" Pelayo, Clara and Harry Ahn, Roy Yasamura, astronaut Ellison Onizuka, Lawndale mayor Sarann Kruse, Harry Marlow, and the chief deputy to supervisor Kenneth Hahn. (Both, courtesy of the Pelayo family.)

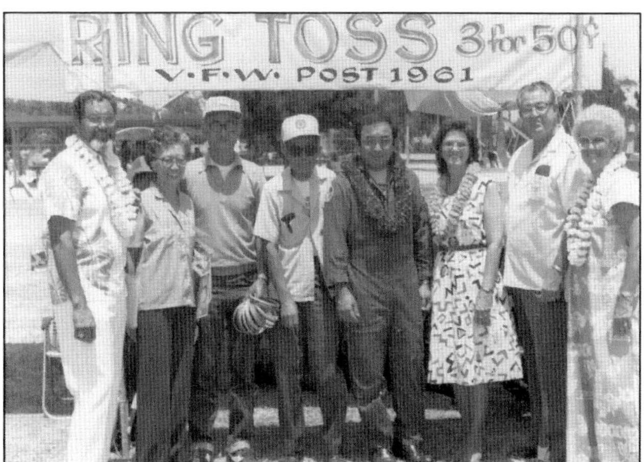

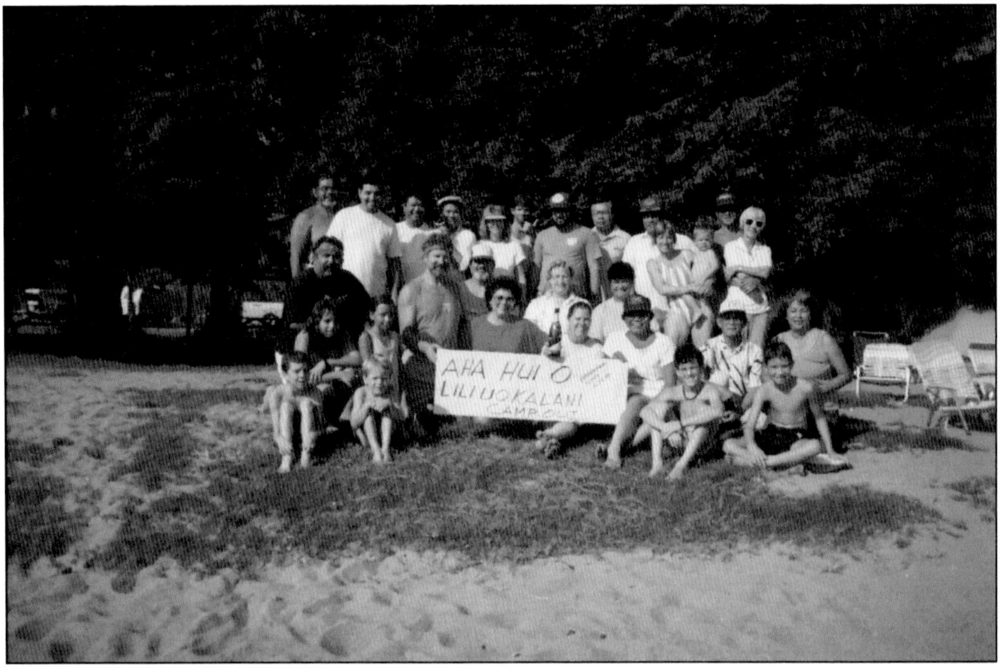

With connections to the nisei and the Gardena VFW, the 'Ahahui o Liliuokalani pooled the resources of various groups to become one of the most impactful civic clubs that supported, educated, and created opportunities for Hawaiian culture to thrive. Chartered in 1977 it was the second Hawaiian Civic Club formed on the continent. The 'Ahahui helps maintain an interest in and preservation of the customs and culture of the Hawaiian people through workshops and college scholarships for Hawaiian youth in Southern California. Shown above, annual campouts were a family event for 'Ahahui, with members bringing their extended ohana to share in weekends of talking story, ono food and good fun. Shown below are three of the 'Ahahui's oldest members, Pat Gandall, John Jensen, and Alcario "Sonny" Pelayo working the 'Ahahui food booth at the Alondra Park Ho'olaule'a. (Both, courtesy of the Pelayo family.)

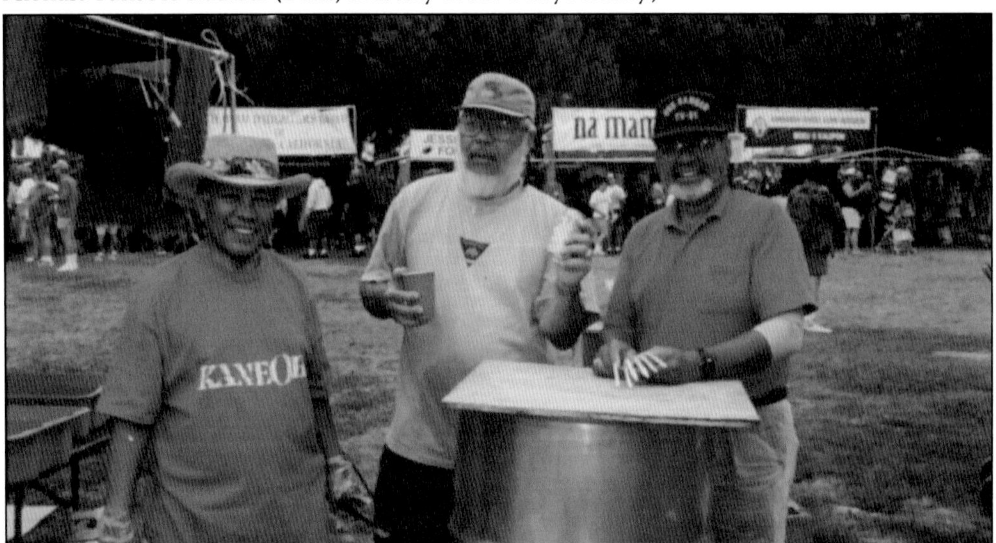

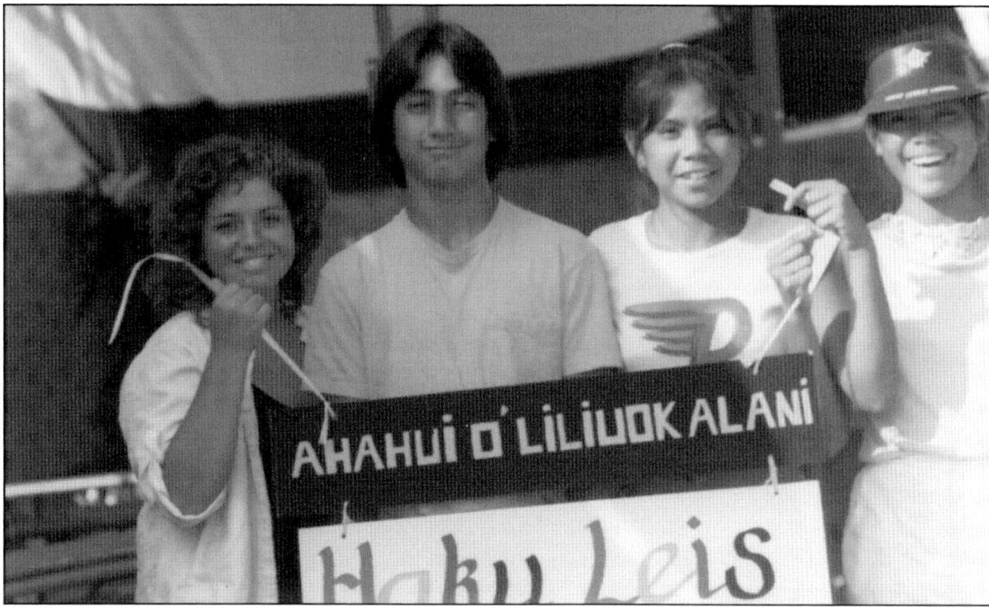

Teaching Hawaiian keiki the key components of being Hawaiian was the underlying purpose of civic clubs. Over time, the children joined *hula halau* (hula schools) and needed performances that would help raise funds. The civic clubs saw this need as an opportunity to showcase Hawaiian talent and awareness and created the first Ho'olaule'a in Northridge. The festival showcases hula dancing from halau all over Southern California, crafts, and Hawaiiana, such as T-shirts, games for children, and delicious food. The early Ho'olaule'a were just a few booths and a few dancers. Pictured above are (left to right) Jeanette, a friend, and Kim and Michelle Rosero, children of Ahahui o Liliuokalani members helping fundraise for scholarships. (Both, courtesy of the Rosero family.)

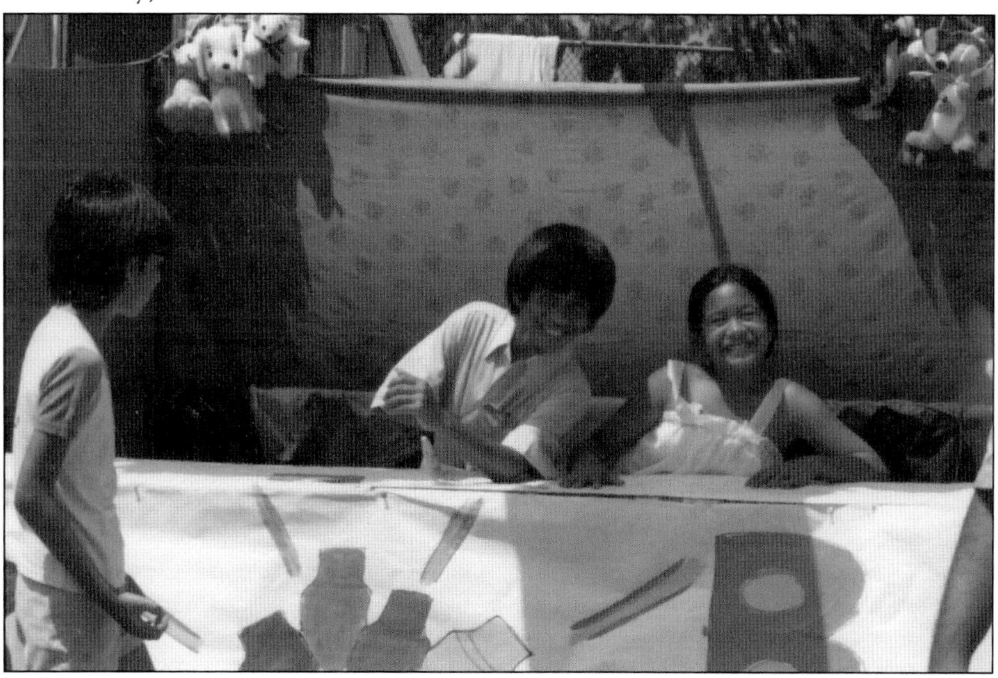

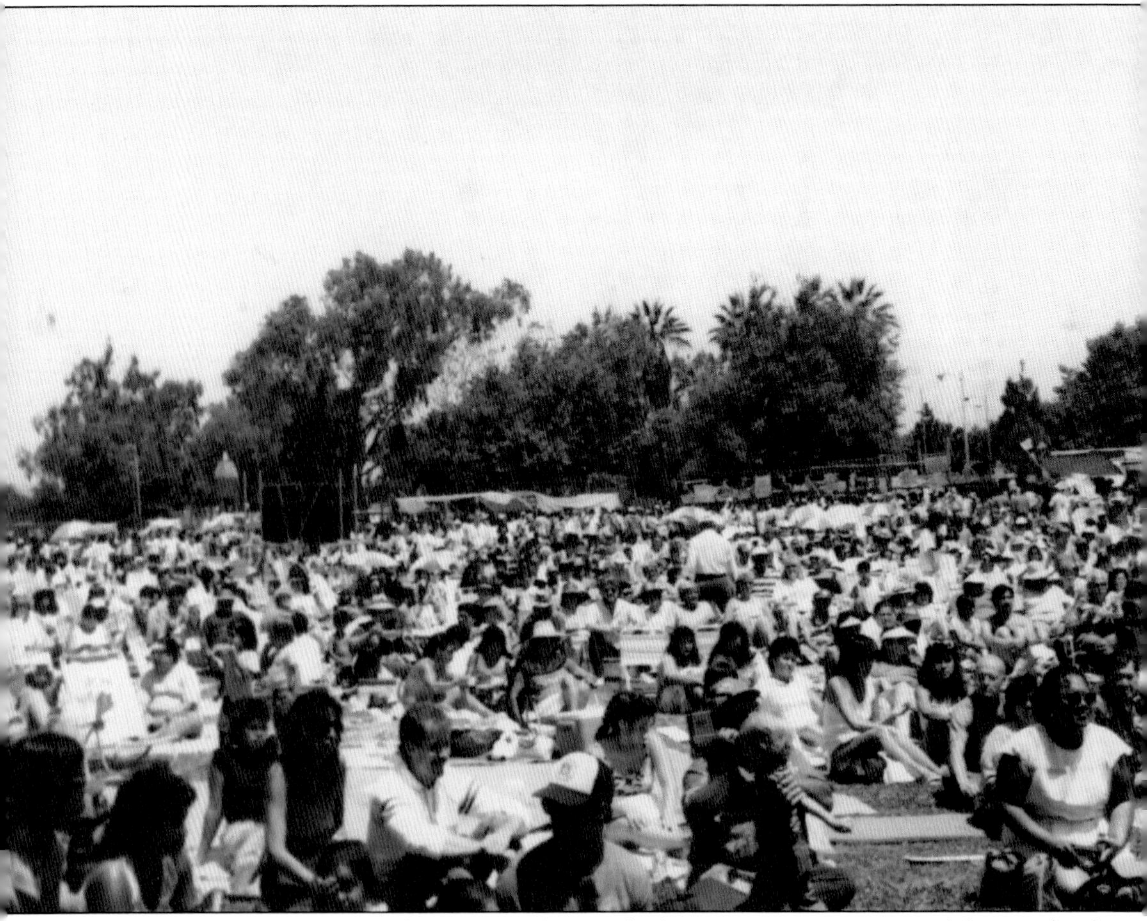

With each successive year, the Los Angeles Ho'olaule'a grew, attracting tens of thousands of people over two days of music. Families picnic and talk story, catch up on old times, and meet new people in an atmosphere based on celebrating aloha. The venue, during those early years, alternated between Northridge and Cerritos before finding a home at Alondra Park in Torrance, California. Alondra Park is a year-round gathering place for many kanaka, locals, and Hawaiians at heart, who use the open space to share music, picnic, and fish. On any given day, one can find someone who, in characteristic Hawaiian fashion, is willing to share his or her skill, knowledge, and stories. (Courtesy of the Rosero family.)

Lorna Samatua was born in Kaneohe, Oahu, and moved to Gardena in 1989, so that her sister could help her raise her children. To stay connected to her homeland and to help educate her grandchildren (shown on the right), Lorna and her family visit the Alondra Park Ho'olaule'a annually. (Courtesy of Lorna and Sanoe Samatua)

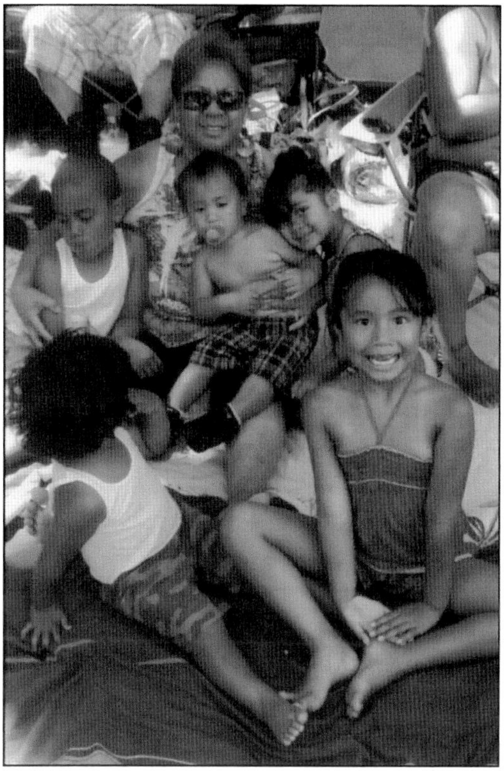

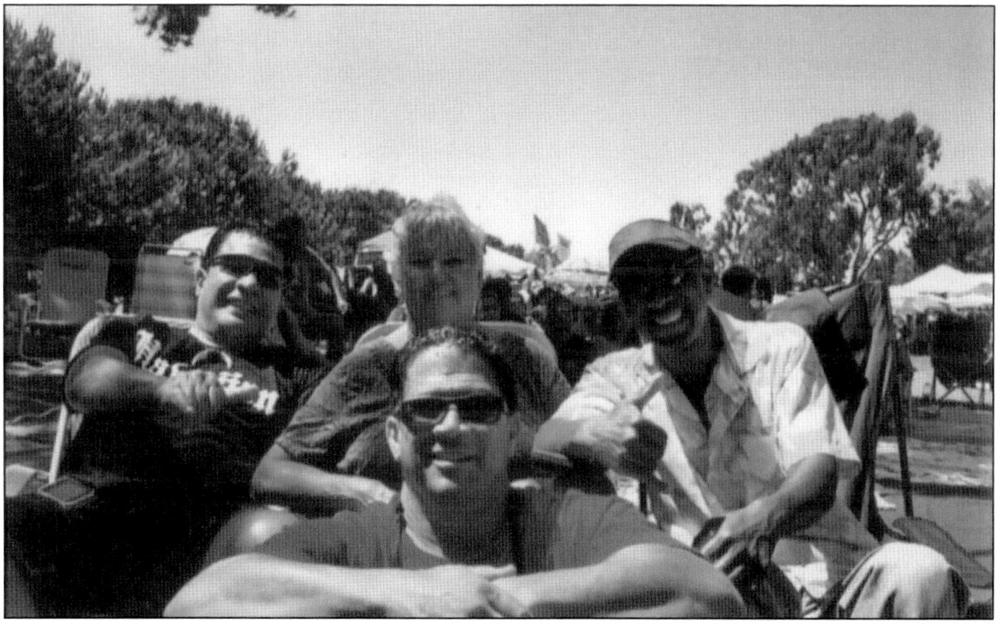

James Caton has attended Ho'olaule'a every year since 1994, when he was brought to one by a Samoan friend. This photograph shows the diversity of people who come to enjoy the celebration. Pictured are Keoki Mokanui (half Samoan and half Native Hawaiian), Mary Ann Mokanui (Caucasian), Charles Ammons (white, black, and Native American), and James Caton (black and Native American). (Courtesy of James Caton.)

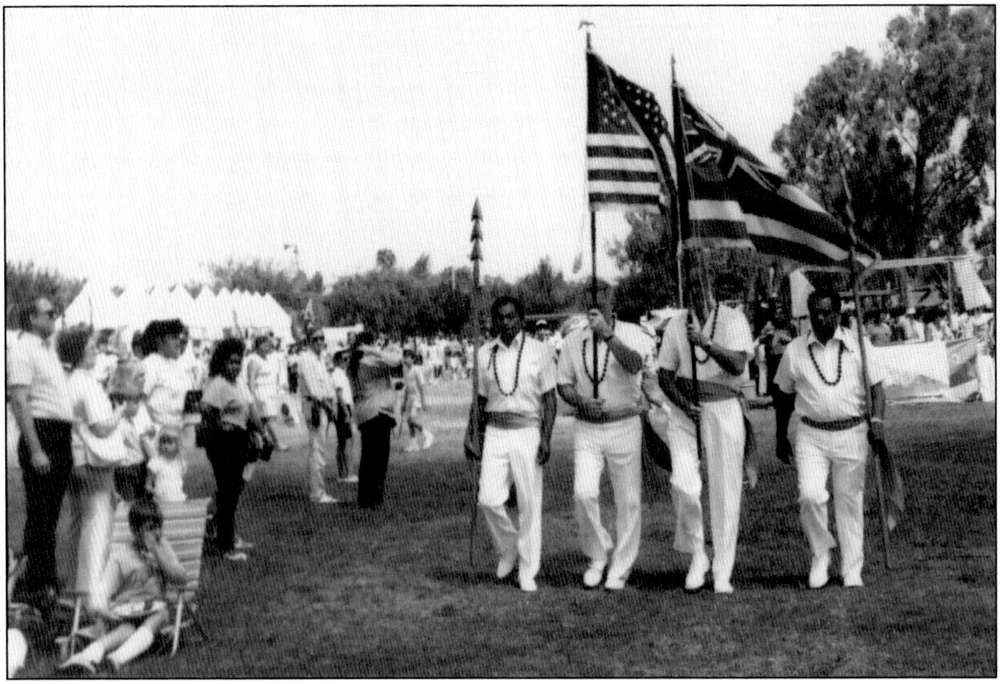

Ho'olaule'a is, if nothing else, a testament to the old and new world the Hawaiians in Los Angeles live in. The opening ceremonies start with two National Anthems, the American anthem and the Hawaiian nation's anthem; a traditional color guard, which normally consisted of men from the VFW; and a presentation of the emblems of ali'i, the feathered kahili, as well as an entrance chant. (Both, courtesy of the Pelayo family.)

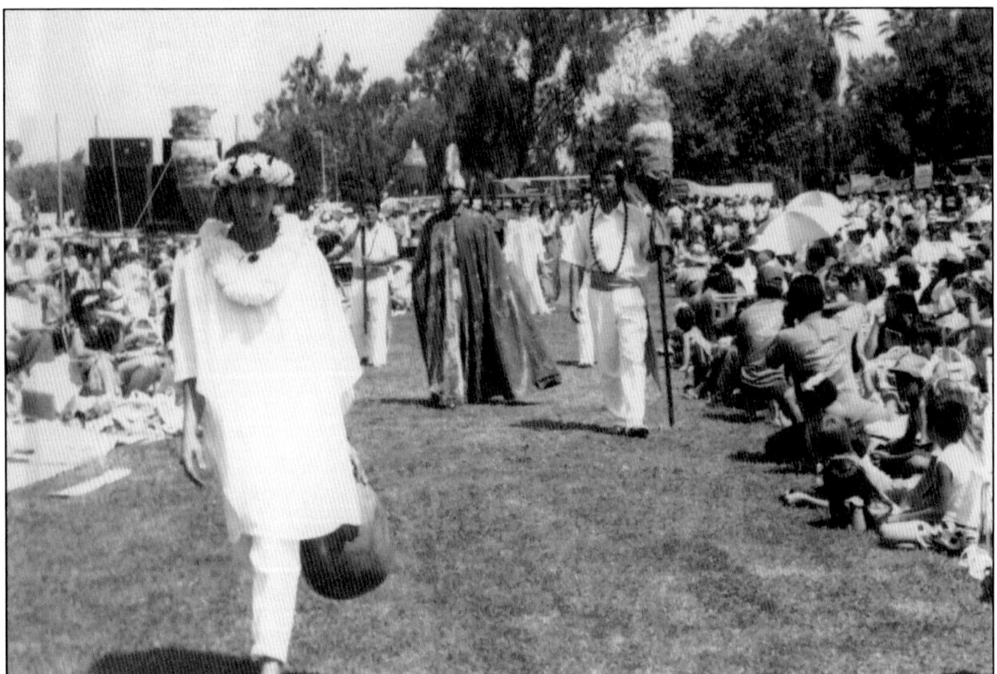

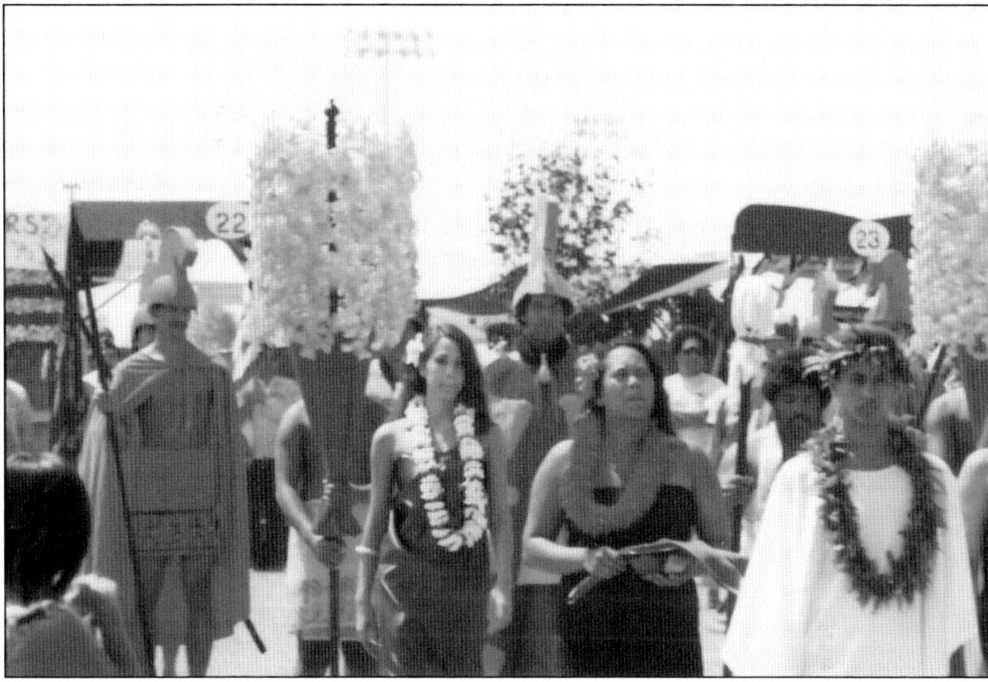

Sometimes lost in the hibiscus decals and bumper stickers, the stuffed *honu* (turtle), the images of surfing and hula, the strumming of the ukulele, and the chants, is the fact that Hawaiian culture is about nature. One can see the influences of nature in many features of the festival, from the ceremonial kahili, whose colors are emblematic of specific royal bloodlines, to the leis and flowers worn by the procession and dancers, and to the flower and plant booths that sell plants from home, from *Hawaii nei* (beloved Hawaii). (Both, courtesy of the Rosero family.)

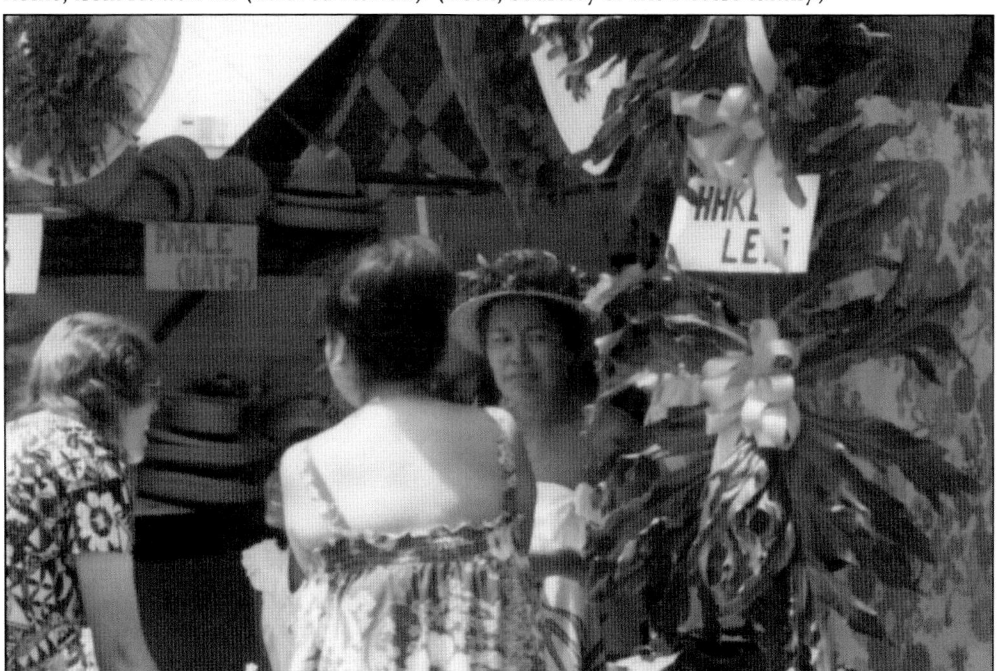

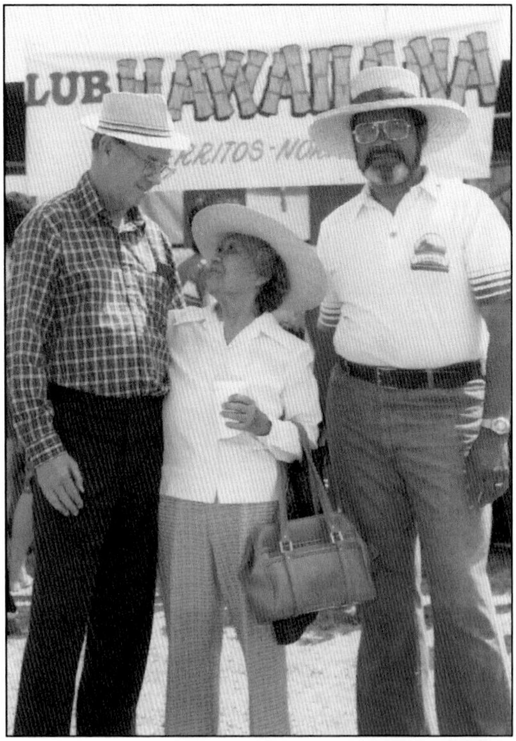

Ho'olaule'a's influence cannot be understated. From its conception, it has attracted more than just Hawaiians and Hawaiians at heart. It was a springboard of Hawaiian culture and introduced the culture into Angeleno consciousness. It raised awareness of a group of people so far from a lost home. Using the success of the festival and the resources of the civic clubs, Native Hawaiians created close ties with local politicians like Kenneth Hahn to help create a foundation for a life in Los Angeles. Hahn and his family continue to be active members in California politics and are equally important in supporting initiatives to keep the Hawaiian culture alive. Pictured here on the left are Kenneth Hahn, Mary Kalama, and Alcario "Sonny" Pelayo at the Cerritos Ho'olaule'a. Below, from left to right, are (first row) Kanani Kalama and Elizabeth and David Kuhia; (second row) Rachel Kam, Kenneth Hahn, and Alcario "Sonny" Pelayo. (Both, courtesy of the Pelayo family.)

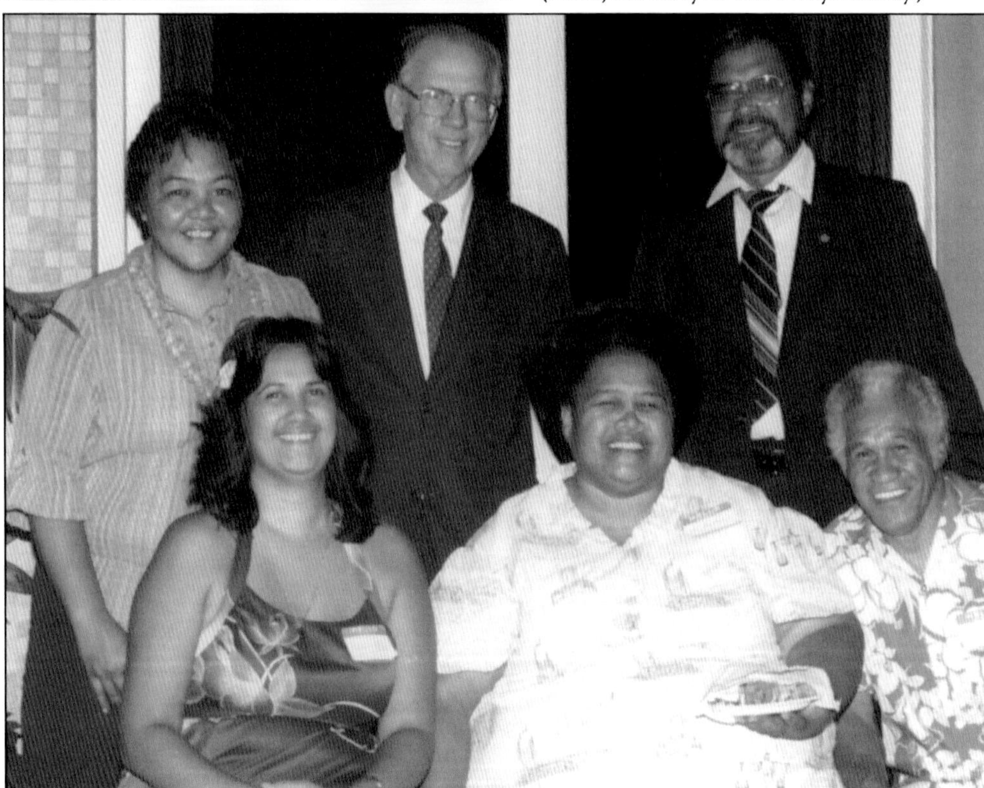

Five

Spreading Aloha

Halau

The face of Hawaiian culture is the *hula halau* (dance school). The halau, with the *kumu* (teacher) at the center, is a key source of Hawaiian tradition and the culture's evolution. More than just a dance studio, the halau teaches its participants a new language, costuming, singing, and making traditional Native Hawaiian instruments. At the same time, like any other place of education, new techniques and movements are learned, shared, and refined. They are gathering places where generations, many times within the same family, meet and learn from each other. While halau are the centers of knowledge, they cannot exist without aloha, kuleana, and malama for each other. Unlike common forms of dance, hula is different because every aspect of it emphasizes the importance of story.

Common ideas of hula revolve around the image of shaking Tahitian hips; however, these ideas focus on the body while hula has a long history that goes beyond entertainment. In *kahiko* (traditional) hula, the dances speak the stories of the gods. In *auana* (contemporary) hula, the dances describe the joys and sadness of life now. Through costumes, hula shows the transition from tapa wraps to pa'u skirts to holoku dresses, telling the story of Christianity's influence. The practice of hula carries with it the tragic years when it was outlawed in public and the triumph of its return.

Halau express all of these stories in individual performances where kumu perfect their style and *haumana* (students) connect with the music, the movement, and each other. As varied as the styles are, halau come together to compete against each other at E Hula Mau, a hula competition in Long Beach. They also showcase their skills at the various festivals and unite to greet representatives from Hawaii and other Polynesian Islands.

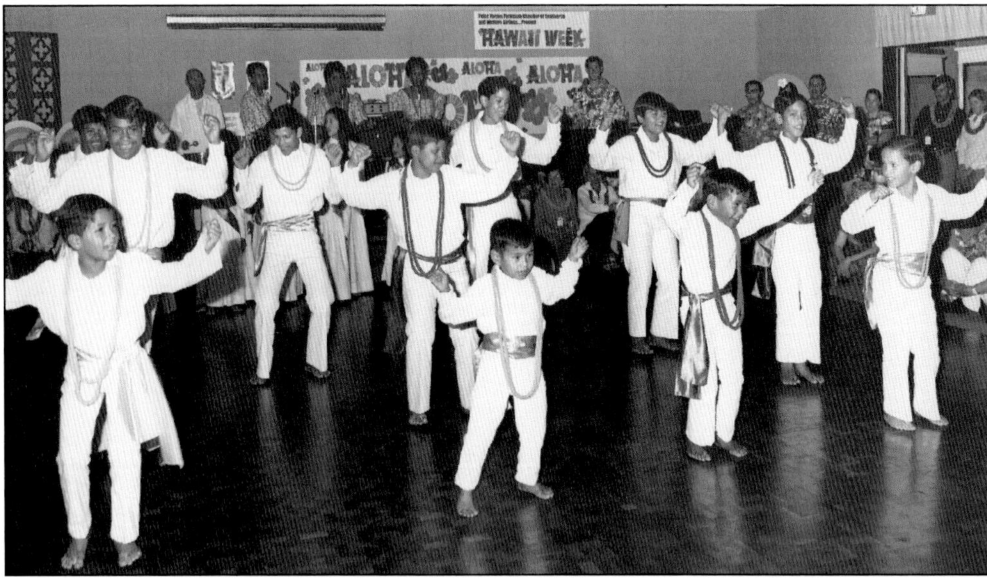

As mentioned in chapter three, the Kalani Islanders played a vital role in the education of California born Native Hawaiians. While the Kalani Islanders taught dances from all cultures, admission into the halau was only allowed for those children with Native Hawaiian blood. Another distinctive feature of the Kalani Islanders that is still rare, even for many halau today, is that all of the music for performances and practices was performed by the Chang family and their haumana (students) themselves. Students learned not only how to dance but also how to sing. The photograph above shows the boys of the Kalani Islanders dancing for the Palos Verdes Chamber of Commerce and Western Airlines Hawaii Week celebration. Below, from left to right, Randy Kaulana Chang, Frank Keli'i Chang, and Kimo Artis dance a hula. (Both, courtesy of Randy Kaulana Chang.)

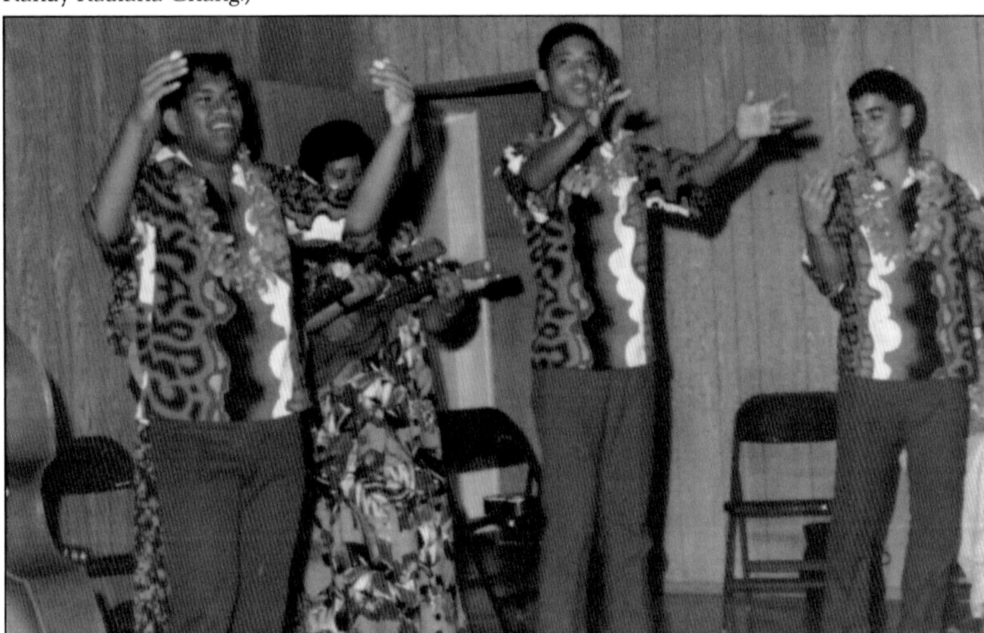

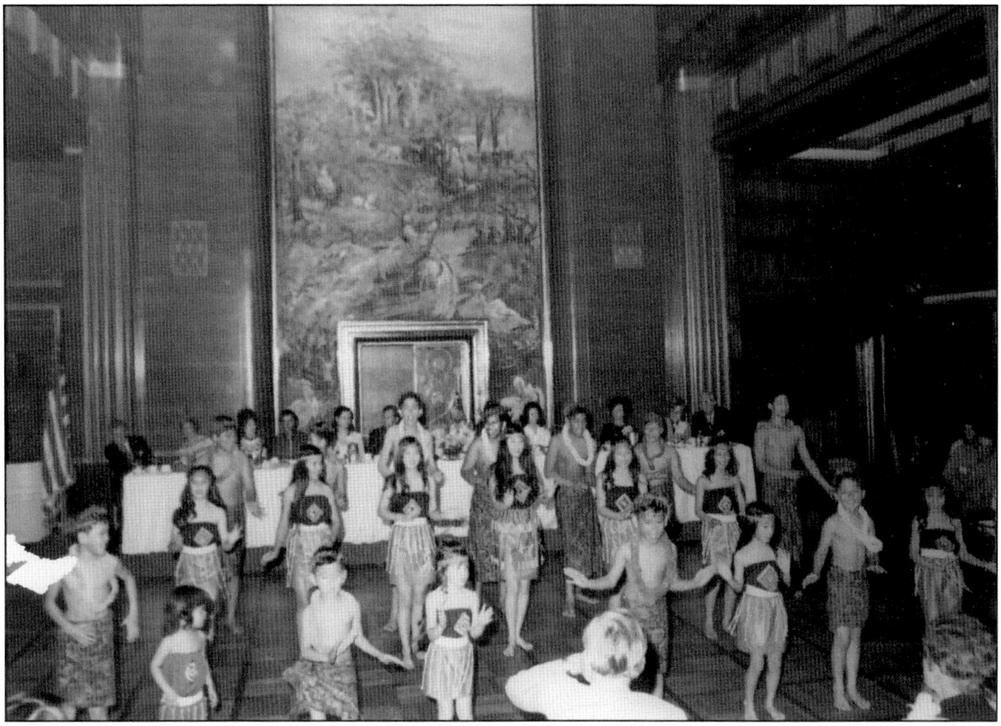

With hula, the Kalani Islanders were able to represent Hawaiian culture in many important historical landmarks. Above is the ballroom on the Queen Mary in Long Beach. Below are the Kalani Islanders performing Polynesian dances at the end of Main Street USA in Disneyland. One of the overall purposes of the hula halau is to remind people that Hawaiian culture is a distinct culture—one that is vibrant and alive. (Both, courtesy of Randy Kaulana Chang.)

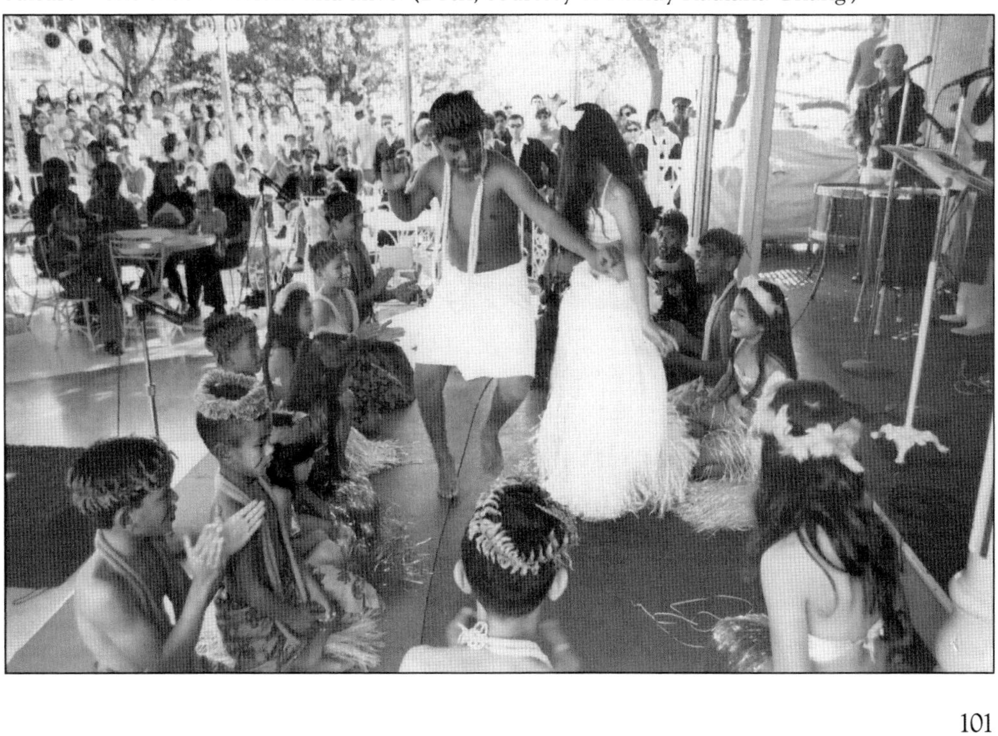

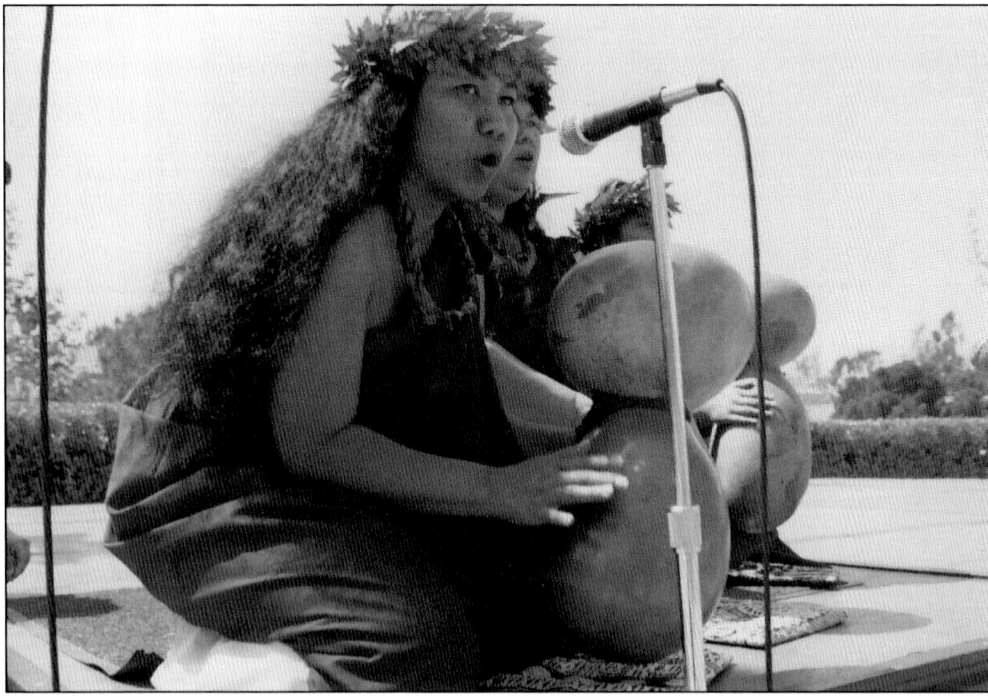

Halau O Lilinoe a me Na Pua Me Kealoha was founded in 1980 by Sissy Lilinoe (above) and Lincoln Kaio in Carson. This decorated halau has garnered many achievements and awards throughout the continental United States as well as Hawaii. The halau mission is to maintain and perpetuate beliefs, cultural practices, philosophies, and traditions of Native Hawaiians. They participate in community events, such as the Alondra Park Ho'olaule'a and competitions like E Hula Mau in Long Beach, California, and the revered Merrie Monarch in Hilo, Hawaii. Below is the halau performing together. (Above, courtesy of Sissy Kaio; below, courtesy of Florante Peter Ibanez.)

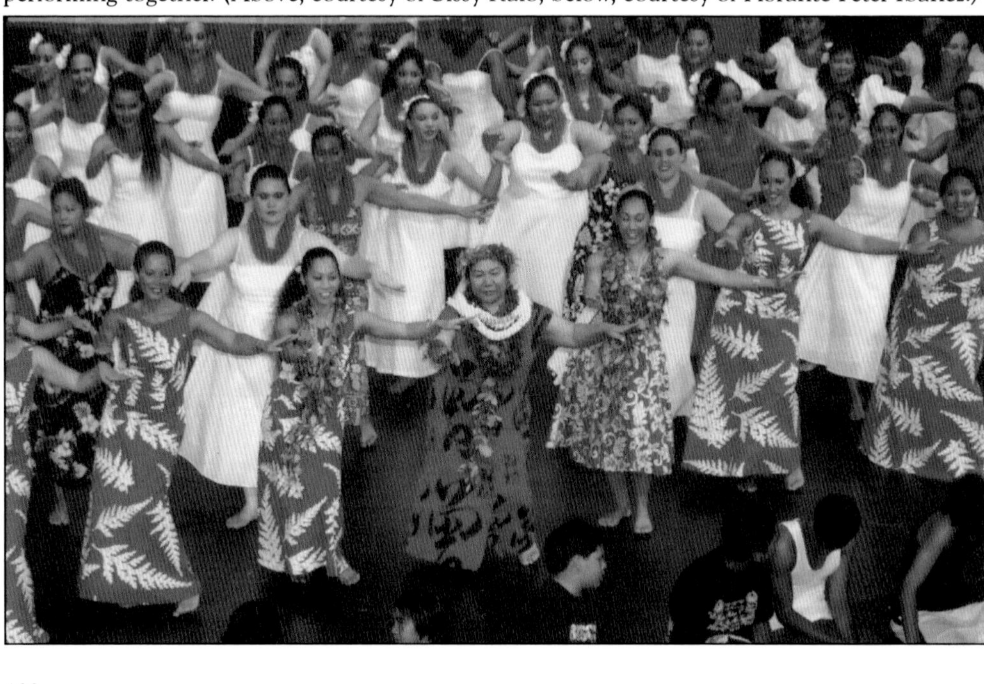

In the 1990s, Sissy Kaio's halau, Na Pua Me Kealoha, based in Carson, gained a reputation for their ability to create entertaining performances while maintaining a dedication to the traditions and values of Hawaiian culture. Kaio's halau, like others, differentiate themselves from hula studios by rooting themselves in tradition. Halau showcase chants, historically accurate costumes, and handmade musical instruments. The techniques they use go past the graceful swaying of auana and demonstrate the violent movements of kahiko. Pictured on the right are members of Halau Na Pua Me Ke Aloha. Below are *wahine* (female) members of Na Pua Me Ke Aloha surrounded by traditional instruments. (Both, courtesy of Sissy and Lincoln Kaio)

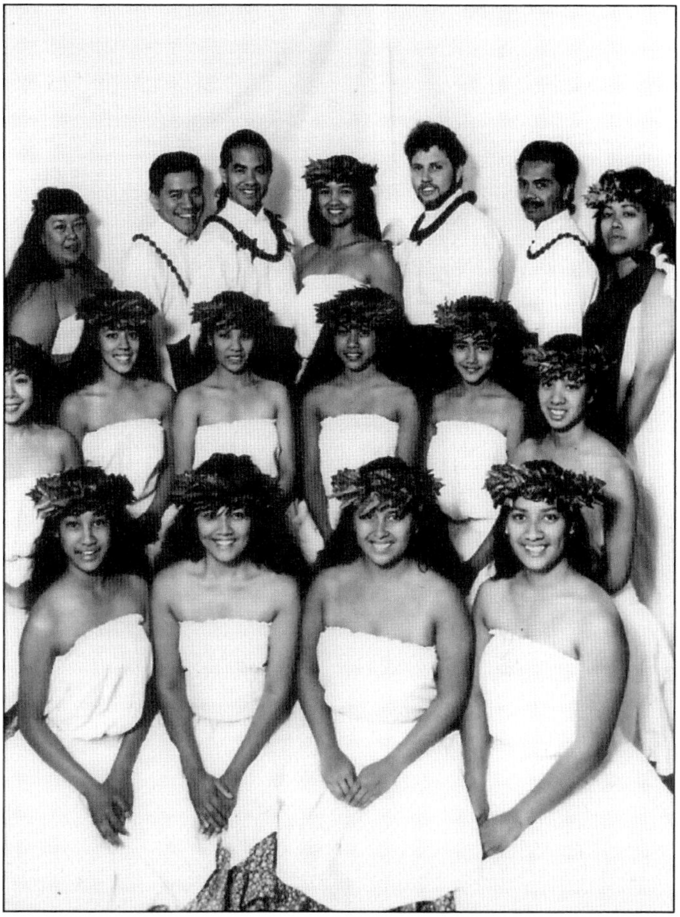

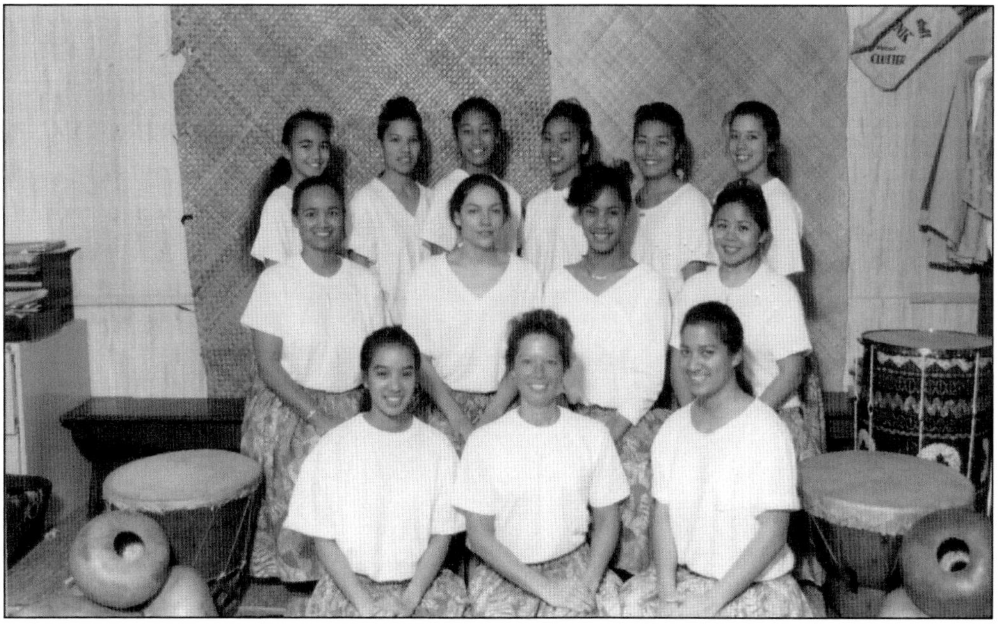

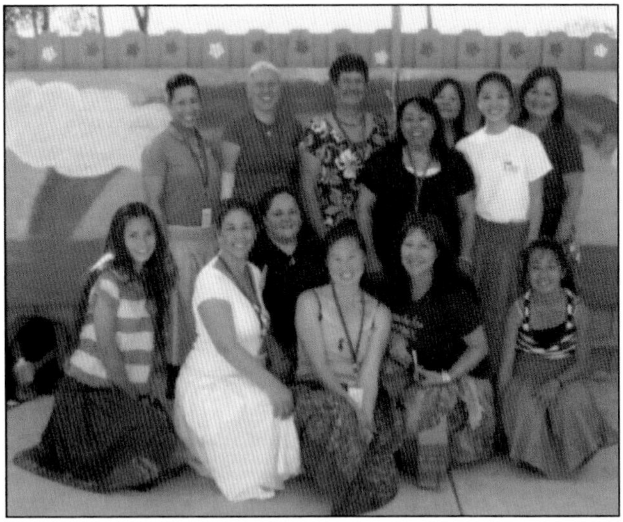

Kulia I Ka Punawai Kumu Hula Association of Southern California was created through the vision of Clarice Wahineali'i Nuhi in 1997. Since then, Kulia I Ka Punawai has been a place for kumu throughout Southern California to come together to share and strengthen their knowledge and understanding of hula. Shown here are students from many different halau who took a class with Kumu Hula Kanani Kalama (back row, third from the left) during a weekend hula retreat in Malibu. (Courtesy of Pi'ilaniwahine Requiro.)

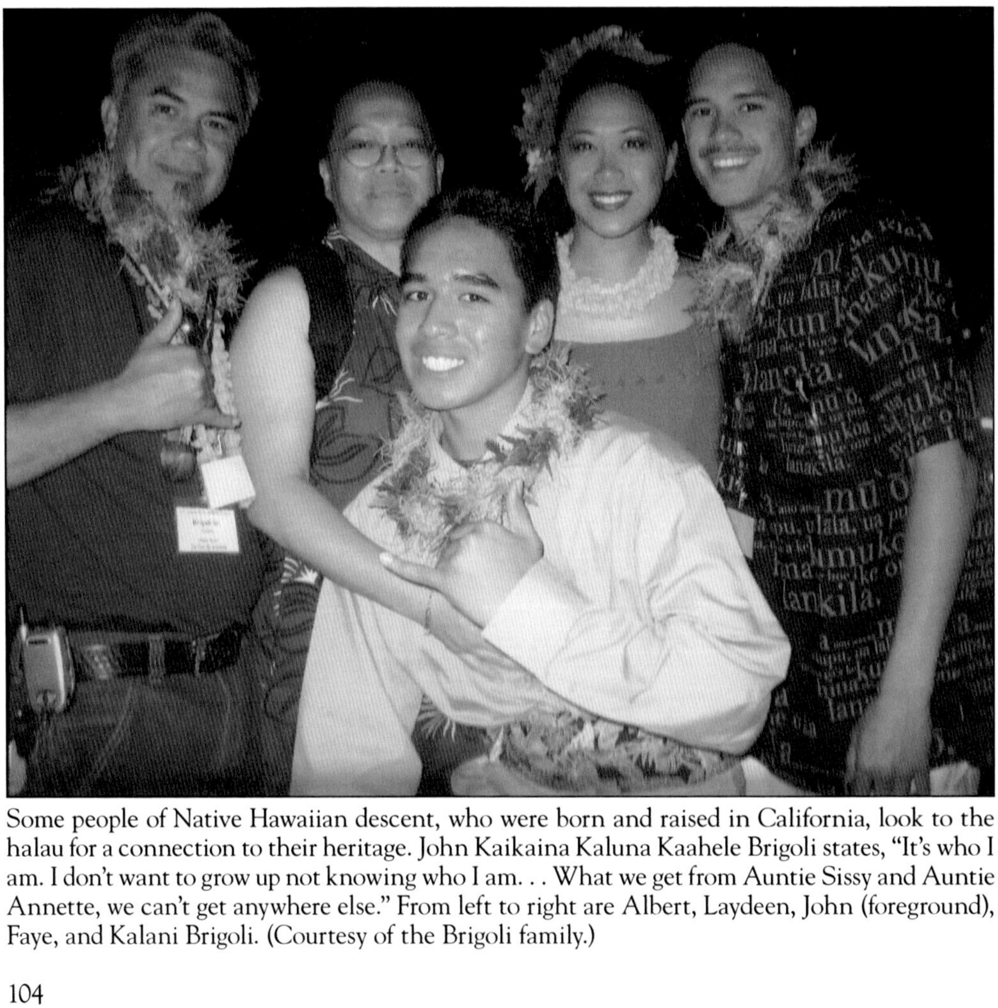

Some people of Native Hawaiian descent, who were born and raised in California, look to the halau for a connection to their heritage. John Kaikaina Kaluna Kaahele Brigoli states, "It's who I am. I don't want to grow up not knowing who I am. . . What we get from Auntie Sissy and Auntie Annette, we can't get anywhere else." From left to right are Albert, Laydeen, John (foreground), Faye, and Kalani Brigoli. (Courtesy of the Brigoli family.)

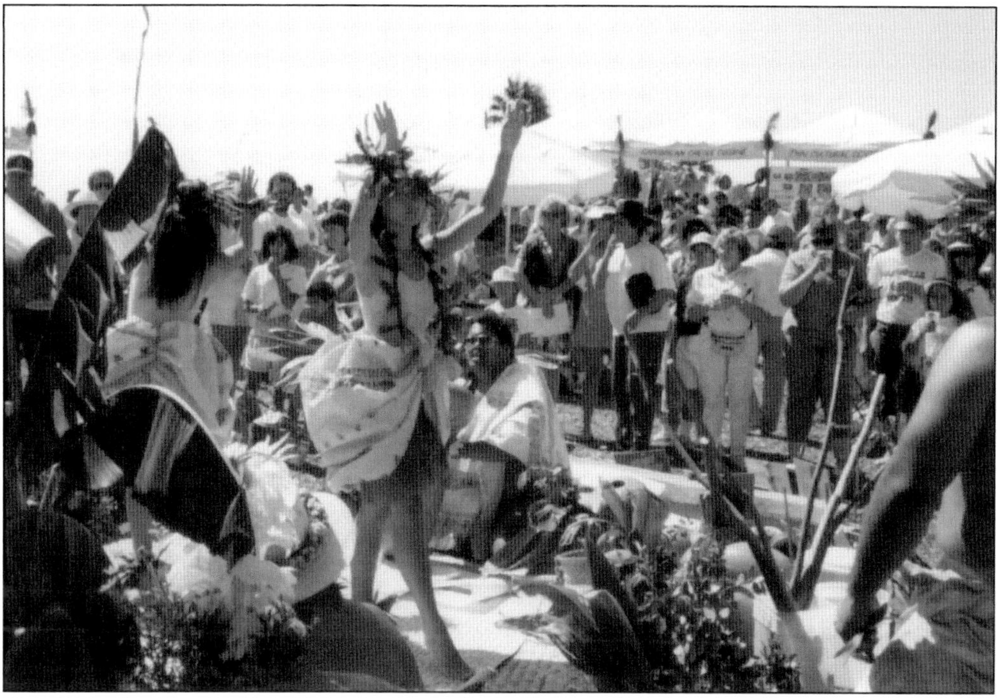

Hula Halau Kaulana Ka Hale Kula 'O Na Pua 'O Ka 'Aina was founded by Kumu Hula Randy Kaulana Chang in Torrance, California. The halau was created to perpetuate Native Hawaiian culture through crafts, dance, music, and history on the continent. The history of the Hawaiian people is perpetuated through formal lecture series on different topics, such as the *kumulipo* (Hawaiian creation story). *Haumana* (students) are taught to make many of their own implements as well as their own leis and attire. The halau participates in community events, such as the Alondra Park Ho'olaule'a and competitions like E Hula Mau in Long Beach, California. The pictures shown are from the Los Angeles Festival in September 1990, where the halau demonstrated Hawaiian culture. (Both, courtesy of Susie Park-Kelly.)

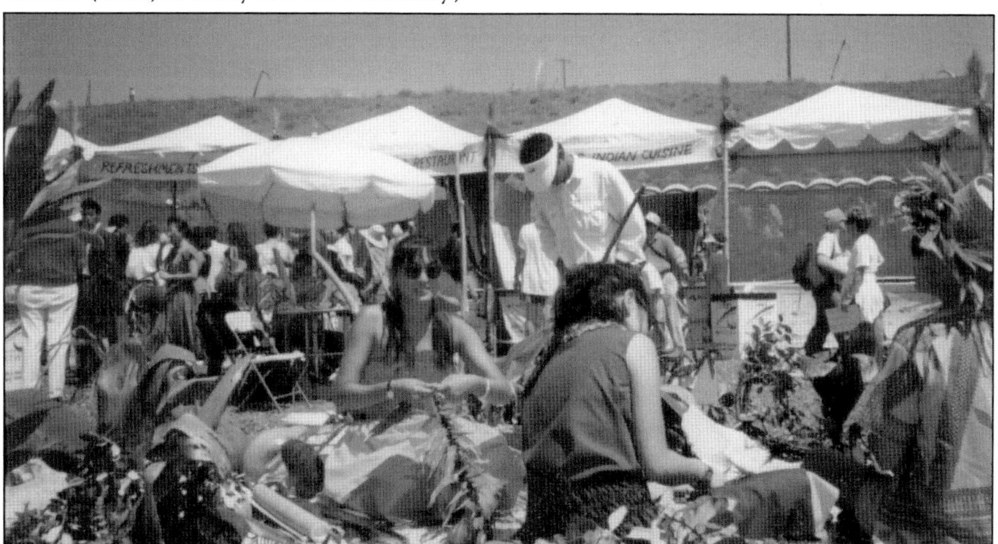

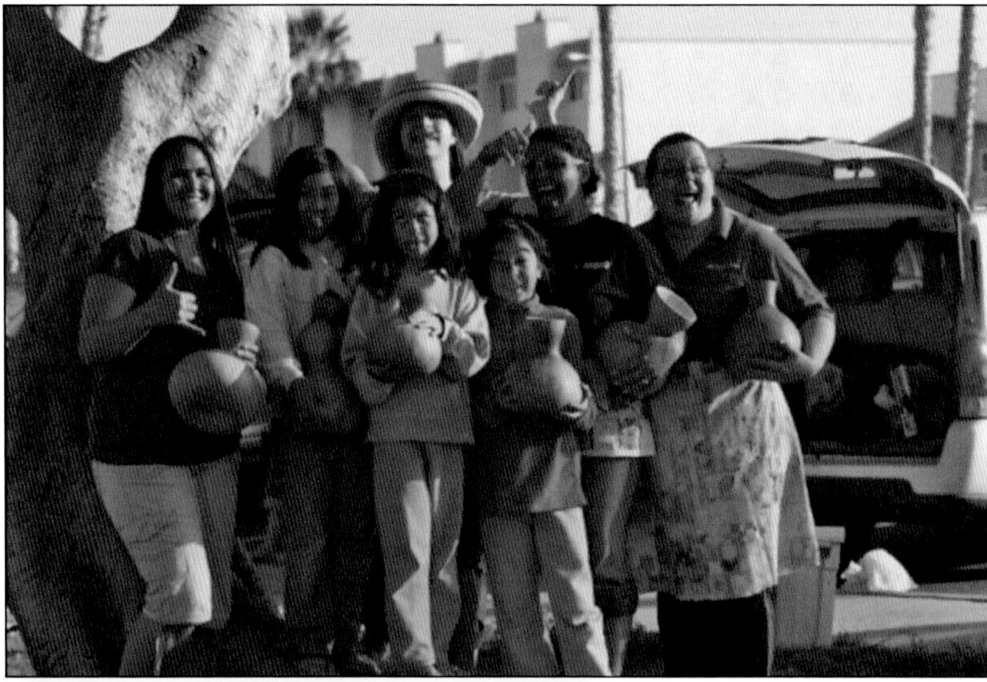

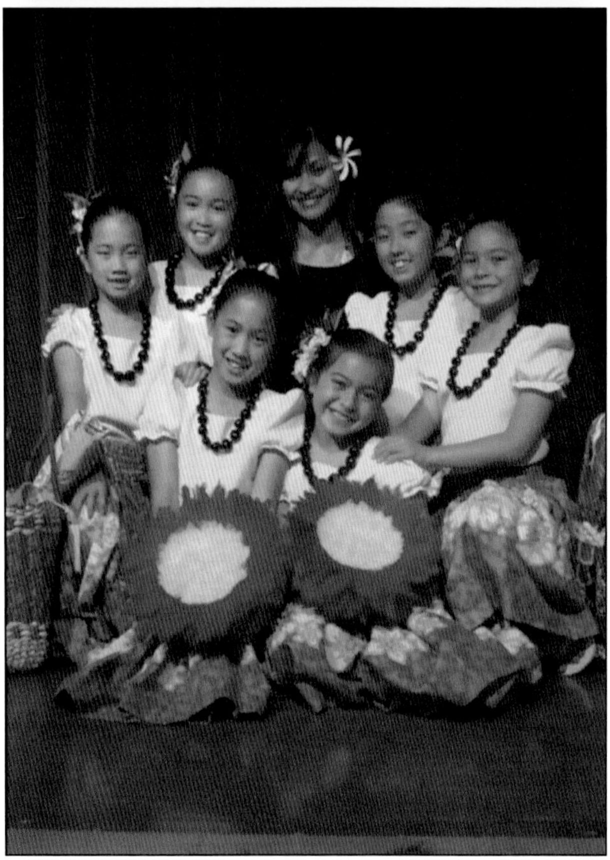

Hula is more than just tradition. It is a living thing that changes with the times, as shown in Kahanuala Coleman's halau. A Gardena resident, Coleman was born on Oahu and raised on Hawaiian Homestead at Kalawahine on Anianiku. She moved to Los Angeles in 1989 and studied hula with Kumu Hula Rolanda Reese and Halau Hula Na Meakanu O Laka O Hawaii. While raising her four children with her husband, David, Kahanuala also became an active member in Hawaii's Daughters Guild of California and began her own hula school, Na 'A'ali'i O Kalamakauikeaouli. Her halau is based on Christian values and maintains a noncompetitive atmosphere. Shown above are some of her adult and keiki *haumana* (students) after cleaning and cutting their ipu. On the left are Kahanuala and her keiki haumana at the first Worship PICC in Wilmington. (Both, courtesy of Kahanuala Coleman.)

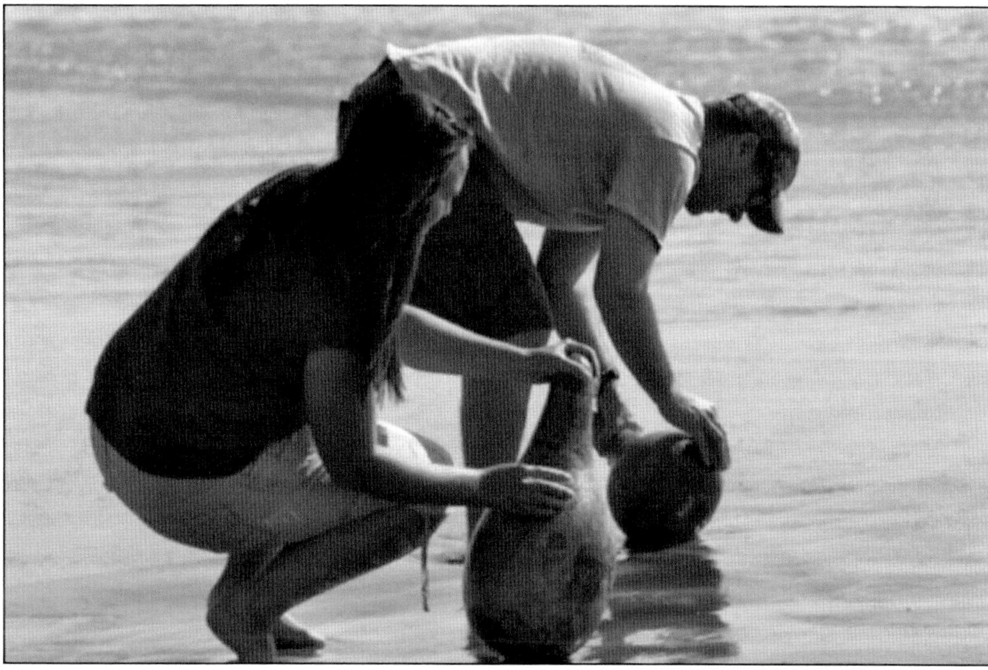

Whether in a hula studio or hula halau, *kumu hula* (teachers of hula) teach more than dance; they also teach tradition and culture. Part of tradition is preparing one's own musical instruments—at least those that can be reproduced on the continent. The ipu, which is used to keep beat and made out of a gourd, is grown somewhat locally near San Diego, California. Many halau and Native Hawaiians visit the gourd farm annually to gather materials for their instruments. Above, haumana clean the dirt off of their ipu in the ocean, using the salt water and sand to make scrubbing easier. Below, haumana clean out the insides of the gourd using spoons and whatever else is handy. (Both, courtesy of Kahanuala Coleman.)

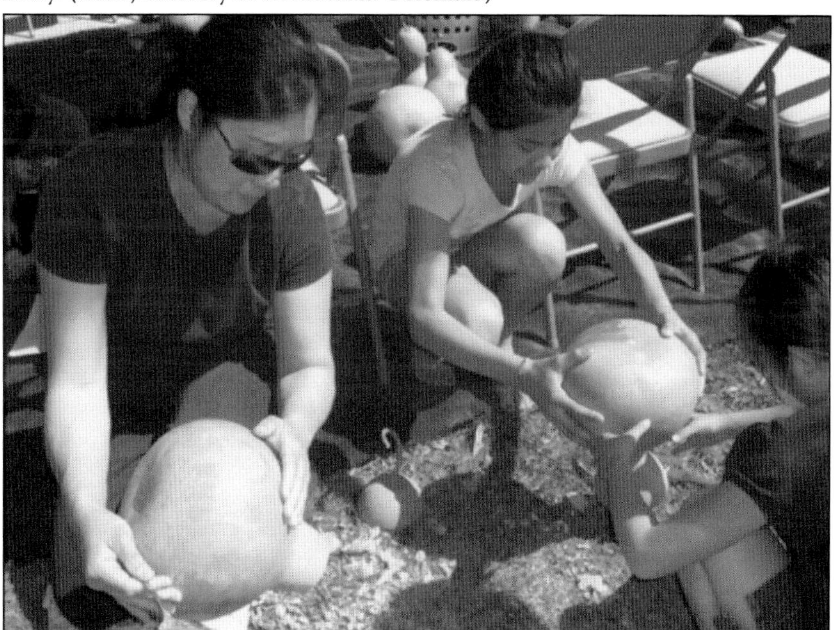

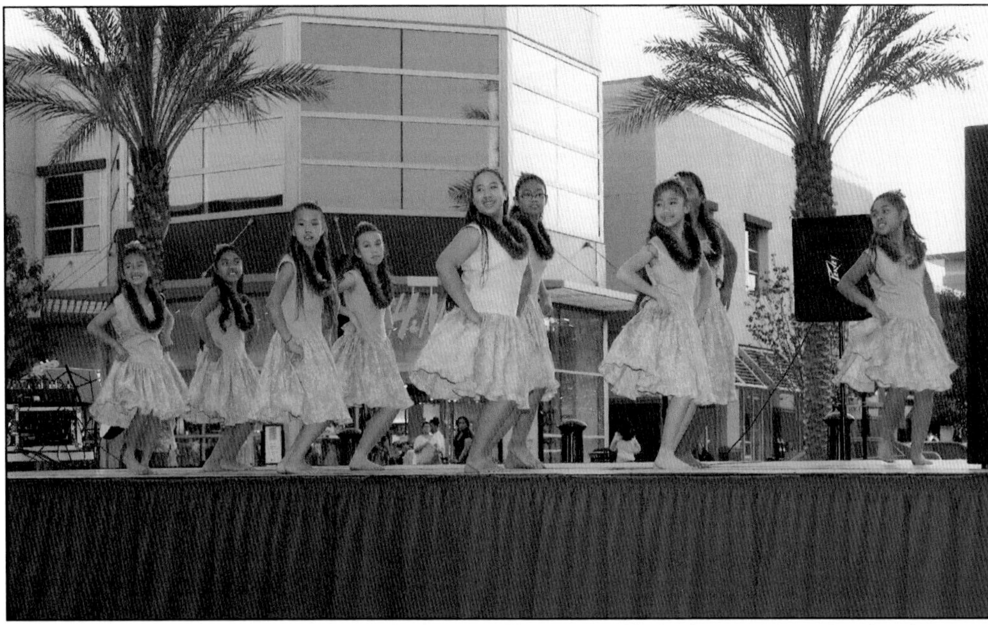

Halau Na Pua Lehua I Ka Ua Noe of Chino Hills was established in 2003 under the direction of Keoni Chang. Keoni Chang is mentored by Nahokuokalani Gaspang, who leads and directs Halau Hula O Kahikilaulani of Hilo. Halau Na Pua Lehua I Ka Ua Noe participates in community events, such as the San Dimas Ho'olaule'a and competitions like the George Na'ope Kane Hula Festival and Keiki Competition in Sacramento, California, and E Hula Mau in Long Beach, California. Like the civic clubs, many halau are created to perpetuate Hawaiian culture for the keiki of Hawaiians as well as the Hawaiian at heart. The children learn the stories of Hawaii before and after annexation. Shown here are the keiki dancing at a community event at the Shoppes in Chino Hills. (Both, courtesy of Joe and Millicent Dypiangco.)

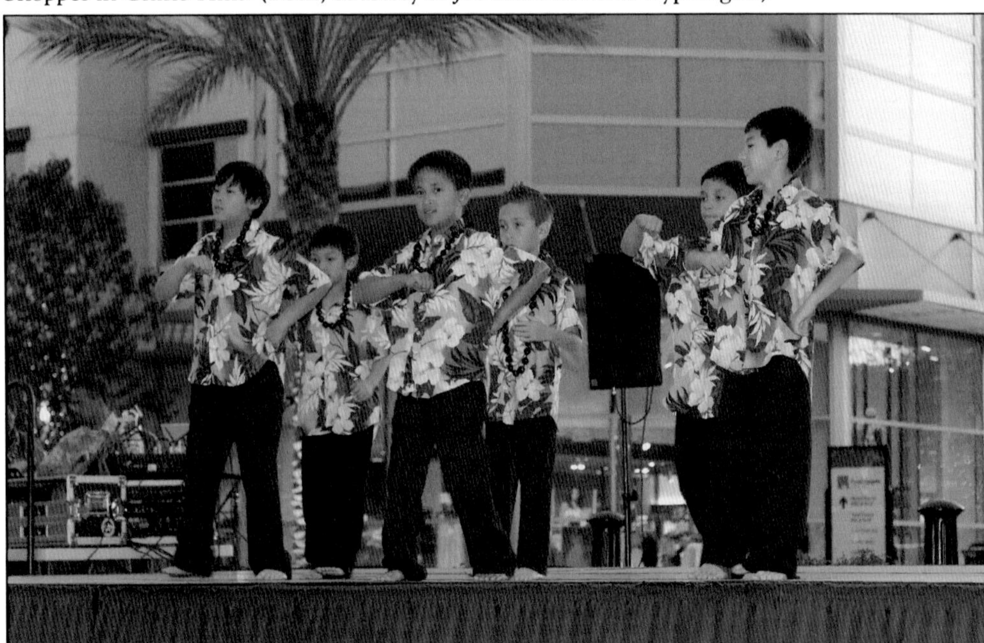

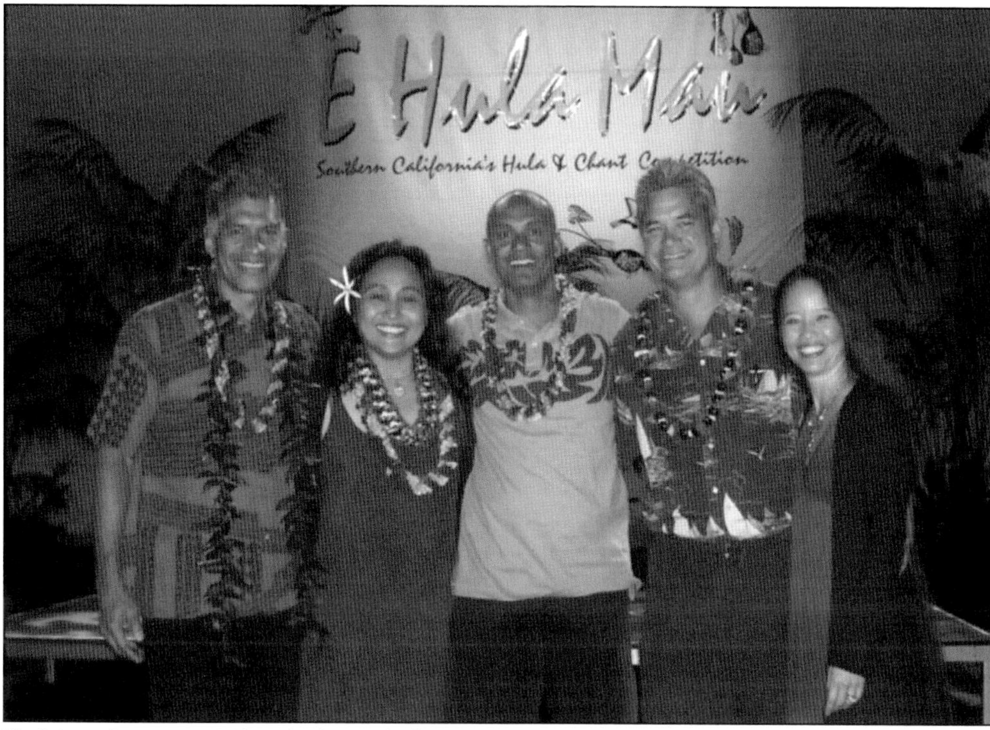

Na Mamo began in 1992 with the goal of perpetuating the "ohana spirit through social interaction and education" and promoting "*lokahi* (family unity) through love and sharing." Na Mamo accomplishes this through community events, particularly the hula and chant competition E Hula Mau, which began in 1995 in Irvine and is currently held in Long Beach, California. During E Hula Mau, Na Mamo presents workshops and lectures featuring lei making, Hawaiian music, cultural practices, genealogy, and Native Hawaiian issues to name a few topics. Shown in the above picture from left to right are some of the past presidents and E Hula Mau chairs as well as some of the founders of Na Mamo: Michael Crabbe (founder), Keikilani Lyons, Iopu Brian Taelefi (founder), Dean Chow (founder), and Kahiwa Chow. The photograph below shows Na Mamo founders Bobby Naluai and Michael Crabbe. (Both, courtesy of Michael Crabbe.)

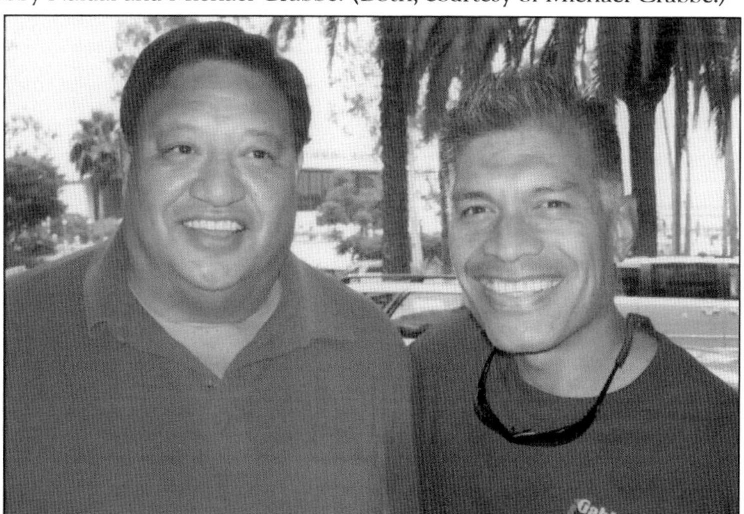

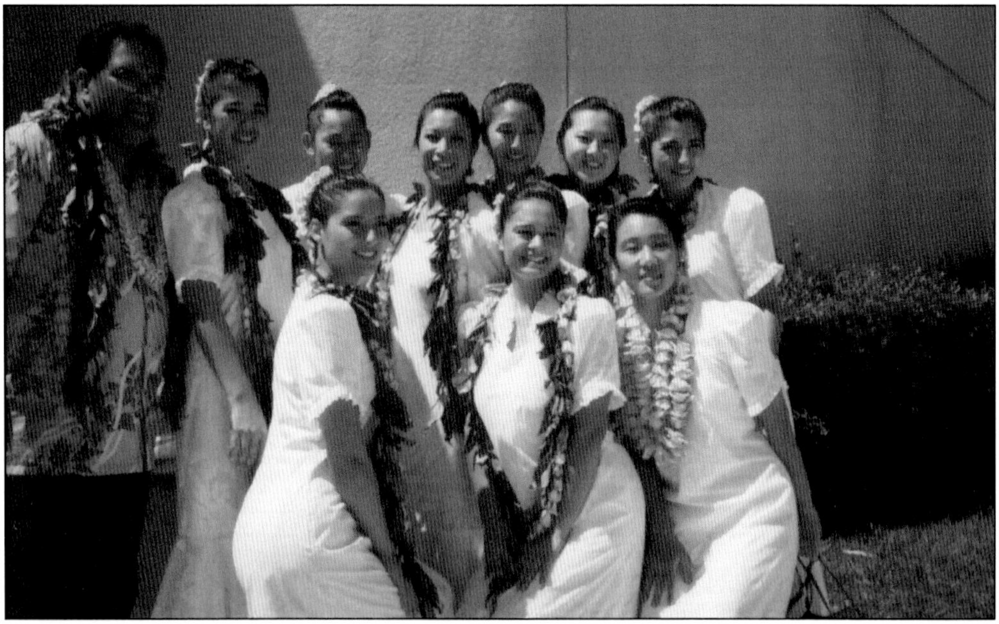

In 1995, the first E Hula Mau occurred in Irvine, California. Shown above are members of Kaulana Ka Hale Kula 'O Na Pua 'O Ka 'Aina, led by Randy Kaulana Chang (far left) during the competition's inauguration. Many of Randy's students at this time were UCLA students who met through Randy's UCLA extension classes. Below are Kane members of Kaulana Ka Hale Kula 'O Na Pua 'O Ka 'Aina rehearsing for their Kahiko number in 2010 at the Long Beach Terrace Theatre. In the picture below are (left to right) Luke Kaimi Haug-Schulz, whose mother, Lehuanani is shown above to the right of Randy Chang; Kalei Devilly, whose mother is active in Na Mamo; Alden Lono Pelayo, who has been dancing with Randy Chang since the Kalani Islanders; Gary Abrajano; and D.J. Taniguchi. (Above, courtesy of Pi'ilaniwahine Requiro; below, courtesy of Lehuanani Tanemura Schulz.)

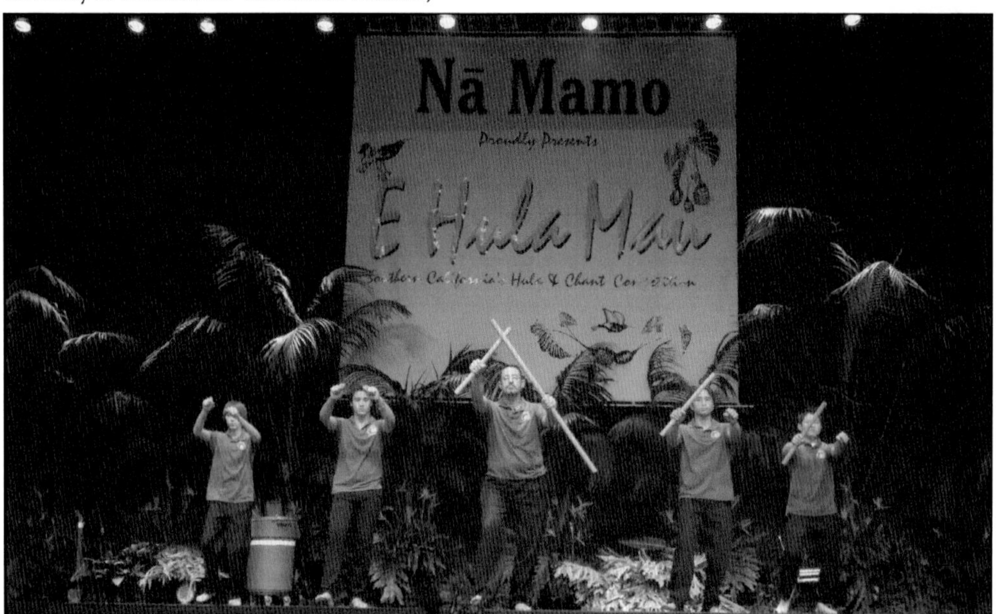

Preparing for E Hula Mau takes months of practice and hours of costume and lei making. The picture to the right shows Carolyn Kimura making leis that the kane will wear on Saturday and the wahine will wear on Sunday. The picture below shows the makua preparing their plumeria leis just hours before they stepped onstage to compete. During preparations, everyone pitches in to help one another as much as possible. All competitors pull together to help get the job done so that everyone can go home and get as much rest as possible before the big day. (Both, courtesy of the Pelayo family.)

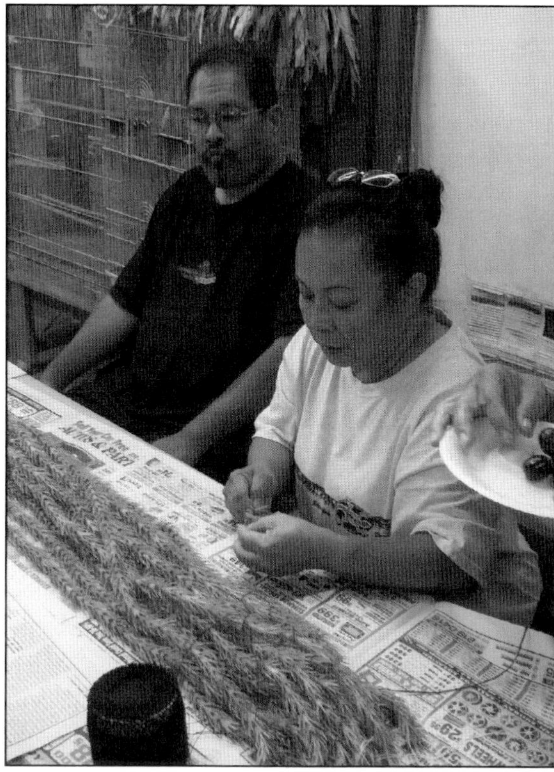

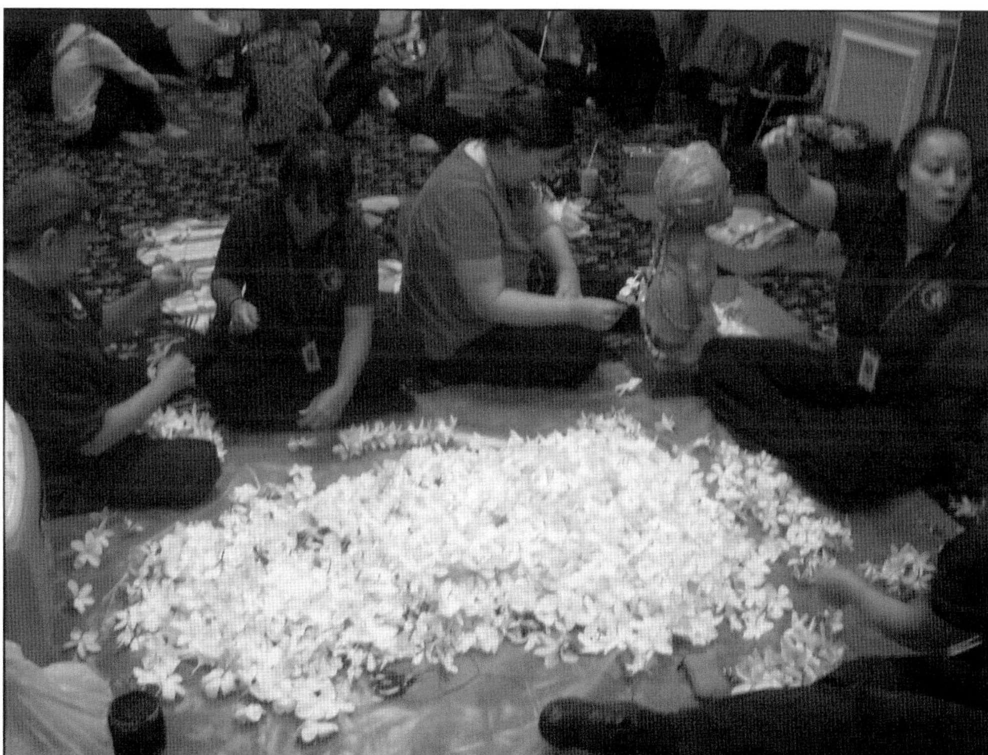

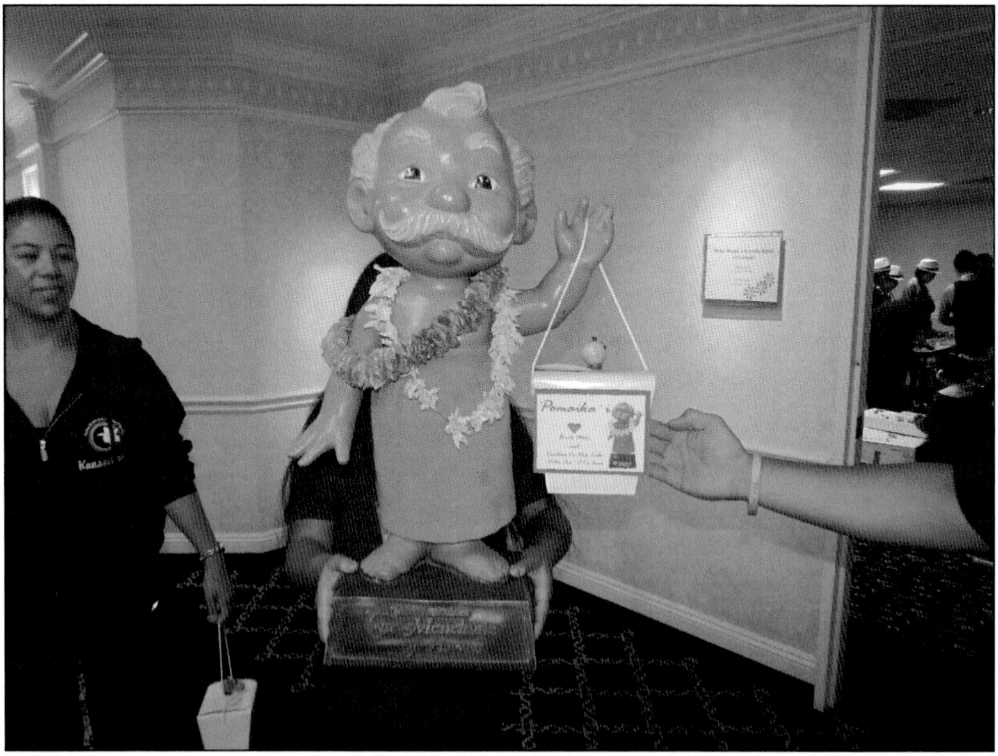

Awards at E Hula Mau are not solely for quality of performance. There is also an Aloha Spirit award. This award is given to the halau that demonstrates the Aloha Spirit through helping other halau, good sportsmanship, and all of the facets of aloha one could think of. Here, Uncle Moki, halau mascot, is delivering kokua baskets to other halau to wish them *po'maika'i* (good luck) on their performances throughout the weekend. Below, Uncle Moki is shown making new friends with some of the 2011 E Hula Mau Staff who come from all over Southern California to help put on the competition. (Both, courtesy of the Pelayo family.)

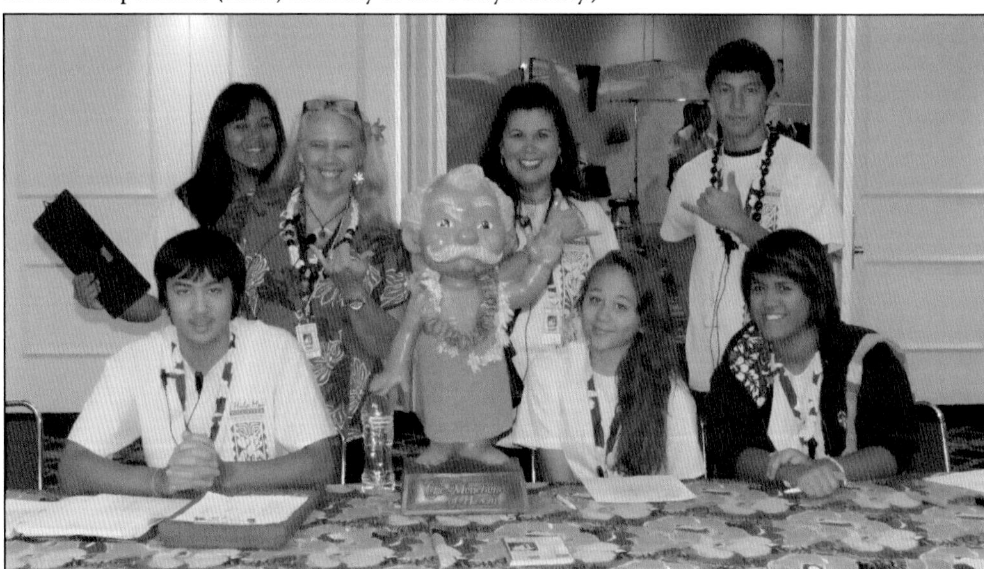

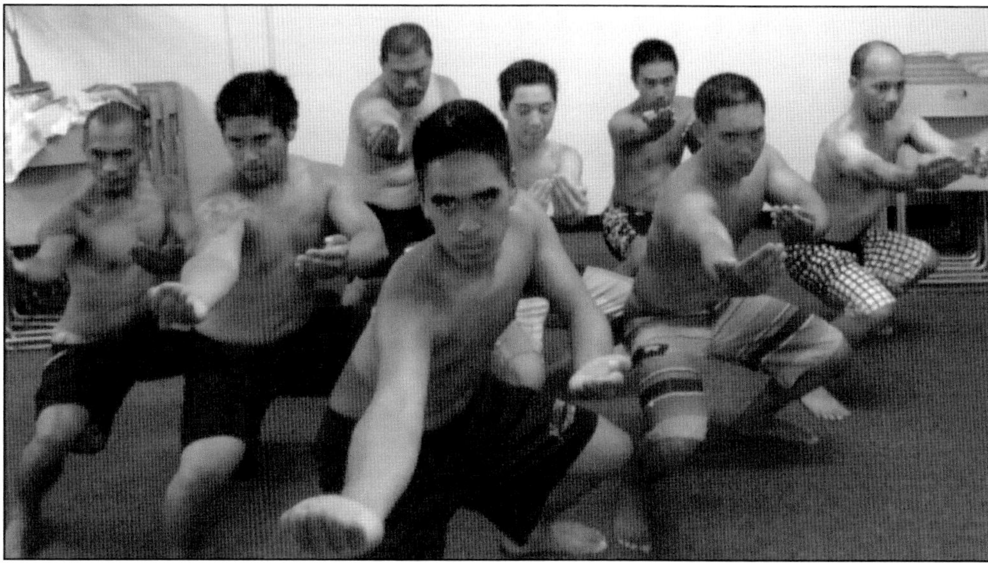

Understated in hula is the participation of men. *Kane* (men) hula becomes not only a cultural outlet but also an outlet for the warrior inside. Kane members of Halau Na Pua Me Ke Aloha, such as Len Moke Hilacion, a Native Hawaiian born and raised in the Los Angeles area, say that through hula they have learned a spiritual connection to those before them. Kane hula is not just limited to Native Hawaiians, and it attracts locals and Hawaiians at heart, such as Kevin Gin and Kevin Villarama, who find that the chants, dances, and lessons are universal. All members of any halau require great sacrifice and commitment, and the kane, who participate in hula, meet those requirements head-on. (Above, courtesy of Sissy Kaio and Annette McCormack; below, courtesy of Florante Peter Ibanez.)

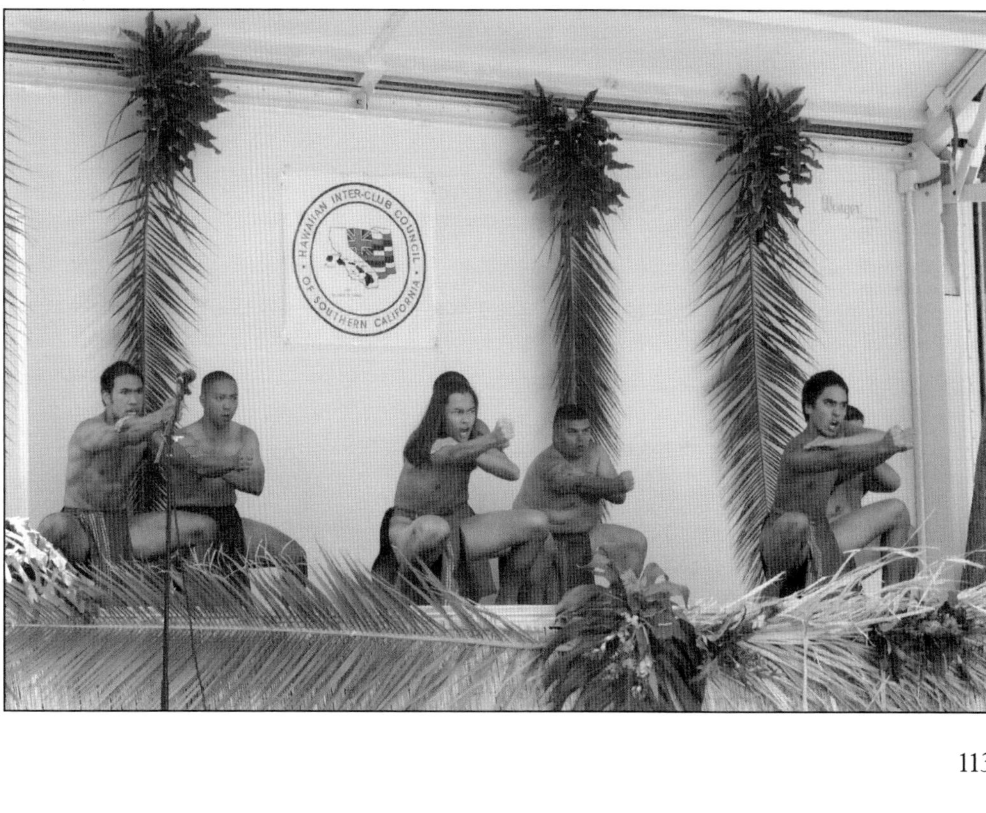

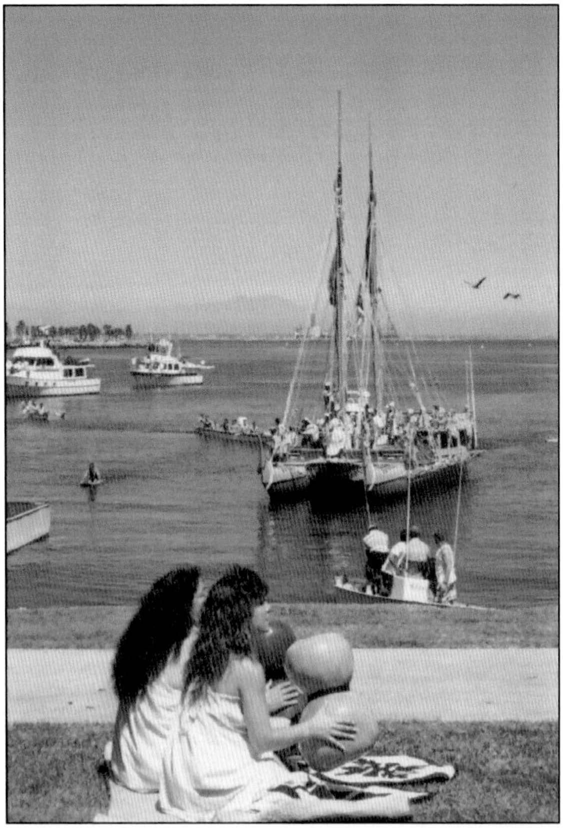

In Aloha Spirit and as the face of Hawaiian culture, hula halau turn out for moments when Hawaii and Polynesia come to California shores. In 1995, Hokule'a sailed up and down the west coast of North America with the purpose of spreading culture and awareness of First Nation issues. The Hokule'a is a traditional Polynesian ship that has been sailing between Tahiti and Hawaii since 1972, using ancient Polynesian technology and navigation. In response to the ship's visit to the West Coast, many people of the First Nations came to greet the ship. When they came to Southern California, Randy Chang's halau, among others, met the ships and treated them to aloha, which included hula performances. In the photograph on the left, women welcome the ship with a chant. Below, a group of *kane* (men) stand ready for a kahiko hula. (Both, courtesy of Pi'ilaniwahine Requiro.)

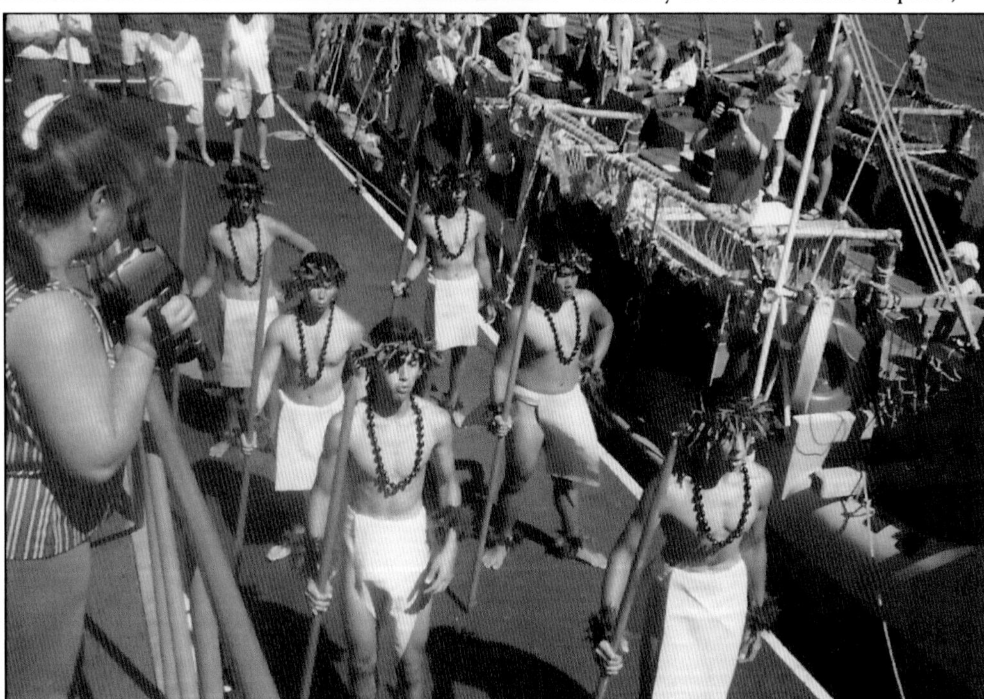

Six

Perpetuating the Culture

Hawaiians Now

In the 21st century, Hawaiians in Los Angeles find themselves occupying a unique space on the border between traditions that effectively ended in the 19th century and a modern community. One tradition is the past that ended with the overthrow of Hawaii's Queen Liliuokalani and America's rise after World War II, and the other is the present that sees them as forerunners to an increasingly racially diverse society. How can a culture that started the previous century with about 30,000 people maintain an identity and culture while dealing with all the issues of now?

The answer, as always, is as practical a one as it is spiritual. Hawaiians accept both cultures and maintain them while always being part of a larger one. Acceptance and adaptation is something they have done since the arrival of Captain Cook, and it is something they will continue to do. When, at one time, Native Hawaiians were warriors, they are now athletes. When they were kumu, they are now teachers and educators. When ohana was broken apart by distance, they have summer schools that teach all the values of family that the Hawaiian culture holds dear.

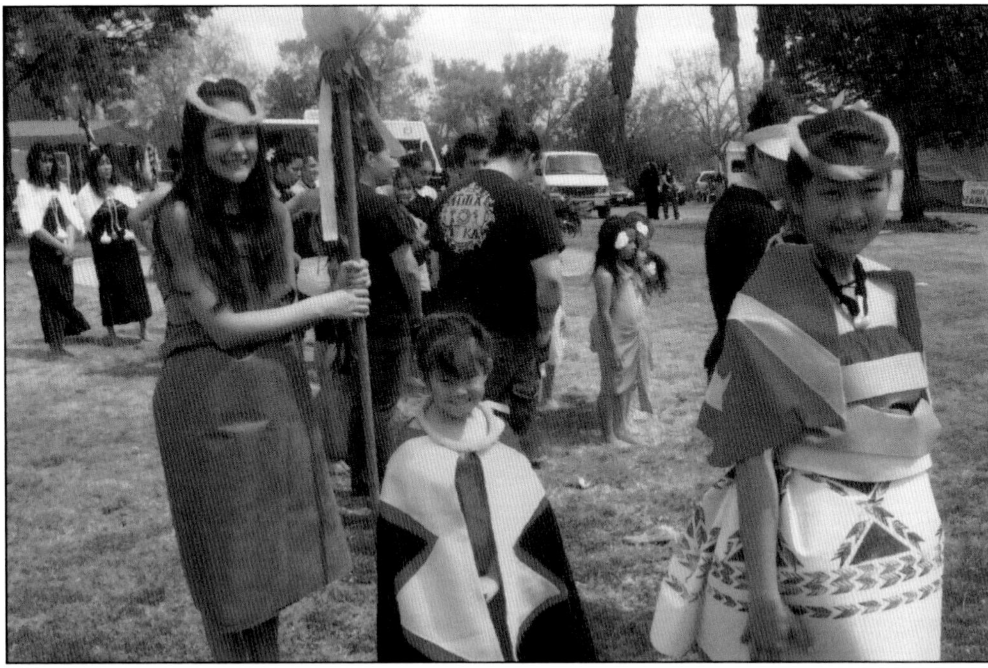

After the Alondra Park Ho'olaule'a became such a success, the Polynesian Interclub Council (PICC) was formed. They decided to put on a Pacific Islander festival at Harbor Regional Park in Wilmington. The festival represented all of the Pacific Islands, and each island had its own booth to help educate the community with demonstrations, workshops, and displays. Shown are representatives for Hawaii (Lessa Kanani'opua Pelayo-Lozada, Noel Taniguchi, and Jade Taniguchi) lining up with the other islands for opening ceremonies. (Courtesy of the Pelayo family.)

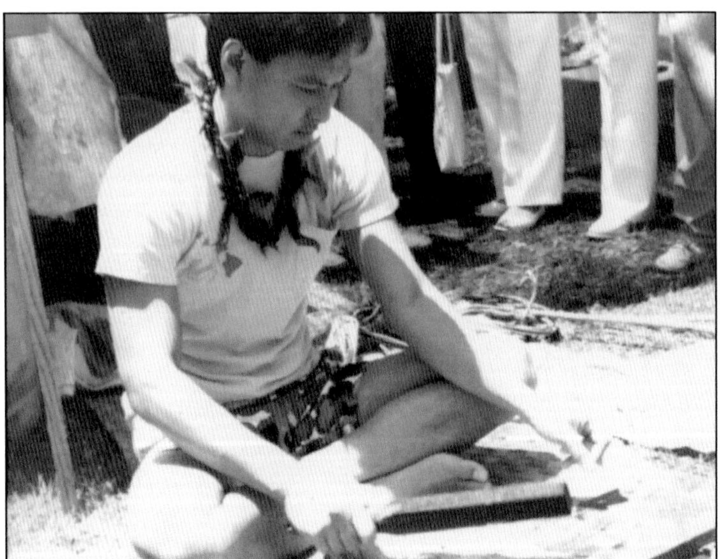

Perpetuating Hawaiian arts is an important part of Hawaiian civic club life and is a common thread in civic club mission statements. Shown here, a man learns how tapa cloth, made out of bark, is made. In ancient Hawaii, tapa or kapa was used for many types of clothing and blankets as well as adornments. Recently, it has also become contemporary art. (Courtesy of the Pelayo family.)

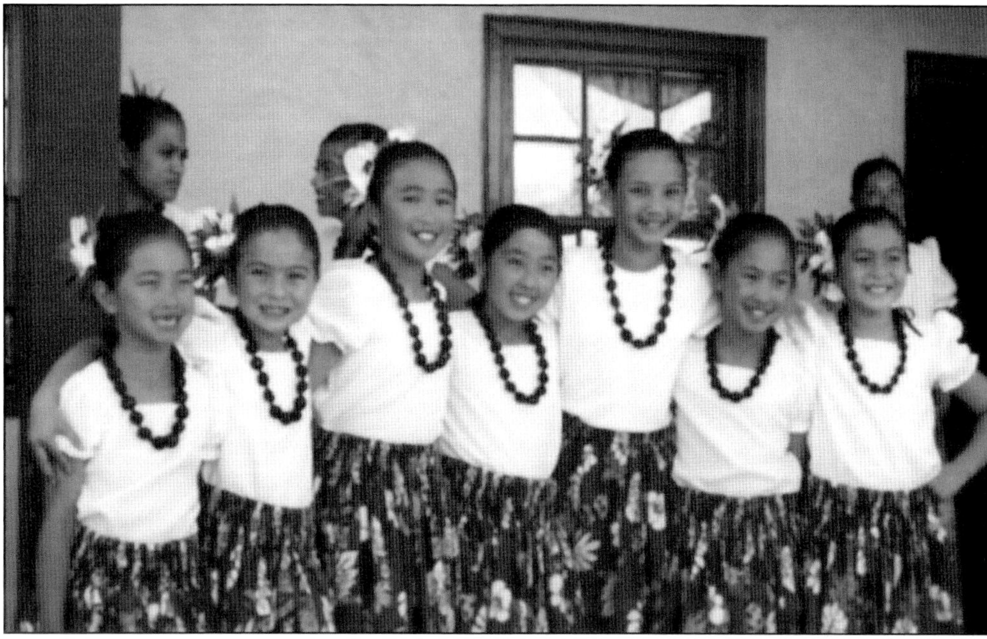

Due to changing city regulations and limitations, in 2011, PICC changed its festival venue and focus. The venue became a church in Wilmington, instead of a park, and each of the islands was invited to help put on a praise and worship festival. Shown are members of Na A'ali'i O Kalamakauikeaouli Hula Praise (keiki above; wahine and keiki below), led by Kahanuala Coleman, who represented the island of Hawaii at the festival. (Both, courtesy of Kahanuala Coleman.)

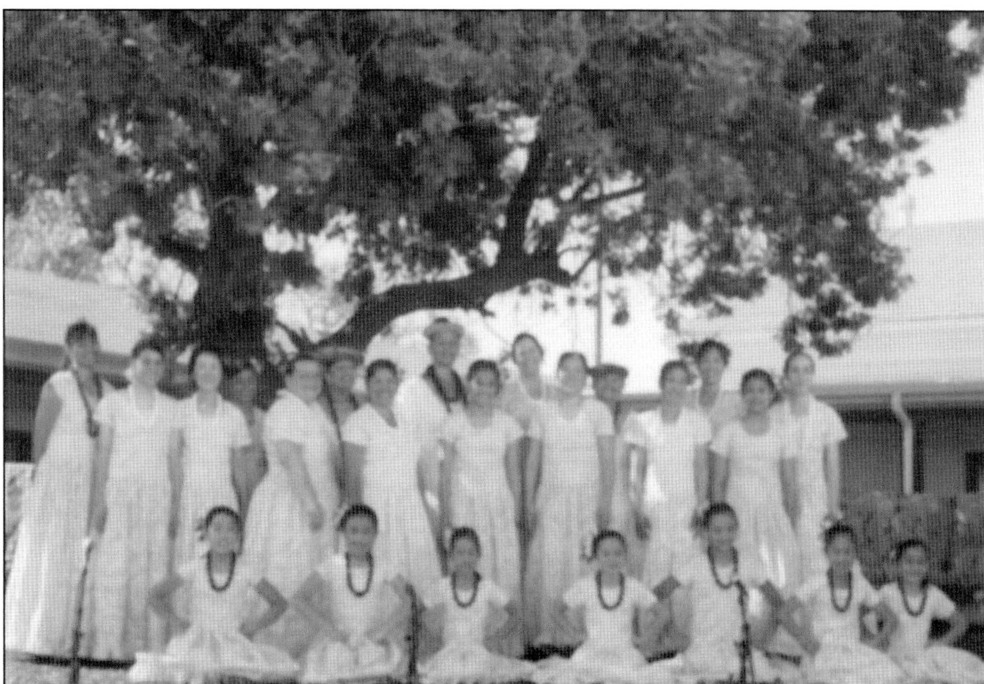

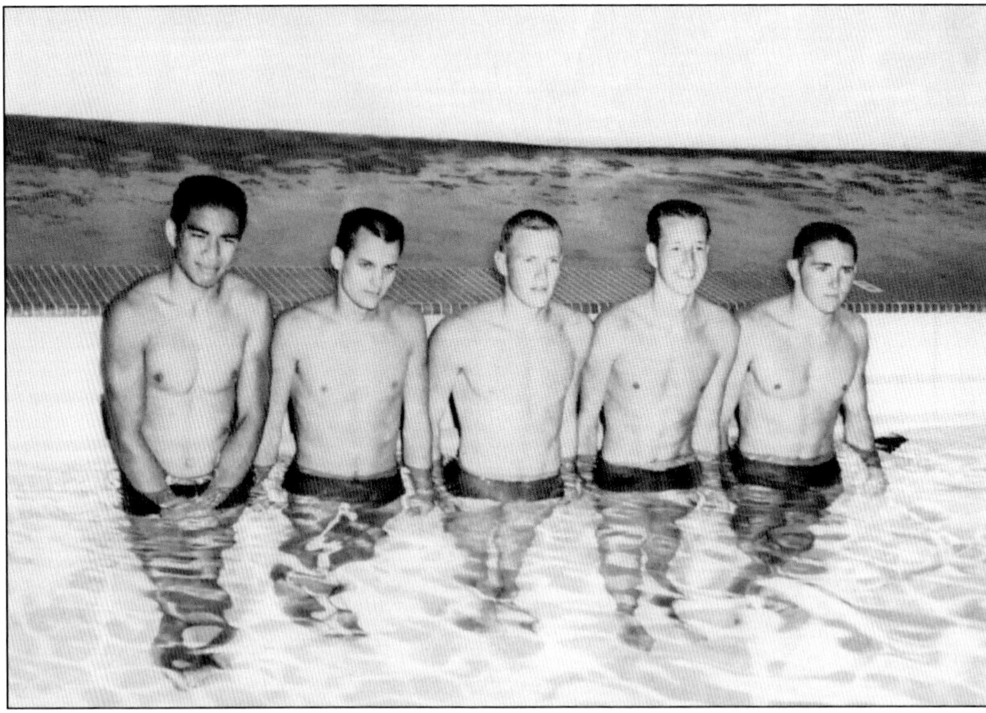

Because many Native Hawaiians recognize the importance of water, swimming is as normal to many kanaka as breathing. As a student at Polytechnic High School in Long Beach, Gus Keolanui (far left), set a school record for the 50-yard freestyle in 1955 and placed 2nd in the CIF Championship in 1955 and 1956. In 1956, Gus qualified as an All-American Top 20, receiving All-City recognition for two years in a row. (Courtesy of Gus Keolanui.)

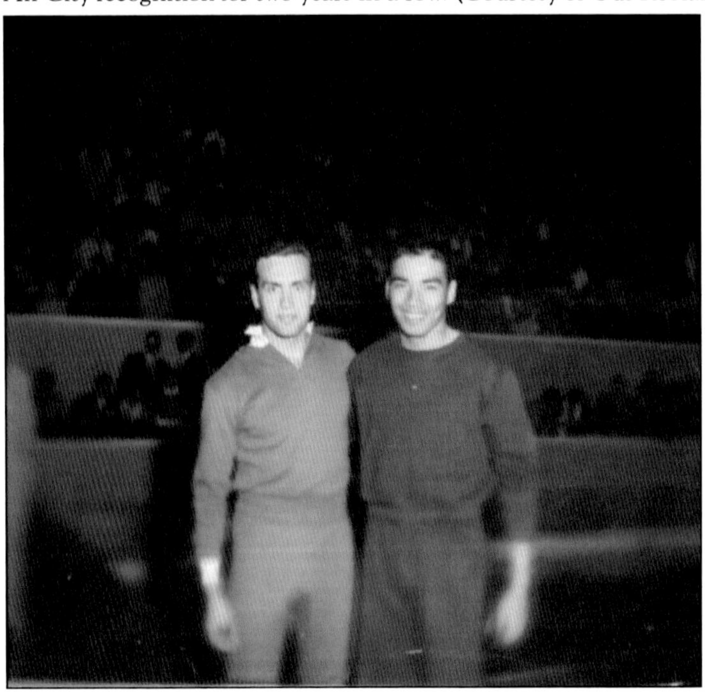

Gus Keolanui, right, was appointed to the US Naval Academy in July 1957. During his first summer cruise in 1958, under the President's People to People Program, the Portuguese Consul arranged for a friendly swim meet against their Olympic Team. Gus placed second in the 50-yard freestyle. He was beaten by their best sprinter, Fernando (shown on the left). (Courtesy of Gus Keolanui.)

In the 1970s , Paul and Nani Nihipali organized the Hawaii Volleyball Association. The organization was originally created for recreational purposes and traveled to different tournaments. They were trying to gain a berth and compete in the Haili Tournament in Hawaii. Later, the organization created scholarship opportunities to support women as they pursued their academic careers. (Courtesy of Elizabeth "Nani" Nihipali.)

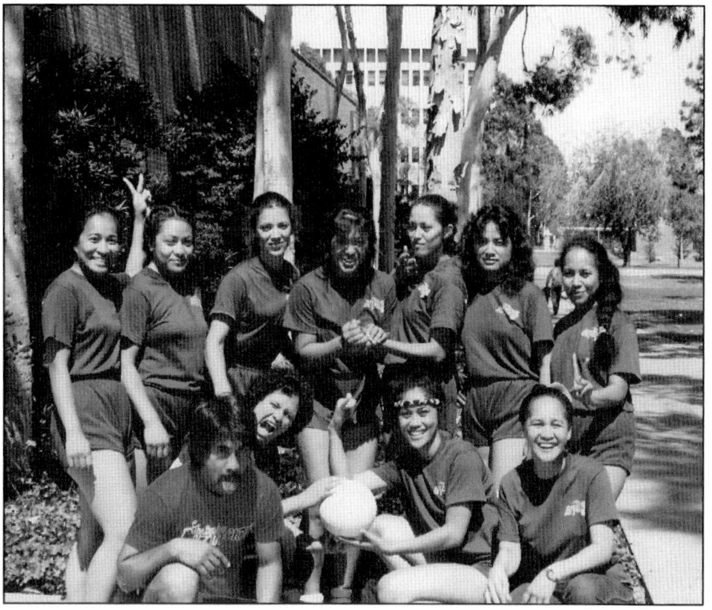

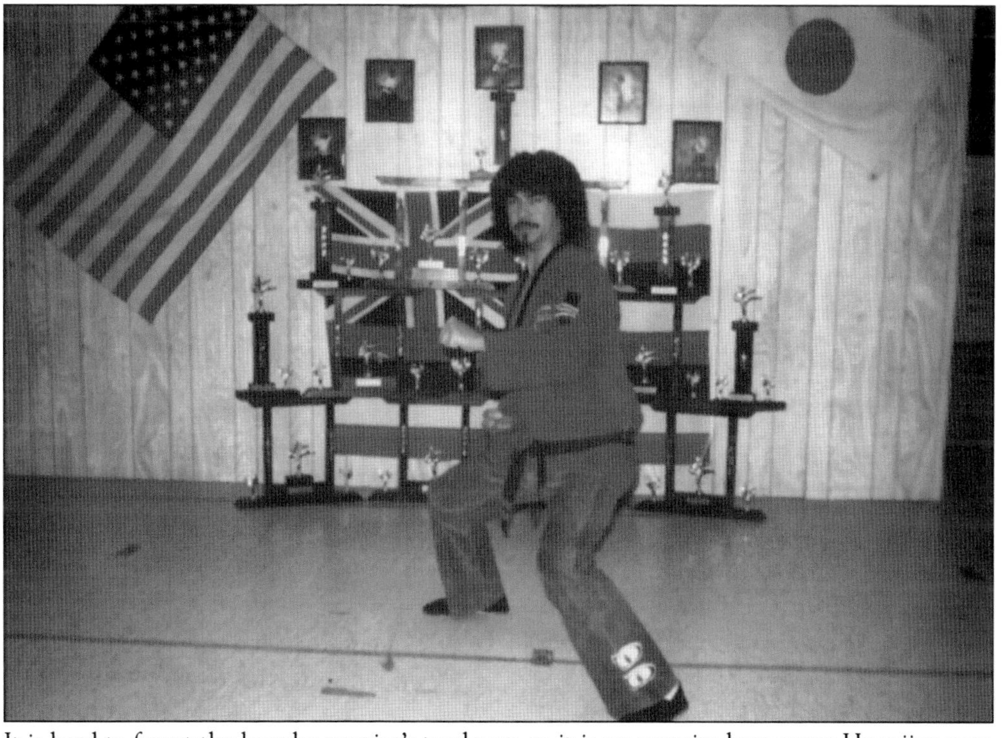

It is hard to forget the kanaka warrior's tendency, so it is no surprise how many Hawaiian men and women look to martial arts as a common past time. Albert Brigoli was born and raised in Kaneohe, Oahu, and is a sixth degree black belt in Goju Kai Karate. Albert and his brothers opened the Brigoli Karate School, where, under the influence of their grandfather Hermenio Brigoli, an eskrimador from Cebu, Philippines, and with permission from the Goju Kai main school in Japan, the brothers incorporated Eskrima into their art, calling the fusion Kaikido. (Courtesy of the Brigoli family.)

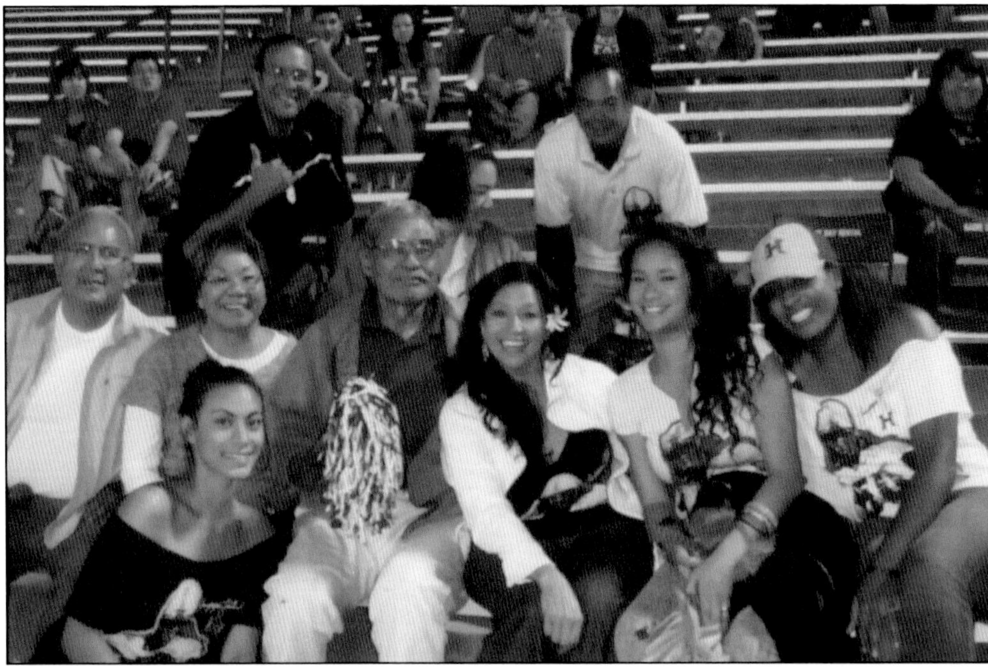

For many Hawaiians, the only way to get back and live in Hawaii is the few years spent in college. Laupepa Letuli, a graduate of North High School, went on to play football for University of Hawaii. The photographs shown here are of his immediate ohana and his extended ohana who took a road trip to see UH play the Fresno Bulldogs. In the top photograph are the Letuli family, Sam and Melanie Rosero, Alcario "Sonny" Pelayo, Keoki Moore, and Stephanie Mahaley. In the bottom photograph are all those who call each other ohana, whether through blood or calabash. The Mahaley family, from Carson, and their son Antoine (back row, far left), who also played for UH, are also with Laupepa Letuli (back row, white shirt) and are included in this extended ohana. (Both, courtesy of the Letuli family.)

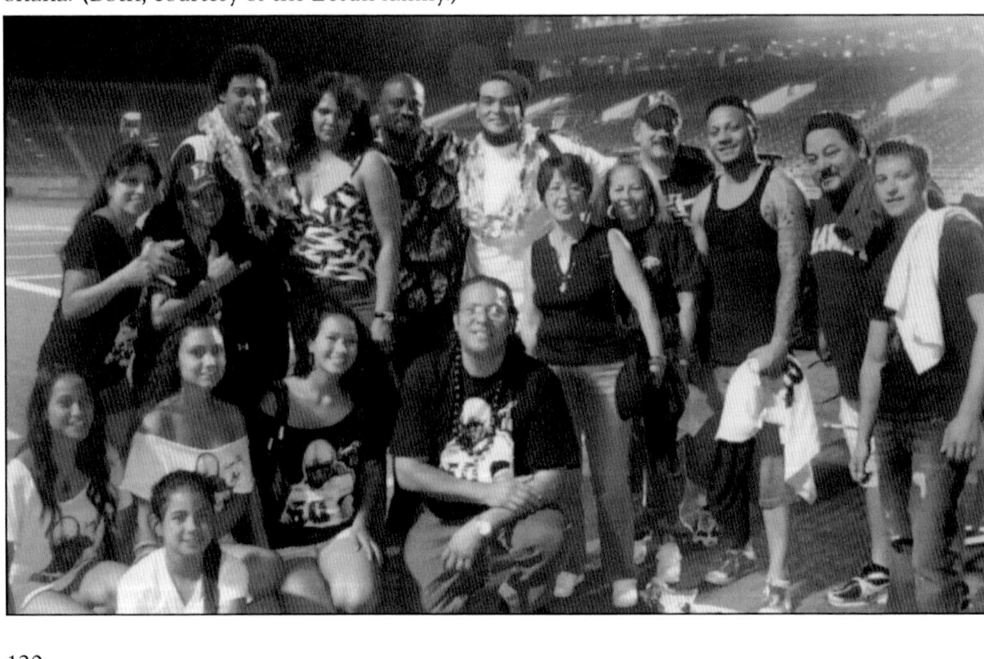

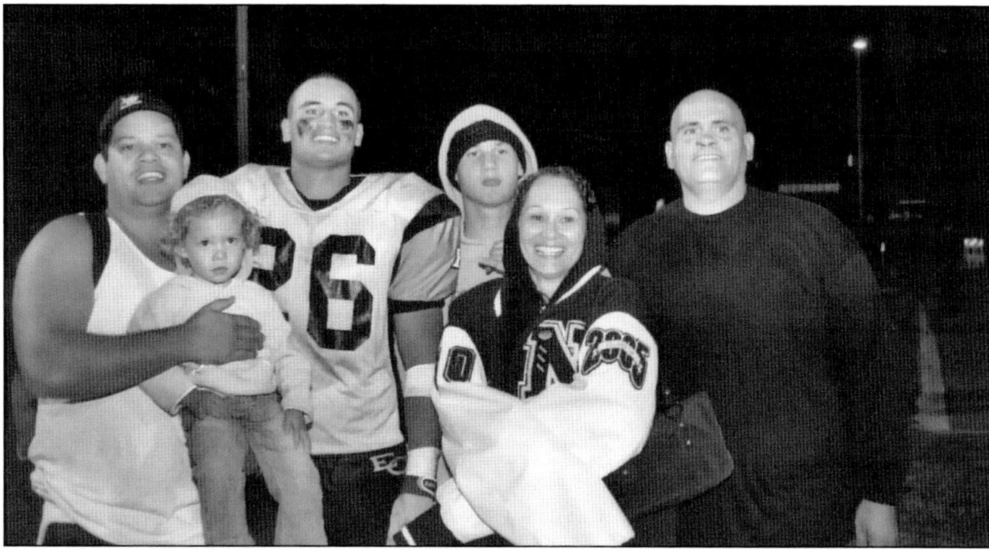

While some Hawaiians find that their only way home is through college, some find college as an opportunity to leave the islands. Student athletes make up an important part of Native Hawaiians in education, since, for many of them, this is one of the only ways to afford college. Kaipo Sarkissian (number 26) and, later, his younger brother Kaimi Sarkissian (pictured in the bottom image, far right), left their home in Waimanalo to live with their extended ohana in Torrance to pursue football and education at El Camino College (ECC). Another Native Hawaiian ECC player, Boo Jackson (pictured below, far left), also lived with his extended ohana while playing football. The above photograph shows the Sarkissian family who would make trips from Waimanalo to Torrance to see their sons play football. Below, Boo stands next to his uncle David Coleman, and Kaipo stands in between his brothers. (Both, courtesy of the Letuli family.)

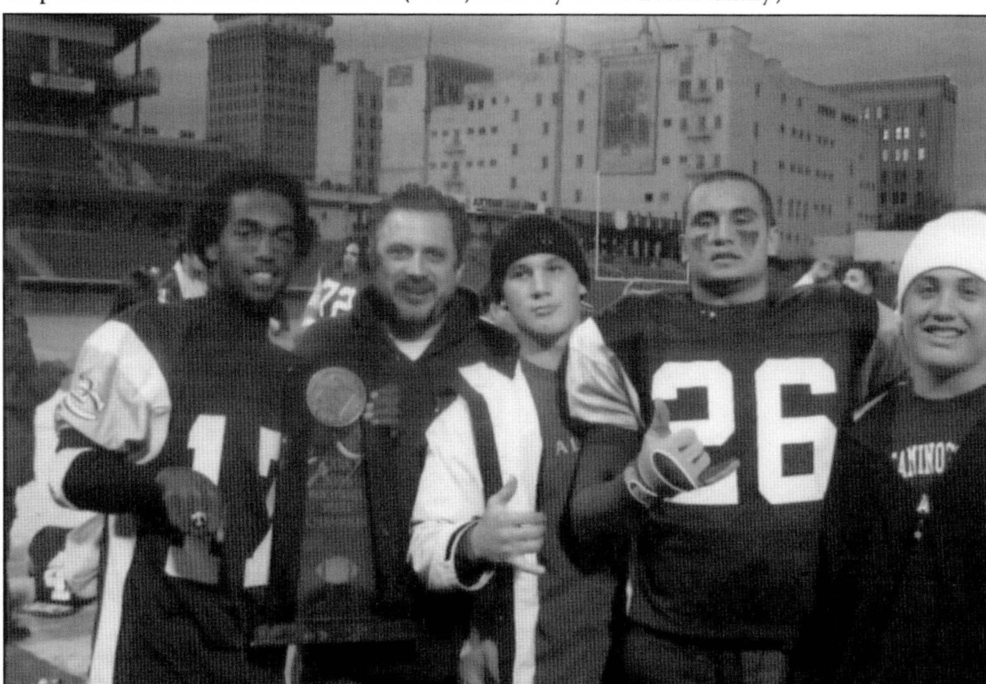

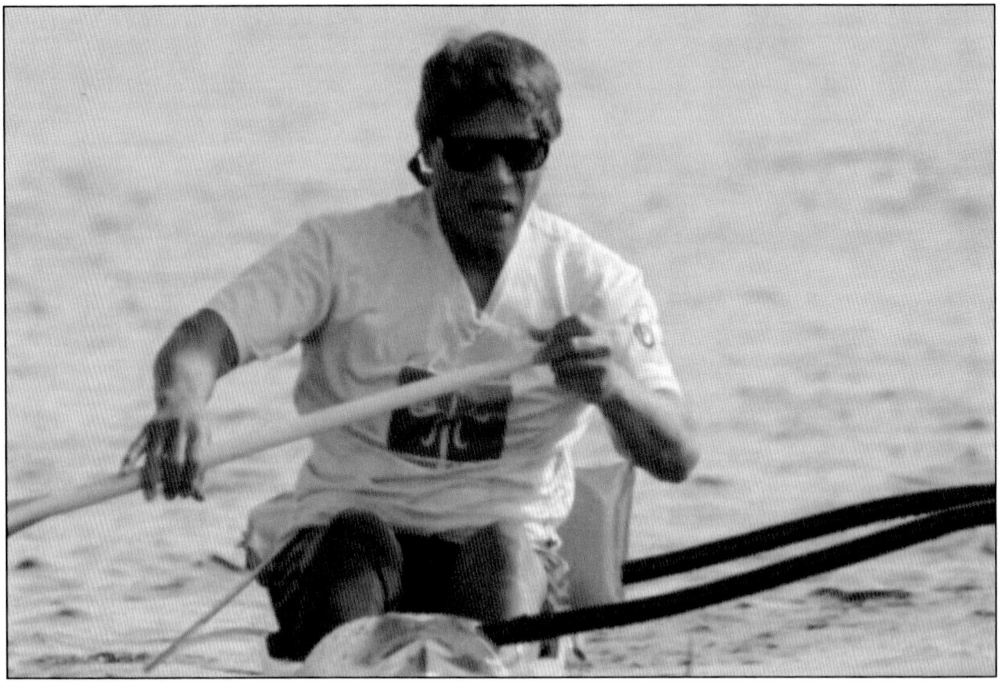

In 1970, Al Ching (shown above), along with Ralph Hanalei, Keith Keillor, Sam Ferrar, Art Hausen, and Mike Jacobs started the Lanakila Outrigger Canoe Club. The canoe club was based in Marina Del Rey and eventually moved to Redondo Beach's King Harbor. The canoe itself is important to Hawaiian culture because it was how the ancient Hawaiians travelled from island to island, spreading news while starting and ending wars. Kamehameha I established the tradition of the broken oar, which charges all Hawaiians to take care of those in need. Outrigger canoe clubs today, like Lanakila, are charged with perpetuating the tradition of paddling as well as taking care of one another. (Above, courtesy of Pi'ilaniwahine Requiro; below, courtesy of Chris Silvester.)

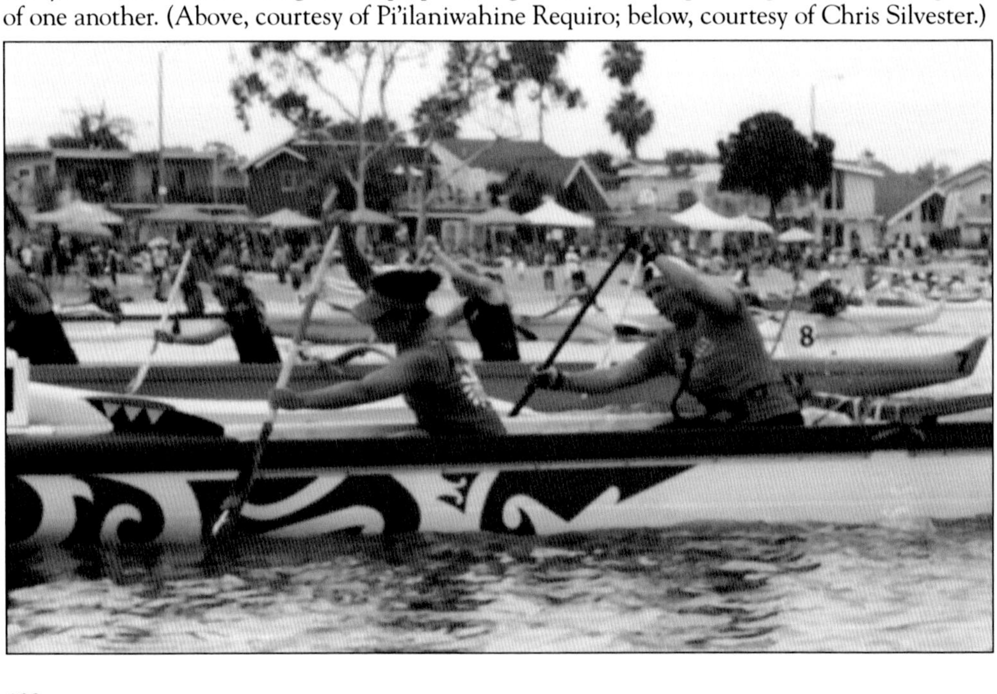

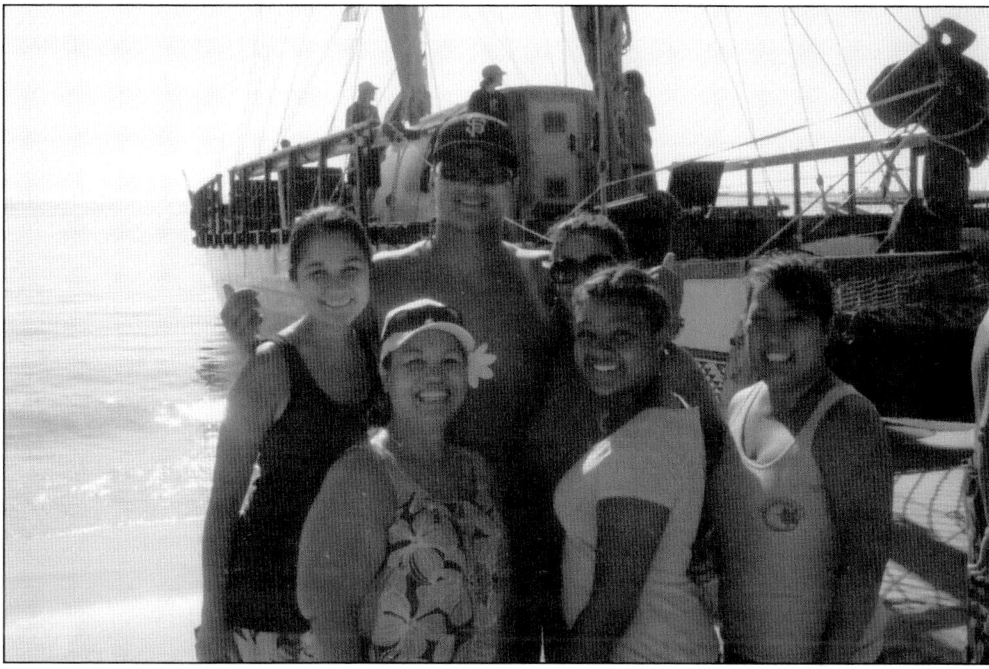

Hawaiians know that education comes from any source and one must be willing to learn from people on distant shores because our experiences, for the most part, are the same. In 2011, the Pacific Island Culture Council entertained the Pacific Voyagers' arrival in San Pedro. The Pacific Voyagers is a small fleet of Polynesian *vaka* (ships) sailing across the Pacific Ocean and down the West Coast. They sail to create awareness about malama 'aina and to honor the ancestors who have sailed before. Pictured above are the girls of Kaulana Ka Hale Kula 'O Na Pua 'O Ka 'Aina posing with a voyager from the Maori vaka, Poihakena Dudley. Below, everyone pulls together to try and get the Samoa vaka offshore and into the ocean. (Both, courtesy of the Pelayo family.)

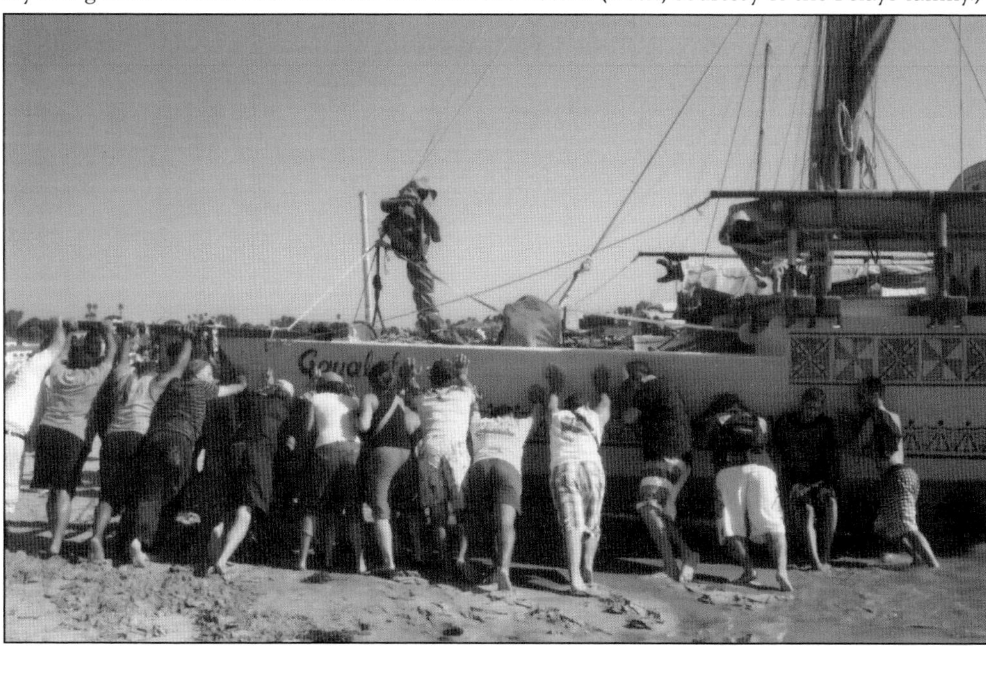

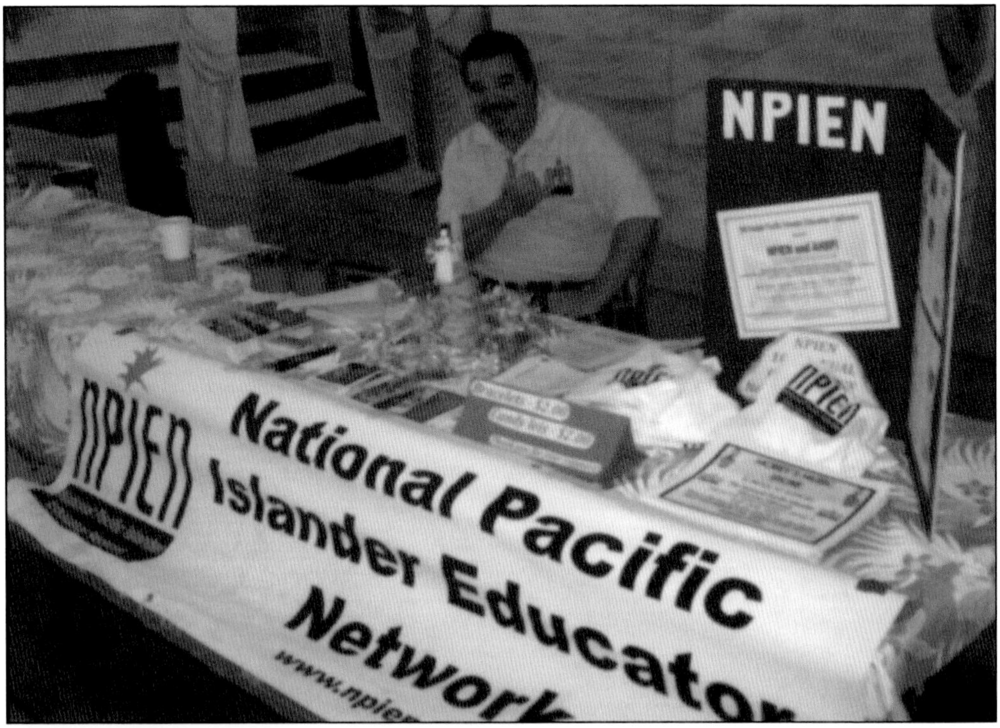

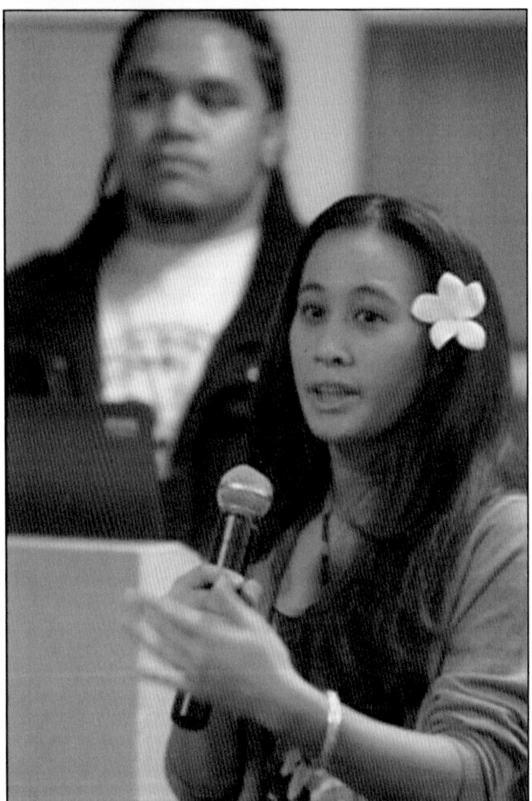

While some find education difficult to maintain, Hawaiians continue to be natural educators. The National Pacific Islander Educator Network (NPIEN) seeks to provide Pacific Islander students with support towards academic achievement, financial aid and scholarships, and mentorship. They provide speakers at academic conferences to introduce research on Pacific Islander students to other educators and support Pacific Islander student club programs. They also give workshops to students at schools in the Los Angeles area. In the above photograph, Lopaka Faria, a member of NPIEN's volunteer staff, mans the NPIEN informational table at a conference. In the next photograph, Brittany Noelani Valdez speaks to students at Lakewood High School on the college admissions process. Noelani also dedicates her time to students in grades 6–12 as an NPIEN guest speaker and mentor. (Both, courtesy of Victor C. Thompson.)

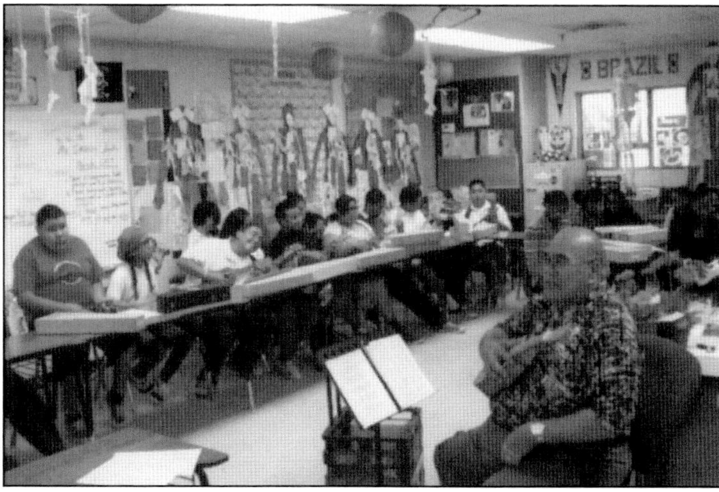

As part of the NPIEN, Uncle Henry Kamae brings ukulele playing to hundreds of students in Los Angeles and Orange Counties every year. Here, he teaches a group of students at Roosevelt Middle School in Compton. Uncle Henry also plays regularly at Bob's Okazuya restaurant in Gardena. (Courtesy of Victor C. Thompson.)

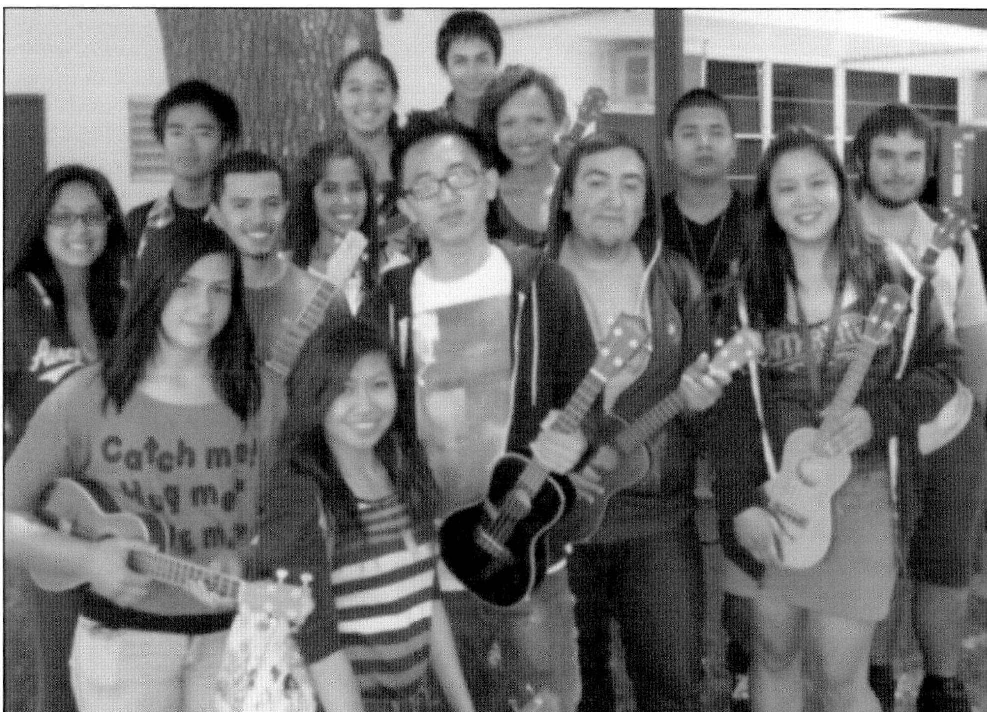

After Tongan ukulele playing students inspired her, Lauren Bowman, a Lawndale High School music teacher, learned to play the ukulele and incorporated the instrument into her music class. The Lawndale High School Ukulele Club, founded by Bowman, held its first Ukulele Festival in May 2011. In this photograph, members of the Lawndale High School Ukulele Club pose with their ukuleles. (Courtesy of Lauren Bowman.)

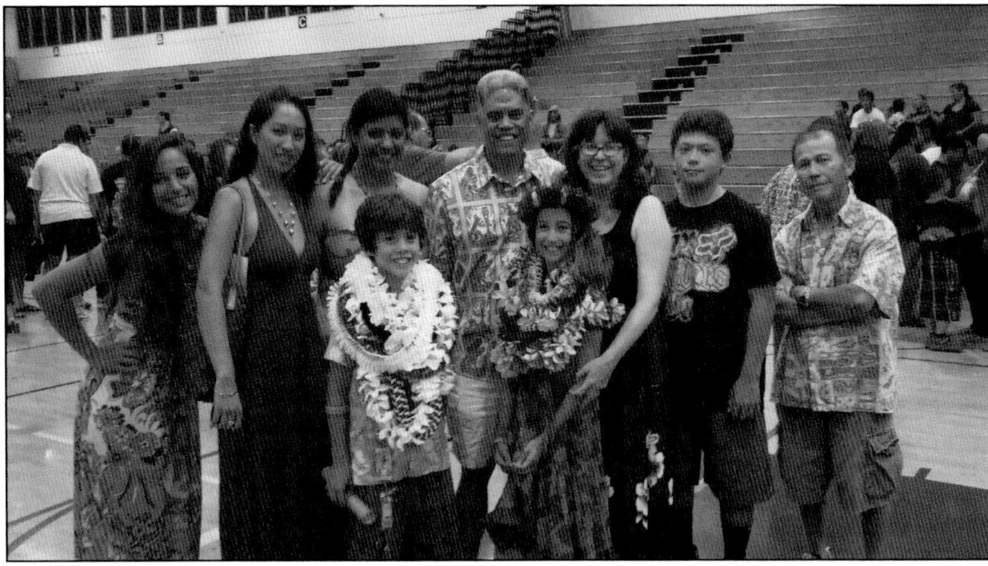

Realizing how hard it is to maintain tradition in a modernizing world, Kamehameha Schools started the program Ho'omaka'ika'i. Every year, in the summer after fifth grade, Native Hawaiian children are invited to learn about their ancestors and the Hawaiian culture. This program has become a right of passage for many Native Hawaiian children on the continent. For many, it is their first airplane ride and their first time visiting Hawaii, as well as their first immersion into the Hawaiian culture. Through this program and others, the next generation of Hawaiians attain the knowledge and tools they need to survive on the borders between tradition, history, and the present. Shown above are Ryan Huggins and Alyse Makana Pelayo, two graduates of Ho'omaka'ika'i. Many of their ohana from California and Hawaii (shown above) came to see their ho'olaule'a on the last day of camp. Below, Ho'omaka'ika'i students demonstrate their new ipu skills. (Both, courtesy of the Pelayo family.)

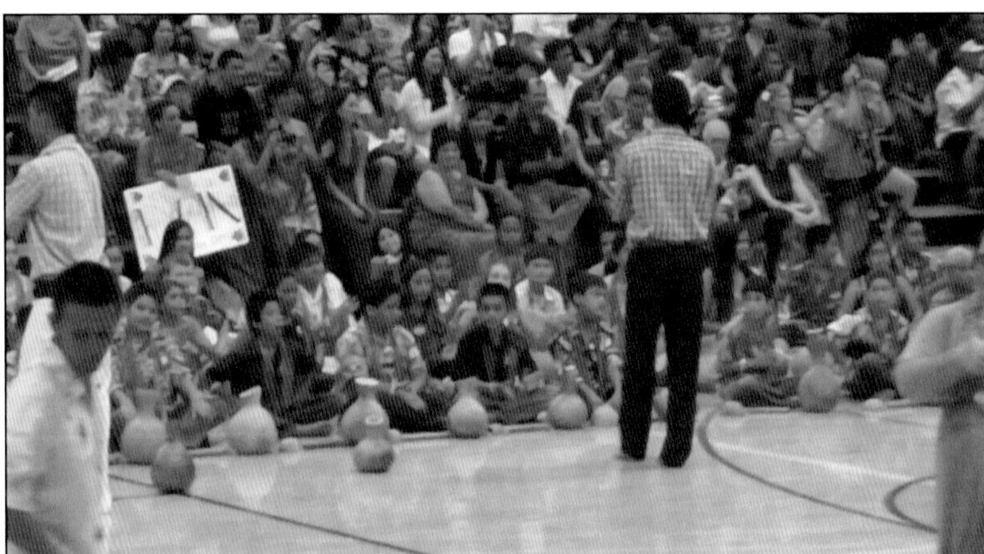

Bibliography

Allen, Helen G. *The Betrayal of Liliuokalani*. Honolulu, HI: Mutual Publishing, 1982.

Barman, Jean. "New Land, New Lives: Hawaiian Settlement in British Columbia." *The Hawaiian Journal of History* 29 (1995): 1–32.

Hall, Lisa Kahaleole. " 'Hawaiian at heart' and other fictions." *The Contemporary Pacific* (2005): 404–413.

Halualani, Rona Tamiko. *In the Name of Hawaiians: Native Identities and Cultural Politics*. Minneapolis, MN: University of Minnesota Press, 2002.

Kauanui, J. Kehaulani. *Hawaiian Blood: Colonialism and the Politics of Sovereignty and Indigeneity*. Durham, NC: Duke University Press Books, 2008.

Kauanui, J. Kehaulani. "Off-Island Hawaiians 'Making' Ourselves at 'Home': A [Gendered] Contradiction in Terms?" *Women's Studies International Forum* (1998): 681–693.

Liliuokalani. *Hawai'i's Story by Hawai'i's Queen*. Honolulu, HI: Mutual Publishing, 1991.

Malo, David. *Hawaiian Antiquities*. Honolulu, HI: Bishop Museum, 1951.

Merry, Sally Engle. *Colonizing Hawai'i: The Cultural Power of Law*. Princeton, NJ: Princeton University Press, 2000.

Okamura, Jonathan Y. "Why There Are No Asian Americans in Hawai'i: The Continuing Significance of Local Identity." *Social Process in Hawaii* (1994): 161–178.

Pelayo, Lessa Kanani'opua. *Ho'omau: The Perpetuation of Hawaiian Culture in Southern California (Master's Thesis)*. Los Angeles, CA: UCLA, 2008.

Silva, Noenoe K. *Aloha Betrayed: Native Hawaiian Resistance to American Colonialism*. Durham, NC: Duke University Press Books, 2004.

Trask, Haunani-Kay. *From a Native Daughter: Colonialism and Sovereignty in Hawaii*. Honolulu, HI: University of Hawaii Press, 1999.

Vowell, Sarah. *Unfamiliar Fishes*. New York, NY: Riverhead Books, 2011.